Intelligent Systems for Security Informatics

Intelligent Systems for Security Informatics

Christopher Yang
Wenji Mao
Xiaolong Zheng
Hui Wang

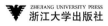

ZHEJIANG UNIVERSITY PRESS
浙江大学出版社

AMSTERDAM • BOSTON • HEIDELBERG • LONDON
NEW YORK • OXFORD • PARIS • SAN DIEGO
SAN FRANCISCO • SINGAPORE • SYDNEY • TOKYO

Academic Press is an Imprint of Elsevier

Academic Press is an imprint of Elsevier
The Boulevard, Langford Lane, Kidlington, Oxford OX5 1GB, UK
225 Wyman Street, Waltham, MA 02451, USA

First edition 2013

Notice
No responsibility is assumed by the publisher for any injury and/or damage to persons or property as a matter of products liability, negligence or otherwise, or from any use or operation of any methods, products, instructions or ideas contained in the material herein. Because of rapid advances in the medical sciences, in particular, independent verification of diagnoses and drug dosages should be made

British Library Cataloguing in Publication Data
A catalogue record for this book is available from the British Library

Library of Congress Cataloging-in-Publication Data
A catalog record for this book is availabe from the Library of Congress

ISBN—13: 978-0-12-404702-0

For information on all Academic Press publications visit
our web site at books.elsevier.com

Printed in the United States of America
Transferred to Digital Printing, 2013

Working together to grow
libraries in developing countries

www.elsevier.com | www.bookaid.org | www.sabre.org

ELSEVIER   BOOK AID   Sabre Foundation
            International

Contents

Preface

The Intelligence and Security Informatics conference series, which includes the IEEE International Conference on Intelligence and Security Informatics (IEEE ISI), the European Intelligence and Security Informatics Conference (EISIC), and the Pacific Asia Workshop on Intelligence and Security Informatics (PAISI), started about a decade ago. Since then, it has brought together many academic researchers, law enforcement and intelligence experts, and information technology consultants and experts to discuss their research and practices. The topics in ISI include data management, data and text mining for ISI applications, terrorism informatics, deception and intent detection, terrorist and criminal social network analysis, public health and bio-security, crime analysis, cyber-infrastructure protection, transportation infrastructure security, policy studies and evaluation, and information assurance, among others. In this book, we have covered the most active research work in recent years.

The intended readership of this book includes (i) public and private sector practitioners in the national/international and homeland security area, (ii) consultants and contractors engaged in ongoing relationships with federal, state, local, and international agencies on projects related to national security, (iii) graduate-level students in Information Sciences, Public Policy, Computer Science, Information Assurance, and Terrorism, and (iv) researchers engaged in security informatics, homeland security, information policy, knowledge management, public administration, and counter-terrorism.

We hope that readers will find the book valuable and useful in their study or work. We also hope that the book will contribute to the ISI community. Researchers and practitioners in this community will continue to grow and share research findings to contribute to national safety around the world.

Christopher C. Yang
Drexel University

Wenji Mao
Chinese Academy of Sciences

Xiaolong Zheng
Chinese Academy of Sciences

Hui Wang
National University of Defense Technology

CHAPTER 1

Revealing the Hidden World of the Dark Web: Social Media Forums and Videos[1]

Hsinchun Chen*, Dorothy Denning[†], Nancy Roberts[†], Catherine A. Larson*,
Ximing Yu*, Chun-Neng Huang*

* Management Information Systems Department, The University of Arizona, Tucson, Arizona, USA
[†] Department of Defense Analysis, Naval Postgraduate School, Monterey, California, USA

Chapter Outline

---

[1] Based on: H. Chen, D. Denning, N. Roberts, C.A. Larson, Y. Ximing, C. Huang, The Dark Web Forum Portal: from multi-lingual to video, IEEE International Conference on Intelligence and Security Informatics (ISI), 2011, pp. 7–14. Used with permission.

Intelligent Systems for Security Informatics.
http://dx.doi.org/10.1016/B978-0-12-404702-0.00001-X

1.1 Introduction

The Internet presence of terrorists, hate groups, and other extremists continues to be of significant interest to counter-terrorism investigators, intelligence analysts, and other researchers in government, industry, and academia, in fields as diverse as: psychology, sociology, criminology, and political science; computational and information sciences; and law enforcement, homeland security, and international policy. Through analysis of primary sources such as terrorists' own websites, videos, chat sites, and Internet forums, researchers and others attempt, for example, to identify who the terrorists and extremists are, how they are using the Internet and for what intent, who the intended audience is, etc. [1]. For example, the United Nation's Counter-terrorism Implementation Task Force in 2009 issued a report describing member states' concerns about continued terrorist use of the Internet for fundraising, recruitment, and cyber attacks, among other things, and analyzed steps to address this use [2]. McNamee et al. [3] examined the message themes found in hate group websites to understand how these groups recruited and reacted to threats through the formation of group identity. Post [4] noted how terrorists had created a "virtual community of hatred" and wrote of the need to develop a psychology-based counter-terrorism program to, in part, inhibit potential participants from joining, reduce support for these groups, and undermine their activities.

In 2002, partly in response to burgeoning interest in terrorist use of the Internet, particularly in the aftermath of 9/11, and partly as a natural expansion of its previous work in border security, and information sharing and data mining for law enforcement, the Artificial Intelligence (AI) Lab of the University of Arizona founded its "Dark Web" project. "Dark Web," as it has become known, is a long-term scientific research program that aims to study international terrorism via a computational, data-centric approach (http://ai.arizona.edu/research/).

Dark Web focuses on the hidden, "dark" side of the Internet, where terrorists and extremists use the Web to disseminate their ideologies, recruit new members, and even share terrorism training materials. Project goals are twofold: (1) to collect, as comprehensively as possible, all relevant web content generated by international extremist and terrorist groups, including websites, forums, chat rooms, blogs, social networking sites, videos, virtual world, etc.; and (2) to develop algorithms, tools, and visualization techniques that will enhance researchers' and investigators' abilities to analyze these sites and their relevance, and that are generalizable to and useful across a wide range of domains.

The next section provides an overview of the genesis and evolution of the Dark Web Forum Portal and includes an examination of the data sources and collection. The following section provides an overview of video portal development. The chapter ends with a conclusion and directions for future work.

1.2 The Dark Web Forum Portal

The Dark Web project has for several years collected a wide variety of data related to and emanating from extremist and terrorist groups. These data have included websites, multimedia material linked to the websites, forums, blogs, virtual world implementations, etc. Forums, as dynamic, interactive discussion sites that support online conversations, have proven to be of significant interest. Through the anonymity of posting under screen names, they allow for and support free expression. They are an especially rich source of information for studying organizations and individuals, the evolution of ideas and trends, and other social phenomena. In forums, ongoing conversations are captured in threads, with each thread roughly corresponding to a subject area or topic. The replies, called postings or messages, are generally time-stamped and attributable to a particular poster (author). Analysis of the threads and messages can often reveal dynamic trends in topics and discussions, the sequencing of ideas, and relationships between posters.

1.2.1 Data Identification and Collection

The forum sites collected for the Dark Web project were identified with input from terrorism researchers, security and military educators, and other experts. They were selected in part because each is generally dedicated to topics relating to Islamic ideology and theology, and range from "moderate" to "extremist" in their opinions and ideologies.

Once identified, semi-automated methods of collection known as "spiders" are used to crawl the forums and capture all messages including metadata, such as author (also known as "poster"), date, and time. The date and time stamps are especially important for helping to maintain the reply network: the order in which messages are posted and replied to. The spiders are described in more detail below.

The forums were originally collected to serve as a research testbed for use in the Lab, particularly to support work in sentiment and affect analysis, and the study of radicalization processes over time.

Access to these forums is now provided to researchers and others through the Dark Web Forum Portal [5]. The portal contains approximately 15,000,000 messages in five languages: Arabic, English, French, German, and Russian. The English- and Arabic-language forums selected include major jihadist websites; some of the Arabic forums have English-language sections. Three French forums, and the single forums in German and Russian, provide representative content for extremist groups producing content in these languages. Collectively, the forums have approximately 350,000 members/authors. The portal also provides statistical analysis, download, translation, and social network visualization functions for each selected forum.

Incremental spidering keeps the content up to date [6]. Tools developed for searching, browsing, translation, analysis, and visualization are described in a later section.

1.2.2 Evolution of the Dark Web Forum Portal

Version 1.0

This section covers the development of the portal and includes references to previous work where certain aspects of the portal research and development are explained in more detail.

As mentioned above, the Dark Web forums were originally collected to serve as a research testbed for the Artificial Intelligence Lab to develop techniques for analyzing the Internet presence and content of hate and extremist groups (e.g. Refs [7−11]). At the time, little previous research had been done on Dark Web forum data integration and searching. Dark Web forums are heterogeneous, widely distributed, numerous, difficult to access, and can mysteriously appear and disappear with no notice or warning. The growing amount of forum material makes searching increasingly difficult [12]. For researchers interested in analyzing or monitoring Dark Web content, data integration and retrieval are critical issues [10]. Without a centralized system, it is labor-intensive, time-consuming, and expensive to search and analyze Dark Web forum data.

Two other characteristics of Dark Web forums create barriers to use. The first is the dynamic nature of the forums, which creates difficulties for analyzing and visualizing interactions between participants. Visualization can reveal hitherto hidden relationships and networks behind online activity [13]. Social Network Analysis (SNA) is a graph-based method that can be used to analyze the network structure of a group or population [14]. SNA has been used to study various real-world networks [15]. Web forums are ideal platforms for social network research because by default they record participants' communications and the postings are retrievable [16]. However, few prior studies had actually incorporated an SNA function into a real-time system.

A second characteristic is the multilingual nature of the forums. Forums can be found in many of the world's languages, and forums collected for Dark Web study were in Arabic and English, initially, with French, German, and Russian forums being added later. It was thus critical that the language barrier be addressed.

Based on the research gaps discussed above, it was clear that a systematic and integrated approach to collecting, searching, browsing, and analyzing Dark Web forum data was needed. We developed these research questions to guide the next steps [5]:

- Q1: How can we develop a Web portal for Dark Web forums which will effectively integrate data from multiple forum data sources?
- Q2: How can we develop efficient, accurate search and browse methods across multiple forum data sources in our portal?
- Q3: How can we incorporate real-time translation functionality into our portal to enable automatic forum data translation from non-English (e.g. Arabic) to English?
- Q4: How can we incorporate real-time, user-interactive social network analysis into our portal to analyze and visualize the interactions among forum participants?

The first iteration of the portal was developed based on the system design shown in Figure 1.1.

The early system design contained three modules:

- Data acquisition — Using spidering programs, web pages from the selected online forums were collected. In the first iteration of the portal, we included six Arabic forums and one English-language forum with a total of about 2.3M messages.
- Data preparation — Using parsing programs, the detailed forum data and metadata were extracted from the raw HTML web pages and stored locally in a database.

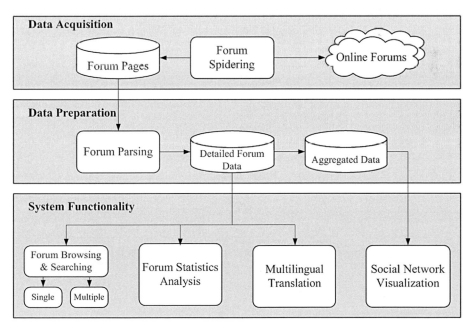

Figure 1.1:
Early system design of the Dark Web Forum Portal.

- System functionality — Using Apache Tomcat for the portal and Microsoft SQL Server 2000 for the database, functions including searching and browsing could be supported. Forums could be searched individually or collectively. For forum statistics analysis, Java applet-based charts were created to show the trends based on the numbers of messages produced over time. The multilingual translation function was implemented using the then-current Google Translation API (http://code.google.com/apis/ajaxlanguage/documentation/#Translation). The social network visualization function provided dynamic, user-interactive networks implemented using JUNG (http://jung.sourceforge.net/) to visualize the interactions among forum members.

Figure 1.2 shows a results screen from a single-forum search using the term "bomb" in the forum Alokab. Alokab is in Arabic; the search term "bomb" was used to retrieve matching threads (shown in the middle column, labeled "Thread Title"), and the translation function was then invoked to translate on the fly from Arabic to English ("Thread Title Translation").

An evaluation was conducted with a small group of users, each of whom performed all tasks related to each function. All search tasks were completed successfully on both our portal and a benchmark system; however, on our system, searching was faster. Users also reacted positively to the translation and SNA functions when queried using a seven-point Likert scale to assess their subjective assessments of their overall satisfaction with the portal, including its usefulness and ease of use.

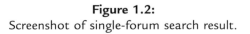

Figure 1.2:
Screenshot of single-forum search result.

This first iteration of the portal was created to address the challenges involved in integrating data from multiple forum data sources in multiple languages, developing search and browse methods effective for use across multiple data sources, and incorporating into a portal real-time translation and real-time social network analysis functions that are typically stand-alone. More details about the first version of the system and the user evaluation can be found in Zhang et al. [5].

Version 2.0

Version 2.0 was developed with several goals in mind:

- Increase the scope of data collection while minimizing the amount of human effort or intervention needed.
- Improve the currency of the data presented in the portal and develop the means to keep it updated in as automated a fashion as possible.
- Enhance searching and browsing from a user perspective.

To increase the scope of data collection and keep the collection up to date, we needed to examine our spidering procedures. Spiders [17] are defined as "software programs that traverse the World Wide Web information space by following hypertext links and retrieving web documents by standard HTTP protocol." As explained in our previous research, there are six important characteristics of spidering programs: accessibility, collection type, content richness, URL-ordering features, URL-ordering techniques, and collection update procedure [18]. A functional spider program must handle the registration requirement of targeted forums (accessibility), extract the desired information from various data types (collection type), filter out irrelevant file types (content richness), sort queued URLs based on given heuristics (URL-ordering features and techniques), and keep the collection up to date (collection update procedure). An incremental spidering process was added to the data acquisition module of the system [6].

The addition of the incremental spidering component allowed the portal to stay up to date within 2 weeks of forum postings. It also enabled us to acquire a great many more forums and to increase the collection from seven forums with 2.3M messages in the first version to 29 forums and more than 13M messages in the second. Tests performed during the development of version 2.0 showed, for example, that the incremental spider allowed us to collect 29,000 messages in less than 45 minutes [6].

Another goal, as listed above, was to improve the searching and browsing experience of users. More flexible Boolean searching was added, to allow users to perform "AND" and "OR" searches. Users could also now enter their search terms in English (or any language) and retrieve matches regardless of the original language of the portal. The display was improved to allow users to comprehend, at a glance, how to view, translate, or download results, whether threads or messages.

Version 2.5

While version 2.0 addressed many of the issues we identified in usability tests, improvements in searching were still needed. Search is one of the most important and well-used functions in the portal and, as of version 2.0, the search results were still not very satisfactory in the following aspects:

- Query parsing: While version 2.0 added some Boolean searching capability, it did not support complex, sophisticated queries.
- Search ranking: The search ranking was problematic when multiple keywords with the "OR" relationship were entered by users.
- Hit highlighting: Matched keywords were not always correctly highlighted; some highlighted words did not match the input search terms.
- Searching efficiency: Searching for messages in more than five forums simultaneously was very slow from a user perspective.

Given these issues, we embarked on a newer version of the portal, version 2.5, based on version 2.0. We adopted Lucene, a popular Java-based full-text indexing framework for the indexing and searching of thread titles and message contents (http://lucene. apache.org/).

Features of Lucene include high-performance indexing that scales well, and accurate and efficient search algorithms. Its index size is roughly 20–30% of the size of the text indexed, and Lucene Java is compatible with Lucene implemented in other programming languages. Incremental and batch indexing are both fast. It offers ranked searching in which the "best" results are returned first, and also offers a wide range of query types.

Implementing Lucene to work for multilingual searching required analysis before proceeding. The Dark Web Forum Portal (DWFP) contains 29 forums in five languages: English, Arabic, French, German, and Russian. We examined the languages contained in the 29 forums manually and found that among the 17 Arabic forums, 16 are purely in Arabic. An exception was the forum Alqimmah, which contains a considerable number of English messages. All seven English-language forums contain Arabic messages. All French, German, and Russian forums also contain Arabic messages. See Table 1.1 for a listing of forums.

Lucene requires different analyzers for different languages. Even for the four languages that use SnowballAnalyzer, the analyzer has to be initialized differently for each language. At the same time, documents representing forum messages have very different fields from documents representing forum threads. We therefore created 10 indices for all the forum threads and messages (five languages times two types of documents (message and thread)). Since it is difficult to identify the underlying language of texts at thread or message level, we chose a coarser granularity when indexing the forums. For all 16 Arabic forums that contain

Table 1.1: Forums Available in Version 2.5 of the Dark Web Forum Portal

Index Language	Forums
English	Alqimmah, Ansar1, Gawaher, IslamicAwakening, IslamicNetwork, Myiwc, TurnToIslam, Ummah
Arabic	Alboraq, AlFaloja, AlFirdaws, Almedad, Alokab, Alsayra, AsAnsar, Atahadi, Hanein, Hawaa, Hdrmut, M3f, Majahden, Montada, Muslm, Shamikh Alqimmah, Ansar1, Gawaher, IslamicAwakening, IslamicNetwork, Myiwc, TurnToIslam, Ummah, Alminhadj, Aslama, Ribaat, DeAnsarnet, KavkazChat
French	Alminhadj, Aslama, Ribaat
German	DeAnsarnet
Russian	KavkazChat

only Arabic texts, we used the ArabicAnalyzer and indexed the threads and messages into corresponding Arabic index. For other forums, which are bilingual, we ran the indexing on each forum twice: once using the ArabicAnalyzer (output to Arabic index) and the second time using the proper SnowballAnalyzer (output to corresponding language index). All 29 forums were indexed into an Arabic index using the ArabicAnalyzer, so that all the Arabic texts in the forums are correctly indexed. For bilingual forums, each forum is further indexed into another language of index, so texts in that language also get properly indexed. With this solution, we guarantee that all texts have been indexed by the correct analyzer at least once. There might be, for example, some English texts indexed into Arabic index, but they have already been correctly indexed into the English index as well. By choosing the proper IndexSearcher at search phase, any incorrectly indexed texts will not affect the search results.

To support searching, we must identify the specific language to use, so that we can choose the correct analyzer for parsing the search query. For example, to search for Arabic content, we first translate the search query into Arabic using Google Translate API (keeping the Boolean operators untranslated). Then the ArabicAnalyzer is used to tokenize the search query. The IndexSearcher searches through the Arabic index and returns a ranked list of hits that are all in Arabic. If a search is performed for all five languages, five IndexSearchers will be created and five lists of hits will be returned. Each of the five lists is sorted by hit score, starting from the highest ranked matching results. To return a single list of search results (as was the case in versions 1.0 and 2.0), we would have to merge the five sorted lists. This kind of merge has the potential to cause two problems: the merge sort is very time consuming for large lists, and the hit scores generated by different IndexSearchers may be in different scales. For example, the top hit in English might become the 1000th result in the combined result list.

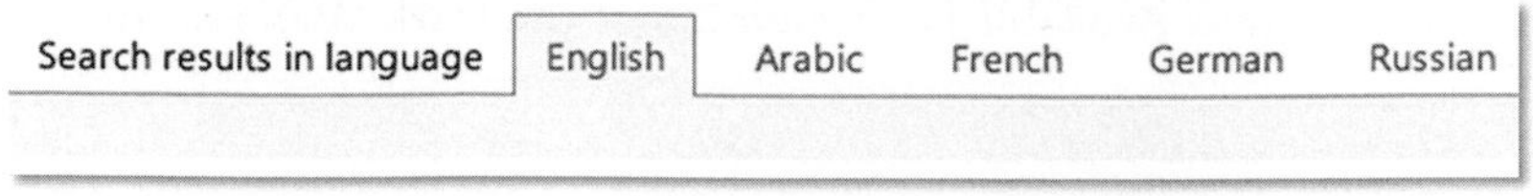

Search results in language	English	Arabic	French	German	Russian

Figure 1.3:
The tab for users to switch between different languages for search results.

To solve this problem, we allow users to choose in which language they would like the search results, instead of trying to return all five languages of results at the same time. Currently, the results default to English-language results; users are able to choose other languages through a tabbed display (see Figure 1.3).

In quick search, users cannot specify the language to use, so English results will be returned first and users may switch to other languages from the search results page. In advanced search, users can directly specify which language to use before starting a search. They can also switch to other languages from the search results page. Using this approach, we only need to search in one index at a time, which helps to produce search results faster.

As mentioned above, Lucene also supports sophisticated Boolean searching: the combination of one or more words or phrases with one or more Boolean operators. Because Boolean logic may be opaque to users, we added in a query builder that would allow users to construct searches using language they were likely to understand.

Implementing Lucene has resulted in both advantages and disadvantages. Through user testing, we can see that searching has been improved through better query parsing, searching ranking, and hit highlighting, but at the cost of maintaining and updating an index separate from the database.

1.2.3 Summary of the Three Versions

Figure 1.4 summarizes the evolution of the DWFP from version 1.0 to 2.5. By developing versions 2.0 and 2.5 of the portal, we have made the portal more useful and a more powerful tool for users looking for topics and trends of interest in the jihadist forums, thus further supporting its potential use as an open source intelligence tool. In the next section of this chapter, we present two case studies by students using the Dark Web Forum Portal while learning to perform intelligence analysis tasks.

1.2.4 Case Studies using the Dark Web Forum Portal

Students taking a Defense Analysis course at the Naval Postgraduate School (NPS) in Monterey, California developed several case studies; two are presented here. The students

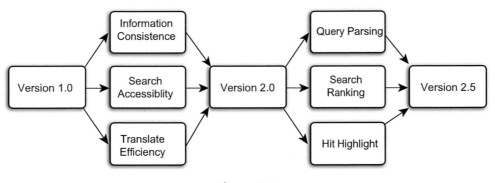

Figure 1.4:
System evolution from version 1.0 through version 2.5.

at NPS are generally mid-career military personnel, often with significant field or battle experience, from the United States or allied countries. They may be from any branch of the military and are seeking a graduate education through any of the 18 departments such as Defense Analysis, Information Sciences, etc. NPS's mission is to provide "high-quality, relevant and unique advanced education and research programs that increase the combat effectiveness of the Naval Services, other Armed Forces of the USA and our partners, to enhance our national security" (NPS website, http://www.nps.edu/About/index.html). In a Defense Analysis course on Conflict and Cyberspace, students examined how cyberspace, particularly the Internet, can serve as a tool, target, and source of conflict for both state and non state actors. As part of the course, the instructor gave a demonstration of the Dark Web Forum Portal in class. The portal was presented as a potential resource for open source intelligence. Following the demonstration, the students were assigned a project to use the portal to investigate a topic of their choice, write a 1200-word paper describing what they did and learned, and discuss their findings in a later class. The following two subsections discuss two of the student projects. In both cases, the students had significant previous military and field experience and expected to continue their military service.

Case study I. Dark Forums in Eastern Afghanistan: How to influence the Haqqani audience

In the first case study, "Dark Forums in Eastern Afghanistan: How to influence the Haqqani audience," the student, who had had previous deployments to Afghanistan, postulated that one reason the war was continuing to drag on was that the USA was "losing the information war" with the people of Afghanistan and Taliban "safe haven" sites, an argument that has also been made by counter-terrorism researchers (e.g. Ref. [19]). The student used the Dark Web Forum Portal to investigate how the Haqqani Network of the Taliban, identified as one of the chief adversaries of the USA, was able to twist US tactical victories into operational defeats in the media and idea battlefields. After investigating relevant forums and postings, he cited, for example, patently false propaganda distributed through the forums that described American deaths that never actually occurred — victories claimed for the Taliban that never happened. The student also learned through forums on the portal that his own patrol had killed the son of a senior Haqqani member while on patrol. This was not information they had access to while in Afghanistan, and was extremely important tactical information that they would have been able to capitalize on while there. Other useful tactical information gleaned through postings on the portal included movements of other Haqqani members in the province, and previously unknown associations and linkages between certain individuals and organizations. According to the student, these are examples of information gaps that, had such intelligence reached them while in-country, would have allowed US patrols to choose different courses of action.

Case study II. Psychological operations

In the second case study, a student familiar with military information support operations (MISO) used the Dark Web Forum Portal to investigate and compare the popularity and use of various media in the Muslim community. Such knowledge can help guide decision-making and communications strategies both in and outside a country of interest. The student examined forum threads and postings related to broadcast media (radio and television) and paper media (brochures, leaflets, and handbills), as all such communication methods may be useful for information operations. He also investigated postings relating to "propaganda," which were often accompanied by very negative perceptions whether attributed to the USA or other Western governments, or to Middle Eastern governments. Much propaganda was attributed to "Zionist" conspiracy groups. Most messages concerning propaganda concerned the message content and the lack of legitimacy of the originator. One interesting and useful finding was that radio was discussed in the forums more than any other media, with comments to the effect that radio, particularly unlicensed or "pirate" radio, was an effective means for reaching Muslims. According to the student, the continuing usefulness of radio outweighs that of other media, although forum participants also expressed interest in using print media such as brochures to spread their messages. Overall, the student thought that the DWFP could be a very useful tool for planning information operations in cyberspace as well as for maintaining situational awareness while in areas dominated by extremists.

Conclusion

By having so many relevant forums readily searchable and translatable through a uniform, easy-to-use interface, the value of these disparate, otherwise inaccessible data sources is increased immeasurably. These two case studies, and others we have on file, demonstrate the potential value of the Dark Web Forum Portal in the context of supplementing and corroborating sensitive intelligence information.

1.3 The Video Portal

The Dark Web Forum Portal was originally constructed to allow the examination, from a broad perspective, of the use of web forums by terrorist and extremist groups. The Video Portal module has been added to facilitate the study of video as it is used by these groups. Both portals are available to researchers on a request basis. Below we provide an overview of the development of the new Video Portal.

As Web 2.0 social media has gained more and more popularity, it has become an inexpensive, effective, and convenient platform for extremists and others to publish and propagate their ideas and point of view. Terrorist-related content can also be obtained from the Internet and has become an important source of information for researchers trying to understand, model, and thwart terrorist behavior.

As shown in Figure 1.5, videos can carry rich image-based (and sound-based) information; we believe identifying and collecting extremist and terrorist-related videos ("dark" videos) will therefore become increasingly important for the Dark Web research community. Online video-sharing websites have attracted less attention than forums and other text-based sources but are nonetheless potentially valuable. Many previous studies have focused on text-based social media such as forums [6] and blogs [20], with little prior work having been published on dark web videos. Huang et al. [21] engaged in dark video identification and proposed a framework for classifying dark videos and segregating them from non-dark videos but this is one of few such studies. Their results implied that dark videos existed on video-sharing websites without being immediately removed by the security mechanisms provided by the websites.

Most publicly accessible video-sharing websites, however, do block illegal, offensive, and terrorism/extremism-related videos from their huge video collections. This is done for the

Eulogy of an "Iraqi Jihadist" – from video No. 2

Experimenting with a highly flammable material – from video No. 4

Posts acetone peroxide experiments – from video No. 6

Figure 1.5:
Examples of screenshots from sample videos.

betterment of society, but can impede access for legitimate research purposes. At the same time, many of these sites lack an effective and accurate means for automatically blocking such videos. YouTube, for example, provides only a flagging mechanism for marking inappropriate videos. Flagged videos are then manually investigated.

To facilitate research of dark videos, we are developing the Dark Video Portal to collect relevant videos from video-sharing sites and provide a user-friendly interface that allows users to search, query, and download the dark video collection. The earlier work on identifying and analyzing dark videos has been described in Salem et al. [22], Fu et al. [23], and Huang et al. [21]. This section describes current progress in portal development.

1.3.1 System Design

The Dark Video Portal consists of three main components: data acquisition, data preparation, and system functionality. Details of each component are shown in Figure 1.6 and described in the following sections.

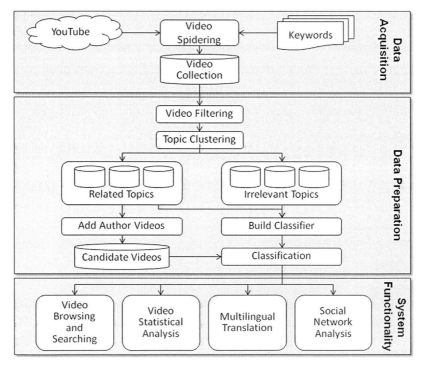

Figure 1.6:
System design of the Dark Video Portal.

Table 1.2: Examples of Terrorist-Related Keywords

Keyword	Translation	Collection
Islamic Jihad	—	Terms used by extremists
Hamas	—	Terms used by extremists
Usbat Al Ansar	—	Terms used by extremists
المجاهدين	Mujahideen	Terms used by extremists
تحضير متفجر	Explosive preparation	Weapons technical terms
موسوعة الأسلحة الكبرى	Great weapons encyclopedia	Weapons technical terms
الحزام الناسف	Explosives belt	Weapons technical terms

1.3.2 Data Acquisition

Data acquisition began first with the identification of keywords by domain experts. Previous investigation in these publicly accessible collections showed that only a small portion of available videos can be classified as "dark." Therefore, we implemented and extended the framework as described in Huang et al [21] to effectively and efficiently identify and collect these dark videos.

To begin identifying dark videos for the portal, we started with two sets of terrorist-related keywords identified by our domain experts: terms used by extremists and technical terms related to weapons. We started searching using 71 terms used by extremists (22 in English and 49 in Arabic) and 57 weapons-related terms (two in English and 55 in Arabic). Table 1.2 gives several examples from each set.

We developed focused crawlers to collect the videos from publicly accessible video-sharing sites and created a Candidate Video Collection. Videos, and their metadata, were identified and collected through three streams: "query" videos (the top 100 videos returned from a given keyword scarch), "related" videos (the top 50 videos recommended when viewing the query video), and "author" videos (the top 50 videos uploaded from each of the authors associated with the query videos). Associated metadata was also collected, including author, video title, description, comments, etc. All of these materials together comprise the Candidate Video Collection.

1.3.3 Data Preparation

Knowing that not all of the collected videos would be relevant, in this step video filtering and topic clustering were implemented to identify potentially "dark" videos from within the Candidate Video Collection.

We first filtered out videos from predefined categories that were irrelevant, such as comedy, education, music, etc. The remaining videos were further clustered into topics using topic clustering. The topics were then classified as either relevant or irrelevant; irrelevant videos were removed from the Candidate Collection. However, because previous work demonstrated that authors are most likely to upload videos within the same or similar topics, the "author" videos of the relevant videos were put together with the relevant videos as the new Candidate Collection.

Further filtering was needed to winnow out all non-dark videos. A training dataset was constructed using the top videos of both relevant and irrelevant topics to serve as positive and negative data points. The training dataset was used to build a classifier using Support Vector Machine (SVM). Videos from the new Candidate Video Collection were fed into the classifier; those deemed irrelevant were removed from the database.

In total, 104,206 videos were collected by using 128 predefined keywords. Of these, 12,728 were classified as "dark" videos. Table 1.3 shows the details of the results for both sets of keyword types: terms used by extremists and weapons technical terms.

Table 1.4 shows a small sampling of selected "dark" videos collected as described above and now stored in the dark video database.

1.3.4 Portal System

In order to be accessible by and useful to users, the dark video data collection needed to have a usable interface constructed to support the kind of searching, browsing, and other functions users would need.

Table 1.3: Number of Videos Collected

Collection Name	No. of Collected Videos	No. of Classified Videos	No. of Authors	No. of Comments	No. of Commentors
Terms used by extremists	90,725	11,355	4743	420,446	172,146
Weapons technical term	13,481	1.373	767	42,210	22,061
Totals	104,206	11,356	5510	462,656	194,207

Table 1.4: Examples of Dark Videos

Video ID	Description
5nK93elltHc	"My sword" jihadi hymn
XADz5-x19bg	Funeral of a "martyred" mujahid
yZlQrOkVeEI	Last minutes of a suicide bomber
KB6anaCj1q8	Suicide bomber farewell
39UbzotlaJQ	Attack in Kirkuk, Iraq
8XG5GInbYzw	Taliban suicide attack
lPoQPQhycS8	Ambush in Afghanistan

The portal's functions can be divided into several main categories:

- Access control
- Browsing
- Searching
- Post-search filtering
- Multilingual translation
- Social network analysis.

Access control

In access control, user account names and passwords are stored to allow validated access to the video portal. All users must be granted accounts and are asked to log in before using the system. A screenshot is shown in Figure 1.7.

Browsing

After logging in to the system, users are taken to the home page (shown in Figure 1.8) which provides a brief introduction to the system and lists current video collections. Users can select a video collection (Terms Used by Extremists and Weapon Technical Terms) and browse it through four points of entry:

- General Information: shows general statistical information about the selected video collection.
- Browse by Videos: lists all the videos, allowing users to select those of interest to view comments and additional details.
- Browse by Authors: lists the authors and the numbers of videos and comments posted.
- Browse by Comments: shows the comments for each author and the video to which the comment belongs.

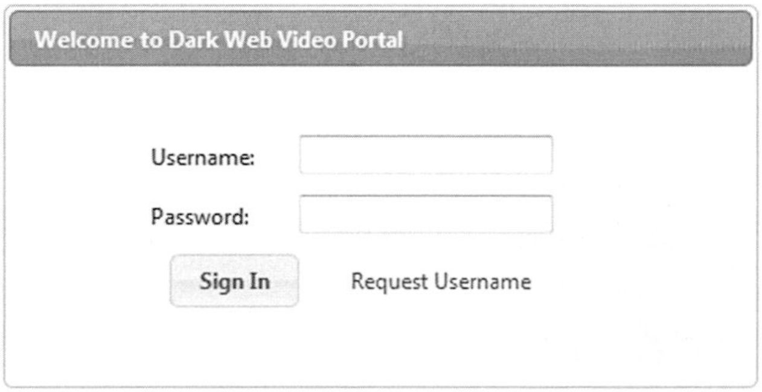

Figure 1.7:
Screenshot of portal log-in.

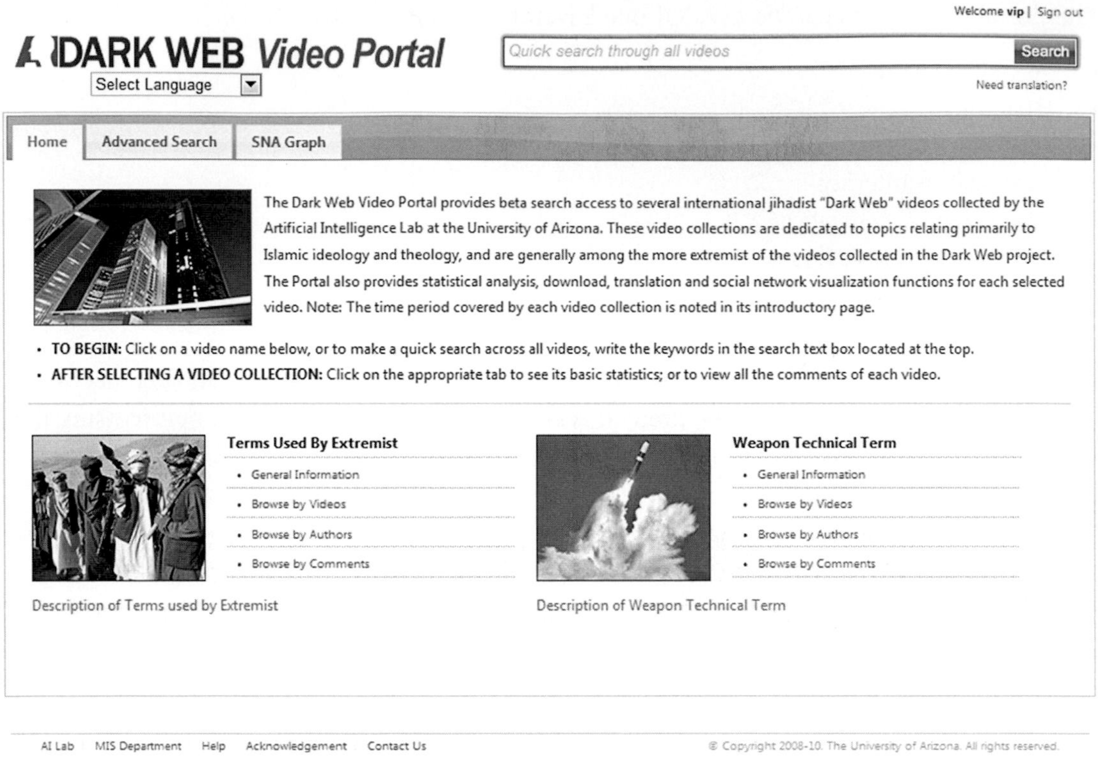

Figure 1.8:
Home page of the Dark Web Video Portal; it provides immediate browsing access for users.

When a collection is selected, statistical information about the collection is first presented, as in Figure 1.9. Users can also see how many videos have been posted for a given video collection, as in Figure 1.10. Other statistical information available through the portal includes the number of comments posted per collection, the top 10 authors who

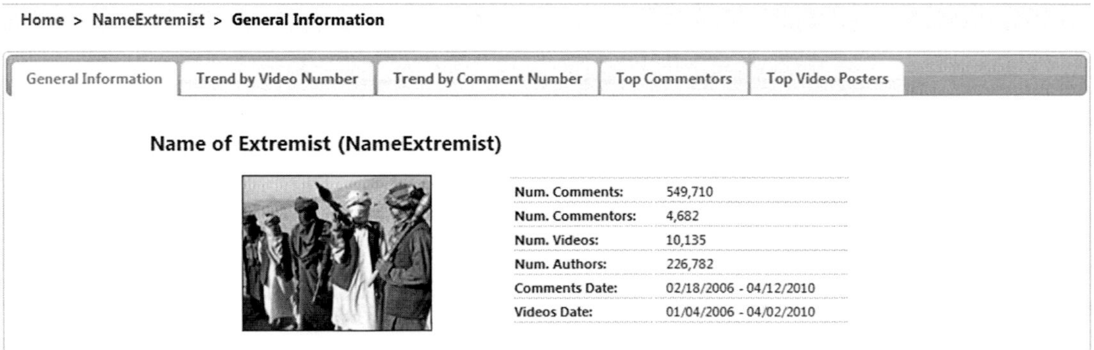

Figure 1.9:
Screenshot of the general information for a video collection including basic statistical information.

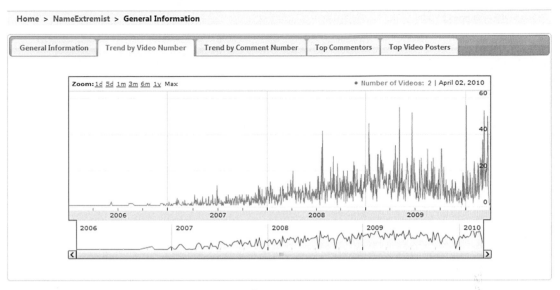

Figure 1.10:
Screenshot of the graph showing the number of videos posted for a specific video collection.

have posted the most videos, and also the top 10 authors posting the most comments for each collection.

In addition to browsing through the general information provided about the collections, authors, and posters, users may also browse directly by video (sorted by the number of video comments, as shown in Figure 1.11) and by author (Figure 1.12).

Searching

Searching is also supported; efforts have been made to identify the ways that users may approach searching the video portal. The following search functions are currently supported by the portal:

- Quick search (in video titles and descriptions)
- Search by Author
- Search by Time
- Search by Topic (Full Text Search).

The next four figures illustrate each of the other search methods available through the portal. Quick search is always available at the top of the portal website, as shown in Figure 1.13. Users enter a keyword of interest; the system returns results from all video titles and descriptions. Users can also search by an author's name (Figure 1.14), by a particular time period (Figure 1.15), and by topic (Figure 1.16).

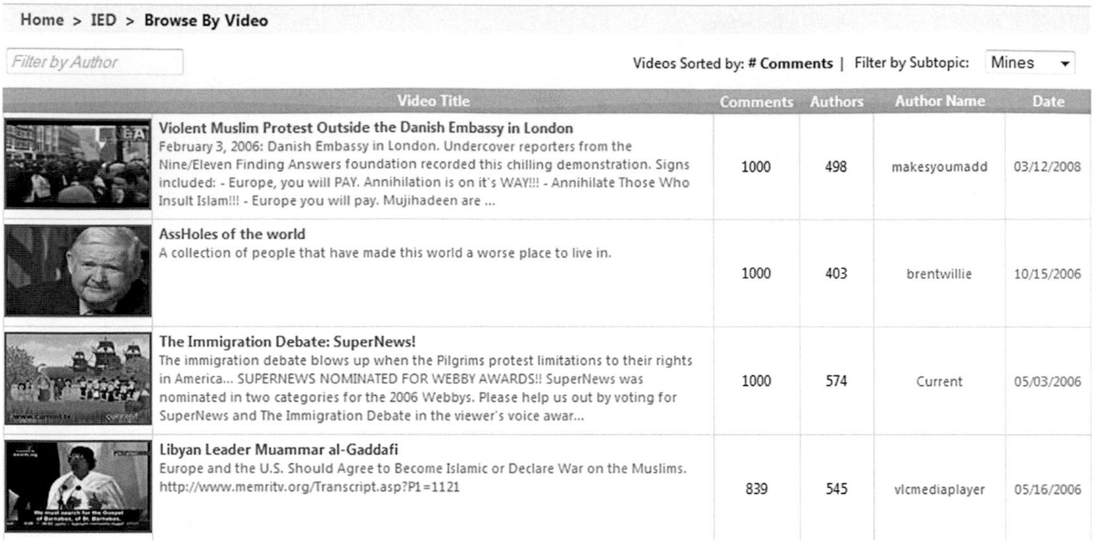

Home > IED > **Browse By Video**

Filter by Author   Videos Sorted by: **# Comments** | Filter by Subtopic: Mines ▾

Video Title	Comments	Authors	Author Name	Date
Violent Muslim Protest Outside the Danish Embassy in London February 3, 2006: Danish Embassy in London. Undercover reporters from the Nine/Eleven Finding Answers foundation recorded this chilling demonstration. Signs included: - Europe, you will PAY. Annihilation is on it's WAY!!! - Annihilate Those Who Insult Islam!!! - Europe you will pay. Mujihadeen are ...	1000	498	makesyoumadd	03/12/2008
AssHoles of the world A collection of people that have made this world a worse place to live in.	1000	403	brentwillie	10/15/2006
The Immigration Debate: SuperNews! The immigration debate blows up when the Pilgrims protest limitations to their rights in America... SUPERNEWS NOMINATED FOR WEBBY AWARDS!! SuperNews was nominated in two categories for the 2006 Webbys. Please help us out by voting for SuperNews and The Immigration Debate in the viewer's voice awar...	1000	574	Current	05/03/2006
Libyan Leader Muammar al-Gaddafi Europe and the U.S. Should Agree to Become Islamic or Declare War on the Muslims. http://www.memritv.org/Transcript.asp?P1=1121	839	545	vlcmediaplayer	05/16/2006

Figure 1.11:

Screenshot of the portal showing the "browse by video" function.

Post-search filtering

Post-search filtering is a useful navigational function allowing users to further refine their search queries while responding to actual results. All of the search results shown above illustrate the filtering methods currently offered by the portal. Users may filter their results by Video Collection, by Author, and by Year.

Home > NameExtremist > **Browse By Video**

sokaboka100 | Remove Filter by Author   Videos Sorted by: **Date** | Filter by Subtopic: All ▾

Video Title	Comments	Authors	Author Name	Date
Grave-worshiper Ahmed Abdou Awad offend literature with the Prophet, peace be upon him	5	4	sokaboka100	05/24/2009
Sufi Abu Nour is guaranteed to his followers Paradise	4	4	sokaboka100	05/22/2009

Page 1 of 1   Go to:

AI Lab   MIS Department   Help   Acknowledgement   Contact Us   © Copyright 2008-10. The University of Arizona. All rights reserved.

Figure 1.12:

When browsing by author, users click on a preceding screen listing each author and his/her number of videos; in clicking on an author's name, the user is taken to this screen, showing the author's videos sorted by date.

Figure 1.13:
The results of a "quick search" on the word "jihad"; the search box is outlined in red.

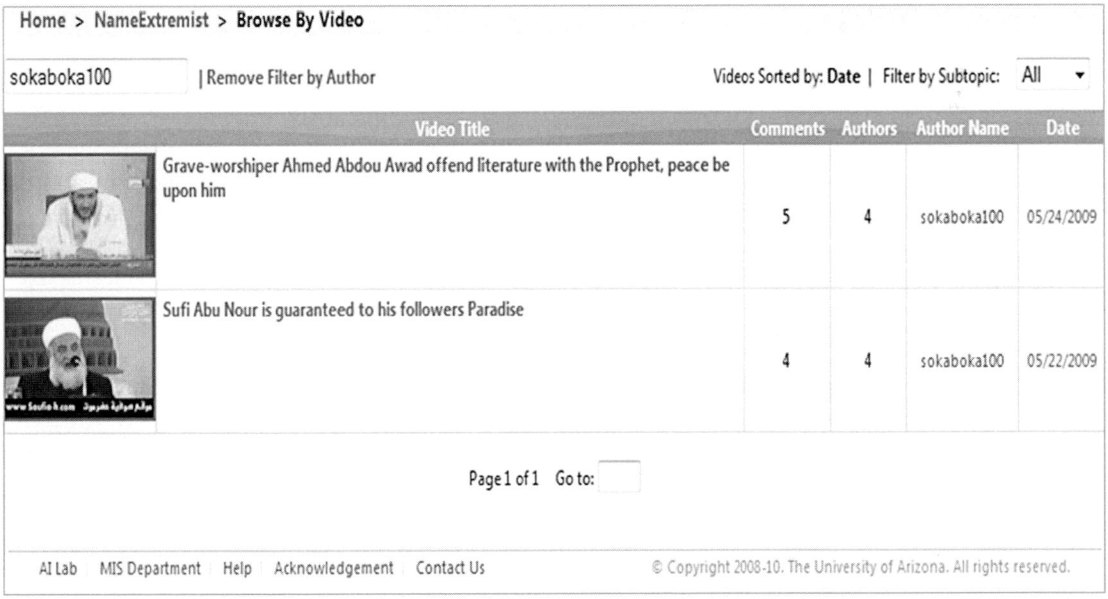

Figure 1.14:
The results of an author search; the search box is outlined in red.

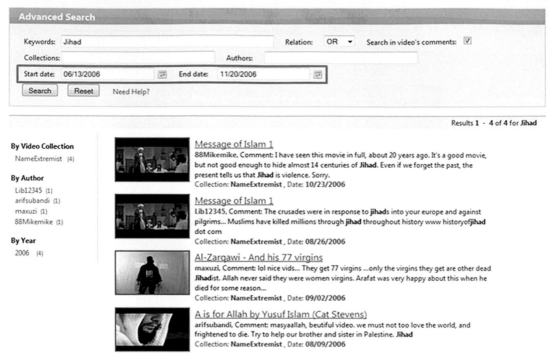

Figure 1.15:
An example of searching for videos posted during a specified time period.

Multilingual translation

The Dark Web Video Portal contains commentary and other text in English as well as in a variety of different foreign languages. To help users who are familiar only with English, a multilingual translation function is built into the portal for use with non-English-language textual content. Non-English text in the system is displayed with translation buttons, which can be used to translate these contents into English. For foreign language texts (such as video titles), a whole-page translation function is provided in the top of the page (see Figure 1.17 for an example).

In addition, multilingual search is supported so that users can use English terms to search multilingual contents. For example, English-language search words input by users are first translated into Arabic, and then both the English and Arabic terms are used together for the search. Figure 1.18 shows the results of one such search; the term "bomb" was used as the search input. Contents containing the word "bomb," whether in English or Arabic, are returned.

Social network analysis

The social network in various kinds of social media, including many publicly accessible collections of videos, can be extended from the definition of the reply network in forums, as illustrated in Figure 1.19.

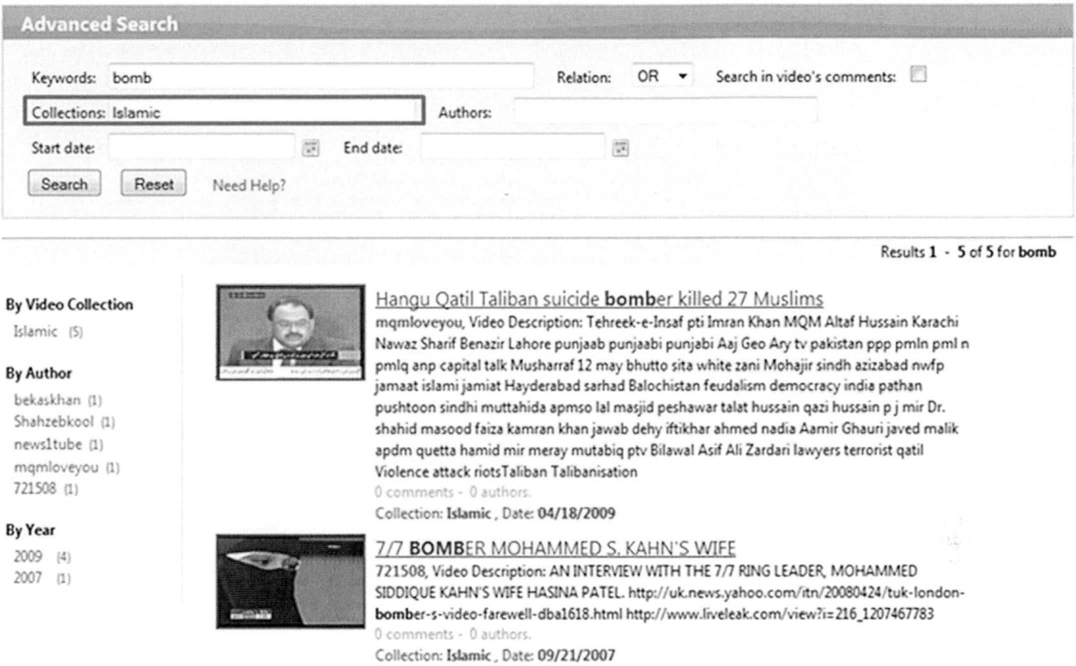

Figure 1.16:
An example of a topical search in video titles and descriptions.

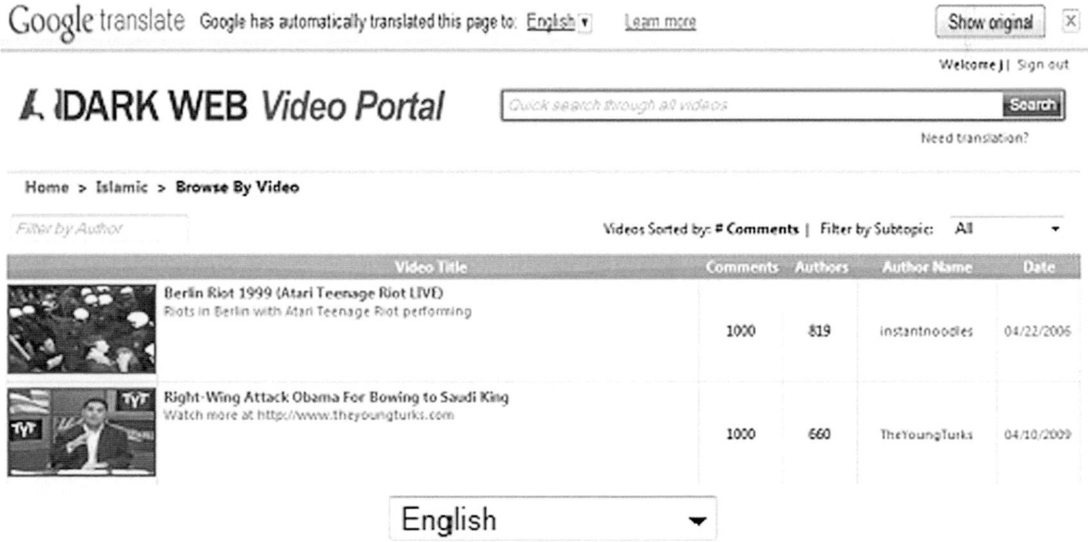

Figure 1.17:
An example of a page, including the video title, translated into English.

DARK WEB *Video Portal*

Select Language ▾

bomb | Search

Need translation?

Advanced Search | Results **1** - **10** of 29 for **bomb**

By Video Collection

NameExtremist (15)
IED (8)
Islamic (5)
WMD (1)

By Author

LionIslam (2)
Smakgakgak (1)
bekaskhan (1)
gedet (1)
NufffRespect (1)
721508 (1)
matcho71 (1)

inside story- Algeria stunned by **bomb**ings- 20 Aug 08- Part 1
AlJazeeraEnglish, Video Description: Algeria is rocked by a series of **bomb** attacks, which kill over 50 people, and injure dozens more. It's the deadliest attack in recent years in the country - and the government's blaming Al Qaeda.
272 comments - 187 authors.
Collection: **NameExtremist** , Date: 08/21/2008

قنبلة حماسية في صوت ابو القعقاع
خطبة حماسية عملاقة للششيخ ابو القعقاع من غرباء ارض الشام :islamy2, Video Description
71 comments - 58 authors.
Collection: **NameExtremist** , Date: 07/08/2008

ارهابين قتلة ومجرمين يزرعون قنبلة في شوارع العراق
iraq العراق :matcho71, Video Description
7 comments - 7 authors.
Collection: **NameExtremist** , Date: 09/20/2007

Figure 1.18:
Video titles containing the word "bomb," whether in English or Arabic, are returned as results from the search for the English-language word "bomb."

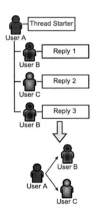

Figure 1.19:
An example of a reply network.

In a reply network, every node represents a user and every link represents a reply relationship. If B replies to A, as in the example, a directed link is added in the social network, pointing from A to B. A directed reply network is extracted based on the reply-to relationship in the thread discussion. Similar relationships proliferate in video-sharing sites. Text comments in videos can be mapped to postings in forum threads as follows:

User (Video sharing site) → User (Forum)
Video Description → Thread Starter
Text Comment → Thread Reply.

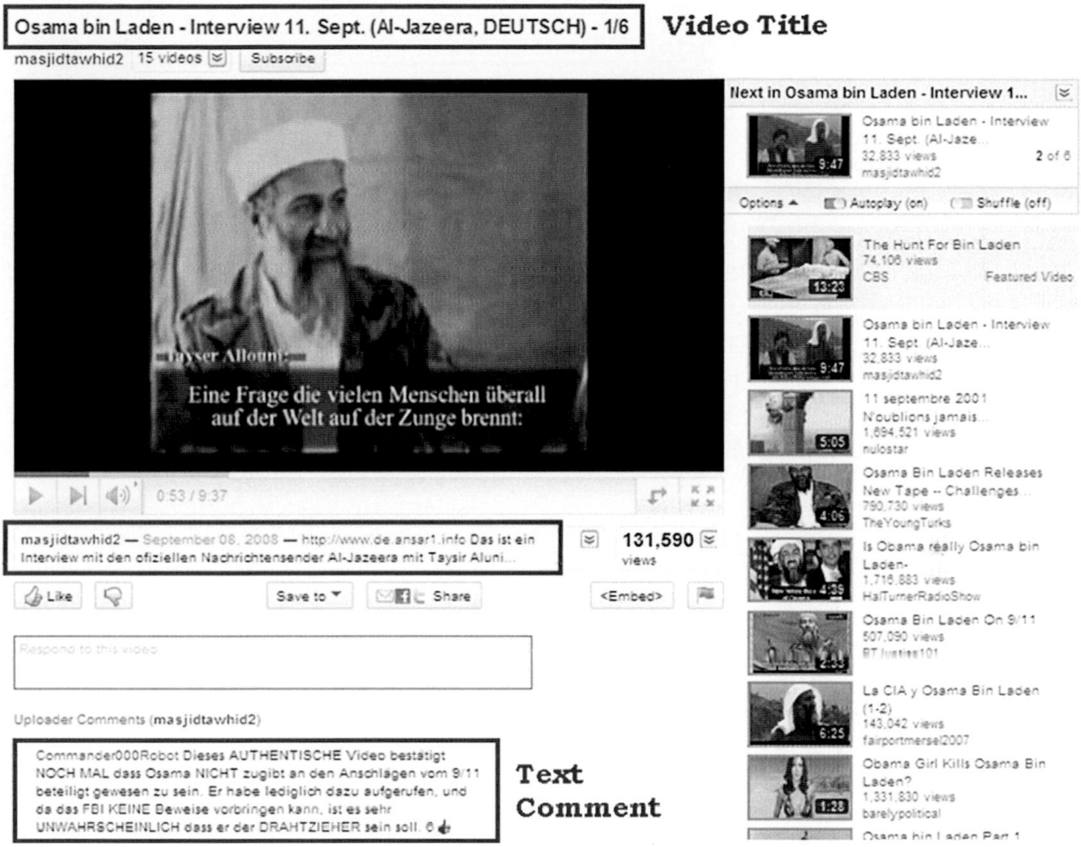

Figure 1.20:
A video and its description linked with a text comment.

In the screenshot in Figure 1.20, a video interview with Osama bin Laden is shown with the description loaded by the poster, followed by a text comment.

In the Dark Web Video Portal, a Social Network Analysis Interface allows users of the system to identify and analyze networks of authors and commenters. An example of the interface showing a small social network of videos and comments is shown in Figure 1.21. This figure also shows the various criteria that can be input by users for identifying and selecting networks.

1.4 Conclusion and Future Directions

Dark web forums often contain nuggets of useful, open-source information buried in significant noise. As shown in the case studies, the Dark Web Forum Portal has demonstrable potential utility as both a filtering mechanism and as a source of additional intelligence for

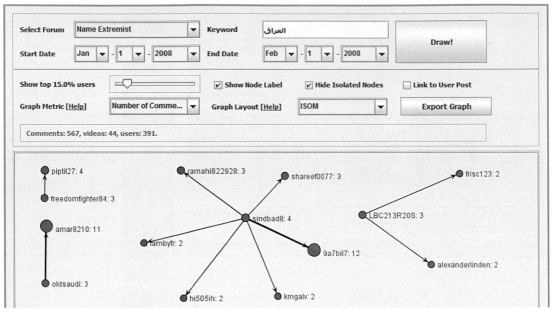

Figure 1.21:
A screenshot of the video portal Social Network Analysis module.

analysis and investigation. Based on recent evaluations, future enhancements will include implementation of the search improvement offered by Lucene, and stabilizing the system such that it can be readily used by larger groups of users.

Dark videos, along with their comments, are usually removed from video-sharing sites. However, these videos can provide important insights into how extremists and terrorists communicate and share information, and may provide important clues about their capability and intent. Given the difficulties of identifying and locating dark videos, and the interest expressed to us by various researchers in accessing them, we believe the intended users will find the Dark Web Video Portal to be useful to their research. Informal feedback received to date has been positive with regard to both content and function. A more formal evaluation will be conducted to ascertain its usefulness and usability.

Acknowledgments

This work has been supported in part by the Counterterrorism Fellowship Program (CTFP), Contract No. N00104-10-C-Q381, the National Science Foundation under Grant Numbers CNS-0709338 and CBET-0730908, and DTRA, under Award No. HDTRA1-09-0-0058.

References

[1] G. Weimann, Terror on the Internet: The new arena, the new challenges, US Institute of Peace, Washington, DC, 2006.

[2] United Nations, Counter-terrorism implementation task force (CTITF). Report of the Working Group on Countering the Use of the Internet for Terrorist Purposes, February 2009. <http://www.un.org/terrorism/pdfs/wg6-internet_rev1.pdf>

[3] L.G. McNamee, B.L. Peterson, J. Peña, A call to educate, participate, invoke and indict: Understanding the communication of online hate groups, Commun. Monogr. 77 (2) (2010) 257—280.

[4] J. Post, 'When hatred is bred in the bone': The social psychology of terrorism, Ann. N. Y. Acad. Sci. 1208 (2010) 15—23.

[5] Y. Zhang, S. Zeng, L. Fan, Y. Dang, C.A. Larson, H. Chen, Dark Web Forum Portal: Searching and analyzing Jihadist forums, Proceedings of the IEEE International Intelligence and Security Informatics Conference, Dallas, TX, 2009, pp. 71—76.

[6] Y. Zhang, S. Zeng, C. Huang, L. Fan, X. Yu, D. Yan, C.A. Larson, D. Denning, N. Roberts, H. Chen, Developing a Dark Web collection and infrastructure for computational and social sciences, 2010 IEEE International Conference on Intelligence and Security Informatics (ISI), Vancouver, BC, Canada, 2010, pp. 59—64.

[7] A. Abbasi, H. Chen, Applying authorship analysis to extremist-group web forum messages, IEEE Intell. Syst. 20 (5; special issue on AI for Homeland Security) (2005) 67—75.

[8] A. Abbasi, H. Chen, CyberGate: A system and design framework for text analysis of computer mediated communication, MIS Q. (MISQ) 32 (4; special issue on Design Science Research) (2008) 811—837.

[9] R. Zheng, J. Li, H. Chen, Z. Huang, A framework for authorship identification of online messages: Writing-style features and classification techniques, J. Am. Soc. Inf. Sci. Technol. 57 (3) (2006) 378—393.

[10] Y. Zhou, J. Qin, G. Lai, H. Chen, Collection of U.S. extremist online forums: A web mining approach, Annual Hawaii International Conference on System Science (2007) 70.

[11] Y. Zhou, E. Reid, J. Qin, H. Chen, G. Lai, U.S. domestic extremist groups on the Web: Link and Content Analysis, IEEE Intell. Syst. 20 (5) (2005) 44—51.

[12] E. Reid, J. Qin, W. Chung, J. Xu, Y. Zhou, R. Schumaker, M. Sageman, II. Chen, Terrorism knowledge discovery project: A knowledge discovery approach to addressing the threats of terrorism, Second Symposium on Intelligence and Security Informatics (ISI 2004), Springer-Verlag, 2004, pp. 125—145.

[13] J. Xu, H. Chen, The topology of dark networks, Commun. ACM 51 (10) (2008) 58—65.

[14] D. Liben-Nowel, The Link-prediction problem for social networks, J. Am. Soc. Inf. Sci. Technol. (JASIST) 58 (7) (2007) 1019—1031.

[15] G. Kossinets, D.J. Watts, Empirical analysis of an evolving social network, Science 311 (2006) 88—90.

[16] Y. Yeung, Macroscopic study of the social networks formed in web-based discussion forums, Proceedings of the 2005 Conference on Computer Support for Collaborative Learning, 2005, pp. 727—731.

[17] F.C. Cheong, Internet Agents: Spiders, Wanderers, Brokers, and Bots, New Riders Publishing, Indianapolis, 1996.

[18] T.J. Fu, A. Abbasi, H. Chen, A focused crawler for Dark Web forums, J. Am. Soc. Inf. Sci. Technol. 61 (6) (2010) 1213—1231.

[19] D. Betz, The virtual dimension of contemporary insurgency and counterinsurgency, Small Wars Insurg. 19 (4) (2008) 510—540.

[20] C.C. Yang, T.D. Ng, Terrorism and crime related weblog social network: Link, content analysis and information visualization, IEEE International Conference on Intelligence and Security Informatics (2007) 55—58.

[21] C. Huang, T.J. Fu, H. Chen, Text-based video content classification for online video-sharing sites, J. Am. Soc. Inf. Sci. Technol. 61 (5) (2010) 891—906.

[22] A. Salem, E. Reid, H. Chen, Multimedia content coding and analysis: unraveling the content of Jihadi extremist groups' videos, Stud. Confl. Terror. 31 (7) (2008) 605–626.

[23] T.J. Fu, C. Huang, H. Chen, Identification of extremist videos in online video sharing sites, Proceedings of the IEEE International Intelligence and Security Informatics Conference, Dallas, TX, 2009.

CHAPTER 2

Proactive Cyber Defense

Richard Colbaugh, Kristin Glass

Sandia National Laboratories, Albuquerque, New Mexico, USA

Chapter Outline

2.1 Introduction

Rapidly advancing technologies and evolving operational practices and requirements increasingly drive both private and public sector enterprises toward highly interconnected and technologically convergent information networks. Proprietary information processing solutions and stove-piped databases are giving way to unified, integrated systems, thereby dramatically increasing the potential impact of even a single well-planned network intrusion, data theft, or denial-of-service (DoS) attack. It is therefore essential that commercial and government organizations develop network defenses that are able to respond rapidly to, or even foresee, new attack strategies and tactics.

Recognizing these trends and challenges, some cyber security researchers and practitioners are focusing their efforts on developing *proactive* methods of cyber defense, in which future

Intelligent Systems for Security Informatics.
http://dx.doi.org/10.1016/B978-0-12-404702-0.00002-1

attack strategies are anticipated and these insights are incorporated into defense designs [1–5]. However, despite this attention, much remains to be done to place the objective of proactive defense on a rigorous and quantitative foundation. Fundamental issues associated with the dynamics and predictability of the coevolutionary "arms race" between attackers and defenders are yet to be resolved. For instance, although recent work has demonstrated that previous attacker actions and defender responses provide predictive information about future attacker behavior [3–5], not much is known about which measurables have predictive power or how to exploit these to form useful predictions. Moreover, even if these predictability and prediction issues were resolved, it is still an open question how to incorporate such predictive analytics into the design of practically useful cyber defense systems.

This chapter considers the problem of protecting enterprise-scale computer networks against intrusions and other disruptions. We begin by leveraging the coevolutionary relationship between attackers and defenders to develop two *proactive filter-based methods* for network defense. Each of these methods formulates the filtering task as one of behavior classification, in which innocent and malicious network activities are to be distinguished, and each assumes that only very limited prior information is available regarding exemplar attacks or attack attributes. The first method models the data as a bipartite graph of instances of network activities and the features or attributes that characterize these instances. The bipartite graph data model is used to derive a machine learning algorithm that accurately classifies a given instance as either innocent or malicious based upon its behavioral features. The algorithm enables information concerning previous attacks to be "transferred" for use against novel attacks; crucially, it is assumed that previous attacks are drawn from a distribution of attack instances related *but not identical* to that associated with the new malicious behaviors. This transfer learning algorithm offers a simple, effective way to extrapolate attacker behavior into the future, and thus significantly increases the speed with which defense systems can successfully respond to new attacks.

The second classifier-based approach to proactive network defense represents attacker–defender coevolution as a hybrid dynamical system (HDS) [6,7], with the HDS discrete system modeling the "modes" of attack (e.g. types of DoS or data exfiltration procedures) and the HDS continuous system generating particular attack instances corresponding to the attack mode presently "active." Our algorithm takes as input potential near-future modes of attack, obtained for example from the insights of cyber analysts, and generates synthetic attack data for these modes of malicious activity; these data are then combined with recently observed attacks to train a simple classifier to be effective against both current and (near) future attacks. The utility of these proactive filter-based methods is demonstrated by showing that they outperform standard techniques for the task of distinguishing innocent and malicious network behaviors in analyses of two publicly available cyber datasets.

An alternative approach to proactive network defense is to consider the problem of anticipating and characterizing impending attack events with enough specificity and lead time to allow mitigating defensive actions to be taken. We also explore this approach in the chapter, proposing a novel *early warning method* as a solution to this problem. The proposed warning method is based upon the fact that certain classes of attacks require the attackers to coordinate their actions, often through social media or other observable channels, and exploits signatures generated by this coordination to provide effective attack warning. Interestingly, the most useful early warning indicator identified in this exploratory study is not one of the standard metrics for social media activity, but instead is a subtle measure of the way attack coordination interacts with the *topology* of relevant online social networks. The potential of the early warning approach to proactive cyber defense is illustrated through a case study involving politically motivated Internet-scale attacks.

2.2 Proactive Filters

In this section we propose two filter-based methods for proactive network defense and demonstrate their utility through analysis of publicly available computer network security-related datasets.

2.2.1 Preliminaries

We approach the task of protecting computer networks from attack as a classification problem, in which the objective is to distinguish innocent and malicious network activity. Each instance of network activity is represented as a feature vector $x \in \Re^{|F|}$, where entry x_i of x is the value of feature i: for instance, x and F is the set of instance features or attributes of interest (x may be normalized in various ways [7]). Instances can belong to one of two classes: positive/innocent and negative/malicious; generalizing to more than two classes is straightforward. We wish to learn a vector $c \in \Re^{|F|}$ such that *the classifier orient* $= sign(c^T x)$ accurately estimates the class label of behavior x, returning $+1$ (-1) for innocent (malicious) activity.

Knowledge-based classifiers leverage prior domain information to construct the vector c. One way to obtain such a classifier is to assemble a "lexicon" of innocent/positive features $F^+ \subseteq F$ and malicious/negative features $F^- \subseteq F$, and to set $c_i = +1$ if feature i belongs to F^+, $c_i = -1$ if i is in F^- and $c_i = 0$ otherwise; this classifier simply sums the positive and negative feature values in the instance and assigns instance class accordingly. Unfortunately this sort of scheme is unable to improve its performance or adapt to new domains, and consequently is usually not very useful in cyber security applications.

Alternatively, learning-based methods attempt to generate the classifier vector c from examples of innocent and malicious network activity. To obtain a learning classifier, one can begin by assembling a set of n_l *labeled* instances $\{(x_i, d_i)\}$, where $d_i \in \{+1, -1\}$ is the class label for instance i. The vector $\boldsymbol{c}$ is then learned through training with the set $\{(x_i, d_i)\}$, for example by solving the following set of equations for $\boldsymbol{c}$:

$$\left[\boldsymbol{X}^T \boldsymbol{X} + \gamma \boldsymbol{I}_{|F|} \right] \boldsymbol{c} = \boldsymbol{X}^T \boldsymbol{d} \tag{2.1}$$

where matrix $\boldsymbol{X} \in \Re^{nl \times |F|}$ has instance feature vectors for rows, $\boldsymbol{d} \in \Re^{nl}$ is the vector of instance labels, $\boldsymbol{I}_{|F|}$ denotes the $|F| \times |F|$ identity matrix, and $\gamma \geq 0$ is a constant; this corresponds to regularized least squares (RLS) learning [8]. Many other learning strategies can be used to compute $\boldsymbol{c}$ [8]. Learning-based classifiers have the potential to improve their performance and adapt to new situations, but realizing these capabilities typically requires that large training sets of labeled attacks be obtained. This latter characteristic represents a significant drawback for cyber security applications, where it is desirable to be able to recognize new attacks given only a few (or even no) examples.

In this section we present two new learning-based approaches to cyber defense that are able to perform well with only very modest levels of prior knowledge regarding the attack classes of interest. The basic idea is to leverage "auxiliary" information that is readily available in cyber security applications. More specifically, the first proposed method is a transfer learning algorithm [9] that permits the information present in data from previous attacks to be transferred for implementation against new attacks. The second approach uses prior knowledge concerning attack "modes" to generate synthetic attack data for use in training defense systems, resulting in networks defenses that are effective against both current and (near) future attacks.

2.2.2 Algorithm 1: Transfer Learning

We begin by deriving a bipartite graph-based transfer learning algorithm for distinguishing innocent and malicious network behaviors, and then demonstrate the algorithm's effectiveness through a case study using publicly available network-intrusion data obtained from the KDD Cup archive [10]. The basic hypothesis is simple and natural: Because attacker/defender behavior coevolves, previous activity should provide some indication of future behavior, and transfer learning is one way to quantify and operationalize this intuition.

Proposed algorithm

The development of the proposed algorithm begins by modeling the problem data as a bipartite graph G_b, in which instances of network activity are connected to their features (see Figure 2.1). It is easy to see that the adjacency matrix A for graph G_b is given by

$$A = \begin{bmatrix} 0 & X \\ X^T & 0 \end{bmatrix} \tag{2.2}$$

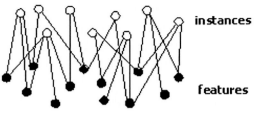

instances

features

Figure 2.1:
Cartoon of bipartite graph model G_b. Instances of network activity (white vertices) are connected to the features (black vertices) that characterize them, and link weights (black edges) reflect the magnitudes taken by the features in the associated instances.

where matrix $X \in \Re^{n \times |F|}$ is constructed by stacking the n instance feature vectors as rows, and each "**0**" is a matrix of zeros. In the proposed algorithm, the bipartite graph model G_b is used to exploit the relationships between instances and features by assuming that, in G_b, positive/negative instances will tend to be connected to positive/negative features. Note that, as shown below, the learning algorithm can incorporate both instance labels and feature labels (if available). In the case of the latter it is assumed that the feature labels are used to build vector $w \in \Re^{|F|}$, where the entries of w are set to $+1$ (innocent), -1 (malicious), or 0 (unknown) according to the polarity of the corresponding features.

Many cyber security applications are characterized by the presence of limited labeled data for the attack class of interest but ample labeled information for a related class of malicious activity. For example, an analyst may be interested in detecting a new class of attacks, and may have in hand a large set of labeled examples of normal network behavior as well as attacks that have been experienced in the recent past. In this setting it is natural to adopt a transfer learning approach, in which knowledge concerning previously observed instances of innocent/malicious behavior, the so-called *source* data, is transferred to permit classification of new *target* data. In what follows we present a new bipartite graph-based approach to transfer learning that is well suited to cyber defense applications.

Assume that the initial problem data consists of a collection of $n = n_T + n_S$ network events, where n_T is the (small) number of labeled instances available for the target domain; that is, examples of network activity of current interest, and $n_S \gg n_T$ is the number of labeled instances from some related source domain, say reflecting recent innocent and malicious activity; suppose also that a modest lexicon F_l of labeled features is known (this set can be empty). Let this label data be used to encode vectors $d_T \in \Re^{n_T}$, $d_S \in \Re^{n_S}$, and $w \in \Re^{|F|}$ respectively. We denote by $d_{T,\text{est}} \in \Re^{n_T}$, $d_{S,\text{est}} \in \Re^{n_S}$, and $c \in \Re^{|F|}$ the vectors of estimated class labels for the target and source instances and the features, and define the *augmented classifier* $c_{\text{aug}} = [d_{S,\text{est}}^T \ d_{T,\text{est}}^T \ c^T]^T \in \Re^{n+|F|}$. Note that the quantity c_{aug} is introduced for notational convenience in the subsequent development and is not directly employed for classification.

We derive an algorithm for learning c_{aug}, and therefore c, by solving an optimization problem involving the labeled source and target training data, and then use c to estimate the class label of any new instance of network activity via the *simple linear classifier orient* = $sign(c^T x)$. This classifier is referred to as *transfer learning-based* because c is learned, in part, by transferring knowledge about the way innocent and malicious network behavior is manifested in a domain that is related to (but need not be identical to) the domain of interest.

We wish to learn an augmented classifier c_{aug} with the following four properties: (1) if a source instance is labeled, then the corresponding entry of $d_{S,est}$ should be close to this ± 1 label; (2) if a target instance is labeled, then the corresponding entry of $d_{T,est}$ should be close to this ± 1 label, and the information encoded in d_T should be emphasized relative to that in the source labels d_S; (3) if a feature is in the lexicon F_l, then the corresponding entry of c should be close to this ± 1 label; and (4) if there is an edge X_{ij} of G_b that connects an instance i and a feature j, and X_{ij} possesses significant weight, then the estimated class labels for i and j should be similar.

The four objectives listed above may be realized by solving the following optimization problem:

$$\min_{c_{aug}} c_{aug}^T L c_{aug} + b_1 \left\| d_{S,est} - k_S d_S \right\|^2 + b_2 \left\| d_{T,est} - k_T d_T \right\|^2 + b_3 \left\| c - w \right\|^2 \qquad (2.3)$$

where $L = D - A$ is the graph Laplacian matrix for G_b, with D the diagonal degree matrix for A (i.e. $D_{ii} = \Sigma_j A_{ij}$), and β_1, β_2, β_3, k_S, and k_T are non-negative constants. Minimizing (2.3) enforces the four properties we seek for c_{aug}. More specifically, the second, third, and fourth terms penalize "errors" in the first three properties, and choosing $\beta_2 > \beta_1$ and $k_T > k_S$ favors target label data over source labels. To see that the first term enforces the fourth property, note that this expression is a sum of components of the form $X_{ij}(d_{T,est,i} - c_j)^2$ and $X_{ij}(d_{S,est,i} - c_j)^2$. The constants β_1, β_2, and β_3 can be used to balance the relative importance of the four properties.

The c_{aug} that minimizes the objective function (2.3) can be obtained by solving the following set of linear equations:

$$\begin{bmatrix} L_{11} + \beta_1 I_{nS} & L_{12} & L_{13} \\ L_{21} & L_{22} + \beta_2 I_{nT} & L_{23} \\ L_{31} & L_{32} & L_{33} + \beta_3 I_{|F|} \end{bmatrix} c_{aug} = \begin{bmatrix} \beta_1 k_S d_S \\ \beta_2 k_T d_T \\ \beta_3 w \end{bmatrix} \qquad (2.4)$$

where the L_{ij} are matrix blocks of L of appropriate dimension. The system (2.4) is sparse because the data matrix X is sparse, and therefore large-scale problems can be solved efficiently. Note that in situations where the set of available labeled target instances and features is *very* limited, classifier performance can be improved by replacing L in (2.4) with the normalized Laplacian $L_n = D^{-1/2} L D^{-1/2}$, or with a power of this matrix L_n^k (for k a positive integer).

We summarize the above discussion by sketching an algorithm for constructing the proposed transfer learning classifier:

Algorithm TL (Transfer Learning)

1. Assemble the set of equations (2.4), possibly by replacing the graph Laplacian L with L_n^k.
2. Solve equations (2.4) for $c_{aug} = [d_{S,est}^T \ d_{T,est}^T \ c^T]^T$ (e.g. using the conjugate gradient method).
3. Estimate the class label (innocent or malicious) of any new network activity x of interest as: orient $= sign(c^T x)$.

Algorithm evaluation

We now examine the performance of Algorithm TL for the problem of distinguishing innocent and malicious network activity in the KDD Cup 99 dataset, a publicly available collection of network data consisting of both normal activities and attacks of various kinds [10]. For this study we randomly selected 1000 normal connections (*N*), 1000 denial-of-service attacks (*DoS*), and 1000 unauthorized remote-access events (*R2L*) to serve as our test data. Additionally, small sets of each of these classes of activity were chosen at random from Ref. [10] to be used for training Algorithm TL, and a lexicon of four features, two positive and two negative, was constructed manually and employed to form the lexicon vector w.

We defined two tasks with which to explore the utility of Algorithm TL. In the first, the goal is to distinguish *N* and *DoS* instances, and it is assumed that the following data is available to train Algorithm TL: (1) a set of $d_S/2$ labeled *N* and $d_S/2$ labeled *R2L* instances (source data), (2) a set of $d_T/2$ labeled *N* and $d_T/2$ labeled *DoS* instances (target data), and (3) the four lexicon features. Thus, the source domain consists of *N* and *R2L* activities and the target domain is composed of *N* and *DoS* instances. In the second task the situation is reversed — the objective is to distinguish *N* and *R2L* activities, the source domain is made up of d_S (*total*) labeled *N* and *DoS* instances, and the target domain consists of d_T (*total*) *N* and *R2L* instances. In all tests the number of labeled source instances is $d_S = 50$, while the number of target instances d_T is varied to explore the way classifier performance depends on this key parameter. Of particular interest is determining if it is possible to obtain good performance with only limited target data, as this outcome would suggest both that useful information concerning a given attack class is present in other attacks and that Algorithm TL is able to extract this information.

This study compared the classification accuracy of Algorithm TL with that of a well-tuned version of the RLS algorithm (1) and a standard naïve Bayes (NB) algorithm [11]; as the accuracies obtained with the RLS and NB methods were quite similar, we report only the RLS results. Algorithm TL was implemented with the following parameter values: $\beta_1 = 1.0$,

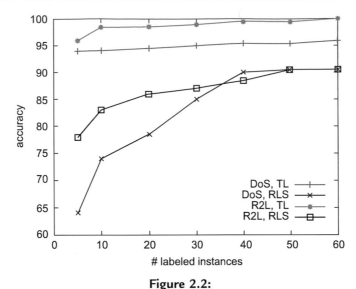

Figure 2.2:
Performance of Algorithm TL with limited labeled data. The plot shows how classifier accuracy (vertical axis) varies with the number of available labeled target instances (horizontal axis) for four tasks: distinguish *N* and *DoS* using *RLS* classifier, distinguish *N* and *DoS* using Algorithm TL, distinguish *N* and *R2L* using RLS classifier, and distinguish *N* and *R2L* using Algorithm TL.

$\beta_2 = 3.0$, $\beta_3 = 5.0$, $k_S = 0.5$, $k_T = 1.0$, and $k = 5$. We examined training sets which incorporated the following numbers of target instances: $n_T = 5, 10, 20, 30, 40, 50, 60$. As in previous studies (see, for example, Ref. [10]), only the 34 "continuous features" were used for learning the classifiers.

Sample results from this study are depicted in Figure 2.2. Each data point in the plots represents the average of 100 trials. It can be seen that Algorithm TL outperforms the RLS classifier (and also the standard NB algorithm, not shown), and that the difference in accuracy of the methods increases substantially as the volume of training data from the target domain becomes small. The performance of Algorithm TL for this task is also superior to that reported for other learning methods tested on these data [12]. The ability of Algorithm TL to accurately identify a novel attack after seeing only a very few examples of it, which is a direct consequence of its ability to transfer useful knowledge from related data, is expected to be of considerable value for a range of cyber security applications.

Finally, it is interesting to observe that the bipartite graph formulation of Algorithm TL permits useful information to be extracted from network data *even if no labeled instances are available*. More specifically, we repeated the above study for the case in which $d_T = d_S = 0$; that is, when no labeled instances are available in either the target or source domains. The

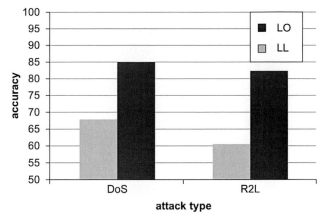

Figure 2.3:
Performance of Algorithm TL when no labeled instances are available. The bar graphs depict classifier accuracy for four tasks: distinguish *N* and *DoS* using a lexicon-only (LO) classifier (left, gray bar), distinguish *N* and *DoS* using lexicon-learning (LL) via Algorithm TL (left, black bar), distinguish *N* and *R2L* using an LO classifier (right, gray bar), and distinguish *N* and *R2L* using LL via Algorithm TL (right, black bar).

knowledge reflected in the lexicon vector w is still made available to Algorithm TL. As shown in Figure 2.3, employing a "lexicon only" classifier, in which the vector *w* is used to build a knowledge-based scheme as described in Section 2.2.1, yields a classification accuracy that is not much better than the 50% baseline achievable with random guessing. However, using this lexicon information together with Algorithm TL enables useful classification accuracy to be obtained (see Figure 2.3). This somewhat surprising result can be explained as follows: The "clustering" property of Algorithm TL encoded in objective function (2.3) allows the domain knowledge in the lexicon to leverage latent information present in the *unlabeled* target and source instances, thereby boosting classifier accuracy.

2.2.3 Algorithm 2: Synthetic Attack Generation

In this section we derive our second filter-based algorithm for distinguishing normal and malicious network activity and demonstrate its effectiveness through a case study using the publicly available Ling-Spam dataset [13]. Again the intuition is that attacker/defender coevolution should make previous activity somewhat indicative of future behavior, and in the present case we operationalize this notion by generating "predicted" attack data and using this synthetic data for classifier training.

Proposed algorithm

The development of the second approach to proactive filter-based defense begins by modeling attacker/defender interaction as a stochastic hybrid dynamical system (S-HDS). Here we present a brief, intuitive overview of the basic idea; a comprehensive description of the modeling procedure is given in Ref. [7]. An S-HDS (see Figure 2.4) is a feedback interconnection of a discrete-state stochastic process, such as a Markov chain, with a family of continuous-state stochastic dynamical systems [6,14]. Combining discrete and continuous dynamics within a unified, computationally tractable framework offers an expressive, scalable modeling environment that is amenable to formal mathematical analysis. In particular, S-HDS models can be used to efficiently represent and analyze dynamic phenomena that evolve on multiple time scales [14], a property of considerable value in the present application.

As a simple illustration of the way the S-HDS formalism enables effective, efficient mathematical representation of cyber phenomena, consider the task of modeling the coevolution of spam attack methods and spam filters. At an abstract but still useful level, one can think of spam—spam filter dynamics as evolving on two timescales:

- The *slow timescale*, which captures the evolution of attack strategies; as an example, consider the way early spam filters learned to detect spam by identifying words that were consistently associated with spam, and how spammers responded by systematically modifying the wording of their messages, for instance via "add-word" (AW) and "synonym" attacks [15].
- The *fast timescale*, which corresponds to the generation of particular attack instances for a given "mode" of attack (for example, the synthesis of spam messages according to a specific AW attack method).

We show in Ref. [7] that a range of adversarial behavior can be represented within the S-HDS framework, and derive simple but reasonable models for spam—spam filter dynamics and for basic classes of network intrusion attacks.

In Ref. [14] we develop a mathematically rigorous procedure for predictive analysis for general classes of S-HDS. Among other capabilities, this analytic methodology enables the

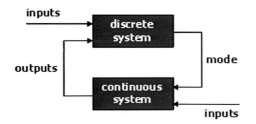

Figure 2.4:
Schematic of basic S-HDS feedback structure. The discrete and continuous systems in this framework model the adversary's selection of attack "mode" and resulting attack behavior respectively, which arise from the coevolving attacker—defender dynamics.

predictability of given dynamics to be assessed and the predictive measurables (if any) to be identified. Applying this predictability assessment process to the adversarial S-HDS models constructed in Ref. [7] reveals that, for many of these models, the most predictive measurable is the *mode* of attack; that is, the state variable for the discrete system component of the S-HDS (see Ref. [7] for a detailed description of this analysis). Observe that this result is intuitively sensible.

This analytic finding suggests the following *synthetic data learning* (SDL) approach to proactive defense: First, identify the mode(s) of attack of interest. For attacks that are already under way, Ref. [7] offers an S-HDS discrete-system state estimation method that allows the mode to be inferred using only modest amounts of measured data. Alternatively, and of more interest in the present application, it is often possible to identify likely future attack modes through analysis of auxiliary information sources (e.g. the subject-matter knowledge possessed by domain experts or "non-cyber" data such as that found in social media [16−18]).

Once a candidate attack mode has been identified, synthetic attack data corresponding to the mode can be generated by employing one of the S-HDS models derived in Ref. [7]. The synthetic data take the form of a set of K network attack instance vectors, denoted $A_S = \{x_{S1}, ..., x_{SK}\}$. The set A_S can then be combined with (actual) measurements of L normal network activity instances, $N_M = \{x_{NM1}, ..., x_{NML}\}$, and P (recently) observed attacks, $A_M = \{x_{M1}, ..., x_{MP}\}$, yielding the training dataset $TR = N_M \cup A_M \cup A_S$ of real and synthetic data. Note that one effective way to generate a set A_S of synthetic attacks is to use the S-HDS formalism to appropriately *transform* attack instances sampled from the observed attack set A_M, rather than to attempt to construct synthetic attacks "from scratch." It is hypothesized that training classifiers with dataset TR may offer a mechanism for deriving defenses that are effective against both current and near-future malicious activity.

We summarize the above discussion by sketching a procedure for constructing the proposed SDL classifier:

Algorithm SDL (Synthetic Data Learning)

1. Identify the mode(s) of attack of interest (e.g. via domain experts or auxiliary data).
2. Assemble sets of measured normal network activity N_M and measured attack activity A_M for the network under study.
3. Generate a set of synthetic attack instances A_S corresponding to the attack mode(s) identified in step 1 (for instance by transforming attacks in A_M).
4. Train a classifier (e.g. RLS, NB) using the training data $TR = N_M \cup A_M \cup A_S$. Estimate the class label (innocent or malicious) of any new network activity x with the classifier trained using data TR.

Algorithm evaluation

We now examine the performance of Algorithm SDL for the problem of distinguishing legitimate and spam emails in the Ling-Spam dataset [13], a corpus of 2412 non-spam emails collected from a linguistics mailing list and 481 spam emails received by the list. After data cleaning and random subsampling of the non-spam messages we are left with 468 spam and 526 non-spam messages for training and testing purposes; this set of 994 emails will be referred to as the *nominal spam* corpus (note that all emails were preprocessed using the *ifile* tool [19]).

We considered three scenarios in this study:

1. NB classifier/nominal spam: For each of 10 runs, the nominal spam corpus was randomly divided into equal-sized training and testing sets and the class label for each message in the test set was estimated with a naïve Bayes (NB) algorithm [11] learned on the training set.
2. NB classifier/nominal plus attack spam: For each of 10 runs, the nominal spam corpus was randomly divided into equal-sized training and testing sets and the test set was then augmented with 263 additional non-spam messages (taken from the Ling-Spam dataset) and 234 spam messages generated via a standard add-word (AW) attack methodology [15]; the class labels for the test messages were estimated with an NB algorithm [11] learned on the nominal spam training set.
3. Algorithm SDL/nominal plus attack spam: For each of 10 runs, the training and test corpora were constructed exactly as in Scenario 2 and the class labels for the test messages were estimated with Algorithm SDL.

In generating the AW attacks in Scenarios 2 and 3, we assume that the attacker knows to construct AW spam to defeat an NB filter but does not have knowledge of the specific filter involved [15]. The synthetic AW attacks generated in Scenario 3 (using step 3 of Algorithm SDL) are computed with no knowledge of the attacker's methodology beyond the mode of attack (i.e. AW).

Sample results from this study are displayed in Figure 2.5. In each case the "confusion matrix" [8] reports the (rounded) average performance over the 10 runs. It can be seen that, as expected, the NB filter does well against the nominal spam but poorly against the AW spam (in fact, the NB filter does not detect a single instance of AW spam). In contrast, Algorithm SDL performs well against both nominal spam and AW spam, achieving ~96% classification accuracy with a low false-positive rate. It is emphasized that this result is obtained using only the (synthetic) estimate of AW spam generated in step 3 of Algorithm SDL.

2.3 Early Warning

In this section we develop an early warning capability for an important class of computer network attacks and illustrate its potential through a case study involving politically motivated *DoS* attacks.

NB Algorithm: Nominal Spam		
class\truth	non-Spam	Spam
non-Spam	262	19
Spam	1	215

NB Algorithm: Nominal and Attack Spam		
class\truth	non-Spam	Spam
non-Spam	524	253
Spam	2	215

Algorithm SDL: Nominal and Attack Spam		
class\truth	non-Spam	Spam
non-Spam	524	40
Spam	2	428

Figure 2.5:

Performance of Algorithm SDL on spam dataset. Each confusion matrix shows number of non-spam messages classified as non-spam and spam (left column) and number of spam messages classified as non-spam and spam (right column). The three matrices, from top to bottom, report the results for: NB against nominal spam, NB against spam that contains add-word attacks, and Algorithm SDL against spam that contains add-word attacks.

2.3.1 Preliminaries

Computer network attacks take many forms, including system compromises, information theft, and denial-of-service attacks intended to disrupt services. In what follows we focus on deriving an early warning capability for distributed denial-of- service (DDoS) attacks; that is, coordinated efforts in which computers are instructed to flood a victim with traffic designed to overwhelm services or consume bandwidth. In particular, we concentrate on politically motivated DDoS attacks, for three main reasons: (1) this class of attacks is an important and growing threat [17], (2) this class is representative of other threats of interest, and (3) it is expected that in the case of politically motivated attacks the coordination among attackers may take place, in part, via social media, thereby enabling an analysis employing only publicly available data.

Consider the task of detecting social media signatures associated with attackers coordinating a politically motivated DDoS. A classic example of the kind of attack of interest is the sequence of DDoS attacks that were launched against government and commercial sites in Estonia beginning in late April 2007. Interestingly, a retrospective study of these events reveals that there was significant planning and coordination among attackers through web forums and blogs prior to the actual attacks [17], supporting the hypothesis that it may be possible to detect early warning indicators in social media *in advance* of such attacks.

Of course, detecting early warning indicators of an impending DDoS attack in social media is a daunting undertaking. Challenges associated with this task include the vast volume of discussions taking place online, the need to distinguish credible threats from irrelevant chatter, and the necessity to identify reliable attack indicators early enough to be useful (e.g. at least a few days in advance of the attack). Recently we have developed a general framework within which to study this class of early warning problem [14,18,20]. The basic premise is that generating useful predictions about social processes, such as the planning and coordination of a DDoS event, requires careful consideration of the way individuals interact through their social networks. The proposed warning methodology therefore exploits information about social network interactions to forecast which nascent online discussions will ultimately lead to real-world attack events and which will fade into obscurity. Interestingly, the features found to possess exploitable predictive power turn out to be subtle measures of the network dynamics associated with the evolution of early attack-related discussions [14,18,20].

We now briefly summarize the early warning framework presented in Refs [14,18,20] and its application to the DDoS warning problem, and then illustrate the implementation and performance of the warning method through a case study involving politically motivated Internet attacks.

2.3.2 Early Warning Method

In social dynamics, individuals are often affected by what others do. As a consequence, social phenomena can depend upon the topological features of the underlying social network, for instance the degree distribution or presence of small world structure, and aspects of this dependence have been characterized (see Ref. [21] for a recent review). We show in Refs [14,18,20] that, for a wide range of social phenomena, useful prediction requires consideration of the way the behavior of individuals interacts with *social network communities*; that is, densely connected groupings of individuals that have only relatively few links to other groups. The concept of network community structure is illustrated in Figure 2.6 and is defined more carefully below. This dependence suggests that in order to derive useful early warning methods for social phenomena, one should consider the topology of the underlying social network; however, standard prediction algorithms do not include such features.

While community structure is widely appreciated to be an important topological property in real-world social networks, there is not a similar consensus regarding qualitative or quantitative definitions for this concept. Here we adopt the modularity-based definition proposed in Ref. [23], whereby a good partitioning of a network's vertices into communities

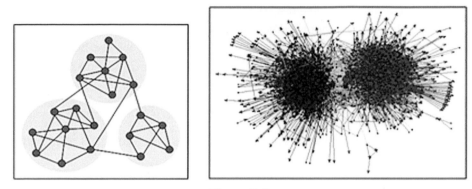

Figure 2.6:
Network community structure. Diagram on the left depicts a network with three communities; graph on the right is a network of political blogs in which community of liberal blogs (left cluster) and community of conservative blogs (right cluster) are clearly visible [22].

is one for which the number of edges between putative communities is smaller than would be expected in a random partitioning. To be concrete, a modularity-based partitioning of a network into two communities maximizes the modularity Q, defined as

$$Q = s^T B s / 4m \tag{2.5}$$

where m is the total number of edges in the network, the partition is specified with the elements of vector s by setting $s_i = 1$ if vertex i belongs to community 1, and $s_i = -1$ if it belongs to community 2, and matrix B has elements $B_{ij} = A_{ij} - k_i k_j / 2m$, with A_{ij} and k_i denoting the network adjacency matrix and degree of vertex i respectively. Partitions of the network into more than two communities can be constructed recursively [23]. Note that modularity-based community partitions can be efficiently computed for large social networks and require only network topology data for their construction.

Despite the fact that community structure is ubiquitous in real social networks, little has been done to incorporate considerations of communities into social prediction methods. In Refs [14,18,20] we present theoretical and empirical evidence that the predictability of social dynamics often depends crucially upon network community structure. More specifically, we show that early dispersion of a social dynamics "activity" across network communities is a reliable early indicator that the ultimate extent of the activity will be significant. (Perhaps surprisingly, this measure is more predictive than the early magnitude of the activity.)

In the context of early warning for politically motivated cyber attacks, the social activity of interest is communication associated with planning and coordinating the attack. Thus, it is of interest to collect data that enable quantification of the extent to which early communications of this type are dispersed across network communities. Such data should therefore include social network information sufficient to allow the identification of network communities as well as the detection of attack-related discussions among individuals in the network. One way to address this challenge is to adopt *online* social activity as a proxy for real-world attack-related discussion and information exchange. More specifically, we use blog posts as our primary dataset. The blog network is modeled as a graph in which the vertices are blogs and the edges represent links between blogs, with two blogs being linked if a post in one hyperlinks to a post in the other. Among other things, this blog graph model enables the identification of blog communities: These are the groups of blogs corresponding to the blog graph partition that maximizes the modularity Q for the graph (see (2.5)); these groups of blogs serve as our proxy for social network communities.

We are now in a position to specify an early warning algorithm for politically motivated DDoS attacks. The algorithm operationalizes the "early dispersion of attack-related discussions" indicator, computing a measure of the magnitude of this dispersion and issuing an alert if and only if the dispersion is "large."

Algorithm EW (Early Warning):

Initialization: Identify a (large) set of cyber security-relevant blogs and forums **B** to be continually monitored; **B** should include sites contributed to and frequented by both attackers (e.g. hacker forums) and defenders (e.g. security blogs).

Procedure:

1. Perform *meme detection* with the blogs in **B** to identify all "memes" that are potentially related to politically motivated DDoS attacks. Characterize the discussion topic(s) associated with each meme.
2. Conduct a sequence of blog graph crawls and construct a time series of blog graphs $G_B(t)$. For each meme/topic M of interest and each time period t, label the blogs in $G_B(t)$ as "active" if they contain a post containing M and "inactive" otherwise.
3. Form the union $G_B = \cup_t G_B(t)$, partition G_B into network communities, and map the communities structure of G_B back to each of the graphs $G_B(t)$.
4. Compute the post volume time series and the post/community entropy (*PCE*) time series for each meme/topic.
5. Construct a synthetic ensemble of *PCE* time series from the post volume dynamics for each meme/topic.
6. Compare the actual *PCE* time series to the synthetic ensemble series for each meme/topic M to determine if the observed early dispersion of activity across communities is "large" for topic M.

We now offer additional details concerning this procedure; a more comprehensive discussion of the methodology is provided in Ref. [7]. Step 1 is performed using the algorithm described in Refs [20,24]. Observe that "memes" in this context are distinctive phrases that propagate relatively unchanged online and act as "tracers" for topics of discussion. It is shown in Refs [20,24] that detecting memes in social media is a useful and general way to discover emerging topics and trends, and we demonstrate in Ref. [7] that meme analysis allows the detection of discussions concerning the planning and coordination of politically motivated DDoS within a day or two of the initiation of these discussions.

Step 2 is by now standard, and various tools exist that can perform these tasks [25]. In step 3, blog network communities are identified with a modularity-based community extraction algorithm applied to the blog graph [23]. In step 4, the post volume for a given meme/topic M, community i, and sampling interval t is obtained by counting the number of posts containing M made to the blogs comprising community i during interval t. PCE for a particular meme/topic M and sampling interval t is defined as follows:

$$PCE_M\left(t\right) = -\sum_i f_{M,i}\left(t\right) \log\left(f_{M,i}\left(t\right)\right) \tag{2.6}$$

where $f_{M,i}(t)$ is the fraction of total posts containing M and is made during interval t, which occurs in community i. Given the post volume time series obtained in step 4, step 5 involves construction of an ensemble of *PCE* time series that would be expected under "normal circumstances"; that is, if meme M propagated from a small seed set of initiators according to standard models of social diffusion [18,20]. Observe that this step enables us to quantify the expected dispersion for $PCE_M(t)$, so that we can recognize "large" dispersion. Step 6 is carried out by searching for memes M and time periods t during which $PCE_M(t)$ exceeds the mean of the synthetic *PCE* ensemble by a user-defined threshold (e.g. two standard deviations).

2.3.3 Case Study: Politically Motivated DDoS

This subsection reports the results of a case study aimed at exploring the ability of Algorithm EW to provide reliable early warning for DDoS attacks. Toward this end, we first identified a set of Internet "disturbances" that included examples from three distinct classes of events:

1. Successful politically motivated DDoS attacks — these are the events for which Algorithm EW is intended to provide warning with sufficient lead time to allow mitigating actions to be taken.
2. Natural events that disrupt Internet service — these are disturbances, such as earthquakes and electric power outages, that impact the Internet but for which it is known that no early warning signal exists in social media.
3. Quiet periods — these are periods during which there is social media "chatter" concerning impending DDoS attacks but ultimately no (successful) attacks occurred.

Including events selected from these three classes in the case study is intended to provide a fairly comprehensive test of Algorithm EW. For instance, these classes correspond to (1) the domain of interest (DDoS attacks), (2) a set of disruptions that impact the Internet but have no social media warning signal, and (3) a set of "non-events" that do not impact the Internet but do possess putative social media warning signals (discussion of DDoS attacks).

We selected 20 events from these three classes:

Politically motivated DDoS attacks

- Estonia event in April 2007
- CNN/China incident in April 2008
- Israel/Palestine conflict event in January 2009
- DDoS associated with Iranian elections in June 2009
- WikiLeaks event in November 2010
- Anonymous v. PayPal, etc. attack in December 2010
- Anonymous v. HBGary attack in February 2011.

Natural disturbances

- European power outage in November 2006
- Taiwan earthquake in December 2006
- Hurricane Ike in September 2008
- Mediterranean cable cut in January 2009
- Taiwan earthquake in March 2010
- Japan earthquake in March 2011.

Quiet periods

Seven periods, from March 2005 through March 2011, during which there were discussions in social media of DDoS attacks on various US government agencies but no (successful) attacks occurred.

For brevity, a detailed discussion of these 20 events is not given here; the interested reader is referred to Ref. [7] for additional information on these disruptions.

We collected two forms of data for each of the 20 events: *cyber data* and *social data*. The cyber data consist of time series of routing updates that were issued by Internet routers during a one-month period surrounding each event. More precisely, these data are the Border Gateway Protocol (BGP) routing updates exchanged between gateway hosts in the Autonomous System network of the Internet. The data were downloaded from the publicly accessible RIPE collection site [26] using the process described in Ref. [27] (see Ref. [27] for additional details and background information on BGP routing dynamics). The temporal evolution of the volume of BGP routing updates (e.g. withdrawal messages) gives a coarse-grained measure of the timing and magnitude of large Internet disruptions and thus offers a simple and objective way to characterize the impact of each of the events in our collection. The social data consist of time series of social media mentions of cyber-related memes

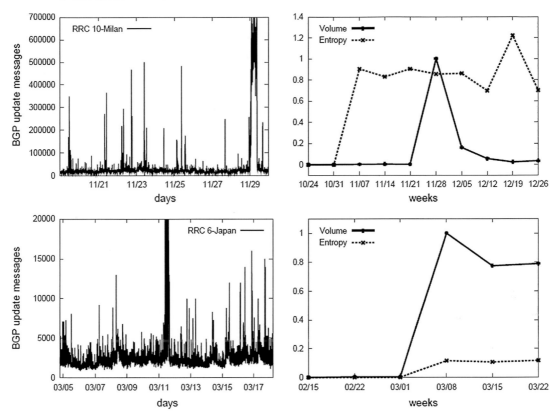

Figure 2.7:

Sample results for the DDoS early warning case study. The illustrative time series plots shown correspond to the WikiLeaks event in November 2010 (top row) and the Japan earthquake in March 2011 (bottom row). For each event, the plot at left is the time series of BGP routing update message counts (note the large increase in updates triggered by the event). The plot on the right of each row is the time series of the social media data, with the solid curve showing blog post volume and the dashed curve depicting blog entropy (in each case, the time series shown are for the meme with largest total volume). Note that while post volume is scaled for convenient visualization, the scale for entropy is consistent across plots to allow cross-event comparison.

detected during a one-month period surrounding each of the 20 events. These data were collected using the procedure specified in Algorithm EW.

Illustrative time series plots corresponding to two events in the case study, the WikiLeaks DDoS attack in November 2010 and Japan earthquake in March 2011, are shown in Figure 2.7. Observe that the time series of BGP routing updates are similar for the two events, with each experiencing a large "spike" at the time of the event. The time series of blog post volume are also similar across the two events, with each showing modest volume prior to the event and displaying a large spike in activity at event time. However, the time series for blog entropy are quite distinct for the two events. Specifically, in the case of the WikiLeaks DDoS the blog entropy (dashed curve in Figure 2.7) experiences a dramatic increase several days before the event (and leads post volume), while in the case of the Japan earthquake blog entropy is small for the entire collection period (and lags post volume). Similar social media behavior is observed for all events in the case study, suggesting that: (1) early dispersion of discussions across blog network communities may be a useful early warning indicator for politically motivated DDoS attacks, and (2) the post volume associated with these discussions does not appear to be a useful early indicator for these attacks.

To investigate this possibility more carefully, we evaluated the predictive performance of two candidate early warning signals on the 20 events in our test set: (1) the "early dispersion" *PCE* indicator computed in Algorithm EW, and (2) a simple volume-based indicator, in which the presence or absence of significant post volume is used as a signal that a DDoS attack is imminent. We found that the *PCE* indicator performed well, correctly classifying all 20 events (seven attacks and 13 non-attacks) and providing an average lead time of 16 days for attack warning. In contrast, blog volume was not found to be useful for early warning, exhibiting essentially identical behavior for DDoS attacks and natural disturbances and spiking slightly *after* the occurrence of the disruption for all events.

2.4 Concluding Remarks

This chapter considers the problem of protecting computer networks against intrusions and other disruptions in a proactive manner. We begin by deriving two new proactive filter-based methods for network defense: (1) a bipartite graph-based transfer learning algorithm that enables information concerning previous attacks to be transferred for application against novel attacks, thereby substantially increasing the rate with which defense systems can successfully respond to new attacks, and (2) a synthetic data learning method that exploits basic threat information to generate attack data for use in learning appropriate defense actions, resulting in network defenses that are effective against both current and (near) future attacks. The utility of these two filter-based methods is demonstrated by showing that they outperform standard techniques for the task of detecting malicious network activity in two publicly available cyber datasets. We then present an early warning method as a solution to the problem of anticipating and characterizing impending attack events with sufficient specificity and timeliness to enable mitigating defensive actions to be taken. The warning method is based upon the fact that certain classes of attacks require the attackers to coordinate their actions, and exploits signatures of this coordination to provide effective attack warning. The potential of the warning-based approach to cyber defense is illustrated through a case study involving politically motivated Internet attacks.

Future work will include application of the proposed proactive defense methods to additional threats, including non-cyber threats that involve attacker—defender coevolution (e.g. counterterrorism), as well as the development of new proactive defense strategies. As an example of one approach toward the latter goal, we have recently shown that adversary activity can be accurately predicted and countered in certain settings by appropriately combining data analysis methods (e.g. machine learning) with behavioral models for adversarial dynamics (e.g. incremental game models) [28].

Acknowledgments

This work was supported by the Laboratory Directed Research and Development Program at Sandia National Laboratories. We thank Chip Willard of the US Department of Defense for numerous helpful discussions on aspects of this research.

References

[1] S. Byers, S. Yang, Real-time fusion and projection of network intrusion activity, Proc. ISIF/IEEE International Conference on Information Fusion, Cologne, Germany, July 2008.

[2] R. Armstrong, J. Mayo, F. Siebenlist, Complexity science challenges in cybersecurity, Sandia National Laboratories SAND Report (March 2009).

[3] R. Colbaugh, Does coevolution in malware adaptation enable predictive analysis? IFA Workshop, Exploring Malware Adaptation Patterns, San Francisco, CA, May 2010.

[4] Y. Mashevsky, Y. Namestnikov, N. Denishchenko, P. Zelensky, Method and system for detection and prediction of computer virus-related epidemics, US Patent 7,743,419 (June 2010).

[5] M. Bozorgi, L. Saul, S. Savage, G. Voelker, Beyond heuristics: Learning to classify vulnerabilities and predict exploits, Proc. ACM International Conference on Knowledge Discovery and Data Mining, Washington, DC, July 2010.

[6] R. Majumdar, P. Tabuada, Hybrid Systems: Computation and Control, LNCS 5469, Springer, Berlin, 2009.

[7] R. Colbaugh, K. Glass, Proactive defense for evolving cyber threats, Sandia National Laboratories SAND Report (September 2011).

[8] T. Hastie, R. Tibshirani, J. Friedman, The Elements of Statistical Learning, second ed. Springer, New York, 2009.

[9] S. Pan, Q. Yang, A survey on transfer learning, IEEE Trans. Knowl. Data Eng. 22 (2010) 1345—1359.

[10] <http://kdd.ics.uci.edu/databases/kddcup99/>, last accessed December 2010.

[11] <http://www.borgelt.net/bayes.html>, last accessed July 2010.

[12] J. He, Y. Liu, R. Lawrence, Graph-based transfer learning, Proc. ACM Conference on Information and Knowledge Management, Hong Kong, November 2009.

[13] <http://labs-repos.iit.demokritos.gr/skel/i-config/downloads/>, last accessed July 2010.

[14] R. Colbaugh, K. Glass, Predictive analysis for social processes I: Multi- scale hybrid system modeling, and II: Predictability and warning analysis, Proc. IEEE International Multi-Conference on Systems and Control, St Petersburg, Russia, July 2009.

[15] D. Lowd, C. Meeks, Good word attacks on statistical Spam filters, Proc. 2005 Conference on Email and Anti-Spam, Palo Alto, CA, July 2005.

[16] L. Cao, P. Yu, C. Zhang, H. Zhang, F. Tsai, K. Chan, Blog data mining for cyber security threats, in: Data Mining for Business Applications, Springer US, 2009.

[17] J. Nazario, Politically motivated denial of service attacks, in: The Virtual Battlefield: Perspectives on Cyber Warfare, IOS Press, Amsterdam, 2009.

[18] R. Colbaugh, K. Glass, Early warning analysis for social diffusion events, Proc. IEEE International Conference on Intelligence and Security Informatics, Vancouver, Canada, May 2010.

[19] <http://www.nongnu.org/ifile/>, last accessed July 2010.

[20] R. Colbaugh, K. Glass, Emerging topic detection for business intelligence via predictive analysis of 'meme' dynamics, Proc. AAAI 2011 Spring Symposium, Palo Alto, CA, March 2011.

[21] D. Easley, J. Kleinberg, Networks Crowds, and Markets: Reasoning About a Highly Connected World, Cambridge University Press, New York, 2010.

[22] L. Adamic, N. Glance, The political blogosphere and the 2004 U.S. election: Divided they blog, Proc. ACM International Conference on Knowledge Discovery and Data Mining, Chicago, August 2005.

[23] M. Newman, Modularity and community structure in networks, Proc. Natl. Acad. Sci. U.S.A. 103 (23) (2006) 8577–8582.

[24] J. Leskovec, L. Backstrom, J. Kleinberg, Meme-tracking and the dynamics of the news cycle, Proc. ACM International Conference on Knowledge Discovery and Data Mining, Paris, France, June 2009.

[25] K. Glass, R. Colbaugh, Web analytics for security informatics, Proc. European Intelligence and Security Informatics Conference, Athens, Greece, September 2011.

[26] <http://data.ris.ripe.net/>, last accessed July 2011.

[27] K. Glass, R. Colbaugh, M. Planck, Automatically identifying the sources of large Internet events, Proc. IEEE International Conference on Intelligence and Security Informatics, Vancouver, Canada, May 2010.

[28] R. Colbaugh, Monsoons, movies, memes, and genes: Combining KD and M&S for prediction, Keynote Talk, KDMS Workshop, ACM International Conference on Knowledge Discovery and Data Mining, San Diego, CA, August 2011.

CHAPTER 3

Privacy-Preserving Social Network Integration, Analysis, and Mining

Christopher C. Yang

Drexel University, Philadelphia, Pennsylvania, USA

Chapter Outline

3.1 Social Network Analysis and Mining

A *social network* is a network of people or other social entities with the edges corresponding to their relationships or associations. A social network is represented as a graph, $G = (V, E)$, in which V is a set of nodes corresponding to people and E is a set of edges ($E \subseteq V \times V$) corresponding to the relationships of the respective people.

Social network analysis and mining (SNAM) has received significant attention in recent years. With the proliferation of online communities and e-commerce services, a large number of social networks can be easily collected in various online settings. For example, a systematic crawling of weblogs on the Internet can identify the interactions of bloggers and different types of relationships, such as friends, subscribers, and ring blog [1]. These social networks are valuable in various application domains, such as marketing, management, sociology, psychology, homeland security, and epidemiology.

Intelligent Systems for Security Informatics.
http://dx.doi.org/10.1016/B978-0-12-404702-0.00003-3

Many social network analysis and mining techniques have been investigated in the literature. Centrality measures and similarity measures are two popular measurements in SNAM. In general, centrality measures determine the relative significance of a node in a social network. Similarity measures compute the similarity between two subgroups within a social network. In centrality measures, degree centrality, closeness centrality, and betweenness centrality are the typical measures. L1-Norm, L2-Norm, mutual information, and clustering coefficient are some common similarity measures.

Recent developments in link mining [2] of social networks focus on object ranking [3−5], object classification [6−8], group detection [9−13], entity resolution [14,15], link prediction [16−19], subgraph discovery [20,21], and graph generative models [22,23]. Some recent applications of SNAM in epidemiology, expert identification, criminal/terrorist social network, academic social network and social network visualization are found in the literature. For example, several models of social networks have been applied in epidemiology [24]. Expert identification [25] develops mechanisms to identify experts in social networks and route queries to the identified experts. Criminal/terrorist social networks [1,26−28] aim to identify the roles of terrorists and criminals by mining the patterns in a social network. Academic social networks [29] model topical aspects of publications, authors and publication venues, and provide a search service of experts and their associations. Co-authorship and co-citation networks are typical networks in this study [30]. Social network visualization [31,32] provides network visualization techniques to analyze the dynamic interactions of individuals in a network.

3.2 Privacy Preservation

As discussed above, many SNAM techniques and applications have been developed. At the same time, there are increasing amounts of social network data for collection in many online settings. It is a good opportunity for harvesting the knowledge from different kinds of social networks since the techniques are becoming more mature and the available data are enormous. On the other hand, there is increasing concern about *privacy preservation* due to the dynamic growth of activities in SNAM. Online users of virtual communities, members of organizations or subscribers of public services may not be aware of their private information being published or shared with other unfamiliar parties. Such concern has motivated a number of research works devoted to privacy preservation of relational data (data represented in a tabular format) in the recent years but there is still a relatively limited amount of work focusing on privacy preservation of social network data.

3.2.1 Privacy Preservation of Relational Data

A number of approaches for *privacy preservation of relational data* have been developed, including *k-anonymity* [33], *l-diversity* [34], *t-closeness* [35], *m-invariance*

[36], δ-*presence* [37], and *k-support anonymity* [38]. Privacy preservation is important in data publishing. The objective is publishing an anonymized version of relational data owned by an organization to the public while the identity of individuals cannot be determined so that no one can recognize the sensitive attribute values of a particular record. Other enhanced techniques of *k*-anonymity and *l*-diversity with personalization, such as personalized anonymity [39] and (α,k)-anonymity [40], allow users to specify the degree of privacy protection or specify a threshold α on the relative frequency of the sensitive data. Versatile publishing [41] anonymizes subtables to guarantee privacy rules.

Privacy preservation of relational data has also been applied in statistical databases. *Query restriction* [42], *output perturbation* [43−45], and *data modification* [39,46,47] are three major approaches. *Query restriction* [41] rejects certain queries when a leak of sensitive values is possible by combining the results of previous queries. *Output perturbation* [43−45] adds noise to the result of a query to produce a perturbed version. *Data modification* [39,46,47] prepares an adequately anonymized version of relational data to a query. The *cryptography approach* of privacy preservation of relational data aims to develop a protocol of data exchange between multiple private parties. It attempts to minimize the information revealed by each party. For example, top-*k* search [48] reports the top-*k* tuples in the union of the data in several parties.

3.2.2 Privacy Preservation of Social Network Data

Current research on privacy preservation of social network data (or graphs) focuses on the purpose of data publishing. A naïve approach removes the identities of all nodes and only reveals the edges of a social network. In this case, the global network properties are preserved for other research applications assuming that the identities of nodes are not of interest in the research applications. However, Backstrom et al. [49] proved that it is possible to discover whether edges between specific targeted pairs of nodes exist or not by active or passive attacks. In order to tackle active and passive attacks and preserve the privacy of node identities in a social network, there are several anonymization models proposed in the recent literature, such as *k*-candidate anonymity [50], *k*-degree anonymity [51], and *k*-anonymity [52]. Such anonymization models are proposed to increase the difficulty of being attacked based on the notion of *k*-anonymity in relational data. For example, *k*-anonymity [52] defines that, for every node v in a graph G, there are at least $k - 1$ other nodes in G, such that their anonymized neighborhoods are isomorphic.

The technique used to achieve the above anonymities is edge or node perturbation [50−52]. By adding and/or deleting edges and/or nodes, a perturbed graph is generated to satisfy the anonymity requirement. Adversaries can only have a confidence of $1/k$ to discover the identity of a node by neighborhood attacks.

Since the current research on privacy preservation of social network data focuses on preserving node identities in data publishing, the anonymized social network can only be used to study global network properties and may not be applicable to other SNAM tasks. In addition, the sets of nodes and edges in a perturbed social network are different from the set of nodes and edges in the original social network. As reported in Ref. [52], the number of edges added can be as high as 6% of the original number of edges in a social network. A recent study [53] has investigated how edge and node perturbation can change certain network properties. Such distortion may cause significant errors in certain SNAM tasks such as centrality measurement, although the global properties can be maintained. In this work, we not only preserve the identities of nodes, but also the social network structures (i.e. edges).

3.3 Information Integration and Privacy Preservation for SNAM

Although social network data are easy to aggregate through online settings or communications, these data are typically distributed and each organization or agent only knows a small piece of the complete network [54]. Using a small piece of data, the SNAM techniques are not able to extract the essential knowledge. In some cases, an inaccurate result will be obtained. For example, each law enforcement unit has its own criminal social network. Mining of an incomplete criminal social network may not be able to identify the link between two criminal subgroups. Unfortunately, due to limits imposed by policy on privacy, different organizations are only allowed to share a small piece of information but not their social networks. As a result, an accurate SNAM cannot be conducted unless integration of the social networks owned by different organizations can be achieved.

3.3.1 Research Problem Definition

Given two or more social networks $(G_1, G_2, \ldots)$ from different organizations $(O_1, O_2, \ldots)$, the objective is achieving *more* accurate social network analysis and mining results by integrating the shared crucial and insensitive information between these social networks whilst at the same time preserving the sensitive information with *a prescribed level of privacy leakage tolerance*. Each organization O_i has a piece of social network G_i, which is part of the whole picture — a social network G constructed by integrating all G_i. Conducting the SNAM task on G, one can obtain the exact SNAM result from the integrated information. However, conducting the SNAM task on any G_i, one can never achieve the exact SNAM result because of the missing information. By integrating G_i and some *generalized information* of G_j, O_i should be able to achieve more accurate SNAM results, although it is not the exact SNAM result. That means that if O_i can obtain generalized information from all other organizations, O_i will be able to obtain an SNAM result much closer to the exact SNAM result than that obtained from G_i alone.

In order to share information for integration and yet not invade individuals' privacy, generalized information that does not contain any private information can be released to another party. The generalized information is a probabilistic model of the general property of a social network. To determine how to generate this generalized information, one may decide what the crucial information for the designated SNAM task is. Not all information is useful for a particular SNAM task.

Since the generalized information is basically a probabilistic model of a social network, it requires some integration points to incorporate the generalized information from multiple social networks to analyze the integrated information. These integration points must be insensitive information to the parties involved in the process. When a particular piece of information is known to both parties, such information is not considered as sensitive to either party. However, other information that is related to such insensitive information is still considered sensitive. For example, when a patient is referred from a medical unit to another medical unit, the identity of this patient is insensitive to both medical units but the identities of other persons who are associated with this patient are sensitive. A piece of information can also be known to both parties when such information is available from a common source. For example, when a swine flu patient is reported to the public health authority, the identity of this patient is known to all medical units.

While sharing and integrating the generalized information for SNAM tasks, we must ensure that a specified tolerance of privacy leakage is satisfied. The measure of privacy leakage must be independent of the techniques used in generating and integrating generalized information of social networks. Privacy means that no party should be able to learn anything more than the insensitive information shared by other parties and the prescribed output of the SNAM tasks. If any adversary attack can be applied to learn any private and sensitive data, there is a privacy leakage. In this problem, the shared insensitive information is the generalized information and the identities of the insensitive nodes are the integration points. The prescribed outputs of the SNAM tasks are the centrality measures or similarity measures such as closeness centrality of a node. The adversary attack can be an active or passive attack. Active attacks refer to planting well-structured subgraphs in a social network and then discovering the links between targeted nodes by identifying the planted structures. Passive attacks refer to identifying a node by its association with neighbors and then identifying other nodes that are linked to this association. These attacks are also called neighborhood attacks.

The leakage of private information includes the identities of sensitive nodes and the adjacency (i.e. edges) of any two nodes regardless of whether any of these nodes are sensitive or insensitive. If any of the active or passive attacks can be applied to the generalized information or the output of the SNAM tasks to learn the above-mentioned private information, there is a privacy leakage. The definitions of tolerance of privacy leakage are given below:

Zero tolerance of privacy leakage:

- No exact identity of sensitive nodes can be identified.
- No adjacency between any two exact nodes can be identified.

τ-tolerance of privacy leakage on a sensitive node:

- The identity of a sensitive node cannot be identified as one of τ or fewer possible known identities.

τ-tolerance of privacy leakage on the adjacency between an insensitive node and a sensitive node:

- The identity of an insensitive node is known but its adjacency with other sensitive nodes is not known.
- The adjacent nodes cannot be identified as one of τ or fewer possible sensitive nodes.

$\tau_1\tau_2$-tolerance of privacy leakage on the adjacency between two sensitive nodes:

- The identity of a sensitive node A cannot be identified as one of τ_1 or fewer possible known identities.
- The adjacent node of this sensitive node A cannot be identified as one of τ_2 or fewer possible known identities.

Zero tolerance means no attack can discover the exact identity of a sensitive node or the adjacency between any two exact nodes. Most attacks cannot discover the exact identity or adjacency given a reasonable privacy preservation technique. However, many attacks are able to narrow down the identity to a few possible known identities. For example, the identity of a sensitive node is John. If an attack discovers the identity to be John, Peter or Mary, it satisfies the 3-tolerance of privacy leakage but not the 4-tolerance or higher. According to these definitions, the higher the value of τ, the tighter the control of privacy leakage.

Zero tolerance is the minimum requirement of any privacy preservation problem. No private information should be discovered. However, to ensure a higher standard to prevent privacy leakage, τ-tolerance is proposed and defined here. Not only can the exact identity of a sensitive node not be discovered, but also the identity cannot be identified as one out of τ or fewer possible identities. Ideally, a privacy-preserving technique should achieve ∞-tolerance, which means no attack can find a clue of the possible identity of a sensitive node. In reality, it is almost impossible to achieve ∞-tolerance due to the background knowledge possessed by adversaries. However, a good privacy-preserving technique should reduce privacy leakage as much as possible, which means achieving a higher value of τ in privacy leakage.

The generalized information in this problem is the probabilistic models of the generalized social networks instead of a perturbed model using the k-anonymity approach. As a result, the τ-tolerance of privacy leakage is independent of the generalization technique. In addition, it preserves both the identities and network structures. By integrating the probabilistic models of multiple generalized social networks, the objective is to achieve better performance of SNAM tasks. At the same time, neither the probabilistic models nor the SNAM results should release private information that may violate the prescribed τ-tolerance of privacy leakage when it is under adversary attacks.

In the previous section, we discussed the existing privacy-preservation techniques of social network data. However, it is not able to solve the problems defined here mainly because of the following limitations:

1. It preserves the identities of nodes in a social network but it does not preserve the network structure (i.e. edges) of a social network.
2. The anonymization approach prohibits the integration of social networks. This is because mapping between social networks cannot be conducted once all nodes of a social network are anonymized. The anonymization approach is useful when one wants to analyze the global network properties of a publicized social network.
3. The perturbation of a social network increases the difficulty of being attacked; however, the perturbation changes the connectivity of nodes and it can significantly distort the SNAM result.
4. The existing privacy preservation techniques have not considered the application of the social network in SNAM. The focus is to utilize the published data to analyze global network properties.

Another approach of privacy-preserving social network analysis related to our research problem is secure multi-party computation (SMC). SMC deals with the problem where a set of parties (P_1, P_2, ..., P_n) with private inputs (x_1, x_2, ..., x_n) wishes to jointly compute some functions of their inputs $f(x_1, x_2, ..., x_n)$. This problem was first proposed in Ref. [55]. If we consider the social networks of individual parties as private inputs and the social network analysis of the integrated social networks as a joint function, the privacy-preserving social network analysis problem can be regarded as a special case of SMC [56]. SMC uses cryptography technology to compute the joint function by taking the encrypted private data as inputs. The key is constructing protocols based on the private input data and the joint function for computation. For example, Brickell and Shmatikov [57] developed the protocols to compute the union set of nodes from multiple social networks and the shortest distances between all pairs of nodes in the combined social network. Frikken and Golle [54] developed a protocol to reconstruct the combined graph but anonymize the nodes and edges. Kerschbaum and Schaad [58] proposed the protocols to compute the closeness and betweenness centralities requiring the parties to agree on a set of nodes. Sakuma and

Kobayashi [59] developed a protocol for computing the ranking algorithms. The advantage of the SMC approach is in using encryption to protect the private data and yet compute the output of the joint function accurately. On the other hand, there are also concerns raised in this approach:

1. The encrypted private data are shared with other parties. There is a risk that the encrypted data are under attack by the malicious party and the private data will be recovered. In our problem, only generalized information is shared and ensured to reach a prescribed tolerance of privacy leakage.
2. The safety of the joint function outputs is usually beyond the scope of SMC. As a result, privacy leakage in the SMC approach has not been investigated.
3. The complexity of SMC is high. It may be computationally infeasible when the input social network data are very large.

3.3.2 A Framework of Integrating Social Networks

We propose the framework of information sharing and privacy preservation for integrating social networks shown in Figure 3.1.

Assuming organization P (O_P) and organization Q (O_Q) have social networks G_P and G_Q respectively, O_P needs to conduct an SNAM task but G_P is only a partial social network for

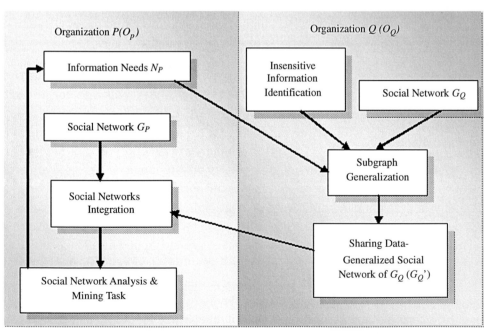

Figure 3.1:
A framework of information sharing and privacy preservation for integrating social networks.

the SNAM task. If there are no privacy concerns, one can integrate G_P and G_Q to generate an integrated G and obtain a better SNAM result. Due to privacy concerns, O_Q cannot release G_Q to O_P but only shares the generalized information of G_Q to O_P. At the same time, O_P does not need all data from O_Q but only those that are critical for the SNAM task. The objectives are to maximize the information sharing that is useful for the SNAM task but to preserve the sensitive information to satisfy the prescribed τ-tolerance of privacy leakage and achieve more accurate SNAM results.

Information sharing

In our framework presented in Figure 3.1, we propose that the information shared between two parties should be based upon the information needs to satisfy the SNAM task, the identification of insensitive information between the two parties, and the information available in the social network. When we perform social network data sharing, we need to consider what kind of information has the highest utility to accomplish a particular SNAM task. We need to determine the insensitive data to be shared and served as the integration points between two social networks so that the generalized information can be integrated.

In k-anonymity privacy-preservation techniques, all identities are assumed to be sensitive but the network structure is insensitive and is published for studying the global network properties. In our research problem, both identities and network structures are considered sensitive but only generalized information is shared. However, we also consider a small number of identities that are insensitive. The identities of these nodes are known to the public or insensitive to both organizations who are sharing the information. For instance, when a patient u is referred from a medical unit O_p to another medical unit O_q, which may be a specialist unit, the identity of u is no longer sensitive to O_p or O_q. However, the acquaintances of u that are known by O_p are still sensitive and their identities cannot be released to O_q. If the identity of patient u has been made available in a common source of O_p and O_q, then it is not sensitive to either O_p or O_q. This common source can be a data source. We define the sensitivity of an identity u between two organizations O_p and O_q as *sensitivity* (u, O_p, O_q):

$$Sensitivity\,(u,\ O_p,\ O_q) = \begin{cases} 0 \text{ if } Refer_{O_p}(u,\ O_q) = 1,\ Refer_{O_q}(u,\ O_p) = 1,\ \text{or } Source_{O_pO_q}(u) = 1 \\ 1 \text{ else} \end{cases}$$

where

$$Refer_x(u,\ y)\ =\ 1 \text{ when } x \text{ makes a referral of } u \text{ to } y \text{ and}$$

$$Source_{x,y}(u)\ =\ 1 \text{ when } u \text{ can be obtained from a common source of } x \text{ and } y.$$

Table 3.1: Examples of Attributes for Generalization

The number of nodes in a social network or a subgroup of a social network
The length of the shortest path in a social network or a subgroup of a social network
The degree of the nodes in a social network or a subgroup of a social network
The number of shortest paths going through an insensitive node between any two nodes in a social network or a subgroup of a social network
The length of the shortest path between two insensitive nodes
The number of the shortest paths between two insensitive nodes
The degree of the insensitive nodes
The eccentricity/k-centricity of the insensitive nodes in a social network or a subgraph of a social graph
The radius/diameter of a social network or a subgraph of a social graph
The center/peripheral/median of a social network or a subgraph of a social graph if it is an (or they are) insensitive node(s)

When information is shared with another organization, some sensitive information must be preserved but the generalized information can be released so that a more accurate estimation of the required information for centrality measures can be obtained. Table 3.1 presents some examples of attributes for generalization.

Subgraph generalization

Given the data that are available to share, we propose the subgraph generalization approach to create a generalized social network G'_Q for distribution to O_P. A subgraph generalization creates a generalized version of a social network, in which a connected subgraph is transformed as a generalized node and only generalized information will be presented in the generalized node. The generalized information is the probabilistic model of the attributes presented in Table 3.1. The edge that links from other nodes in the network to any nodes of the subgraph will be connected to the generalized node. The generalized social network protects all sensitive information while releasing the crucial and nonsensitive information to the information requesting party for social network integration and the intended SNAM task. A mechanism is needed to (i) identify the subgraphs for generalization, (ii) determine the connectivity between the set of generalized nodes in the generalized social network, and (iii) construct the generalized information to be shared.

A subgraph of $G = (V, E)$ is denoted as $G' = (V', E')$ where $V' \subset V, E' \subset E, E' \subseteq V' \times V'$. G' is a connected subgraph if there is a path for each pair of nodes in G'. We only consider connected subgraph when we conduct subgraph generalization.

To construct a subgraph for generalization, there are a few alternatives, including *n-neighborhood*, *k-connectivity*, and *edge-betweenness*:

- **n-neighborhood:** For a node $v \in G$, the ith neighbor of v is $N_i(v) = \{u \in G : d(u,v) = i\}$, where $d(u,v)$ is the distance between u and v. Given a target node, v can be an insensitive node, and the n-neighborhood graph of v is denoted as $n\text{-}Neighbor(v, G)$. $n\text{-}Neighbor$ $(v, G) = (V^i, E^i)$, where $V^i = \{u \in G: d(u,v) \leq n\}$ and $E^i \subset E$, $E^i \subseteq V^i \times V^i$.

- **k-connectivity:** The connectivity $\kappa(G)$ of a graph G is the minimum number of nodes whose removal results in a disconnected graph. The edge connectivity $\kappa'(G)$ of a graph G is the minimum number of edges whose removal results in a disconnected graph. A graph is k-connected if $\kappa(G) \geq k$ and it is k-edge connected if $\kappa'(G) \geq k$. If a graph is k-edge connected, two or more connected subgraphs (components) that are disconnected from each other are created after removing the k edges. Subgraphs can further be generated if the subgraphs being created are also k-edge connected.

- **Edge-betweenness:** The betweenness of an edge is defined as the number of shortest paths between any pairs of nodes in a graph G that pass through it. By sorting the descending order of the betweenness of edges in G, one can remove the edges starting from the ones with the highest betweenness until a predefined number of subgraphs are created. The constructed subgraphs must be mutually exclusive and exhaustive. A node v can only be part of a subgraph but not any other subgraphs. The union of nodes from all subgraphs V'_1, V'_2, ..., V'_n should be equal to V, the original set of nodes in G.

Connectivity of generalized nodes

After subgraphs construction, we convert each subgraph as a generalized node. For each generalized node, we provide the generalized information of the generalized node. The edges between the generalized nodes are retained. However, these edges only correspond to the adjacencies between the generalized nodes but do not release the identity of the nodes in the generalized nodes that produce the adjacency. As a result, it does not directly cause any privacy leakage. Nevertheless, combining such information with other generalized information, an attack can be made to discover sensitive information and thus the development of the subgraph construction techniques must take the prescribed tolerance of privacy leakage into consideration.

Generalized information — probabilistic model

For each generalized node $v'_j \in V'_j$, we determine the generalized information to be shared. The generalized information should achieve the following objectives: (i) be useful for the SNAM task after integration, (ii) preserve the sensitive information, and (iii) be minimal so that unnecessary information is not released. For example, in some SNAM tasks, the distance between nodes is important for its computation. The generalized information of V'_i can be the probabilistic model of the distance between any two nodes v_j and v_k in V'_i, $P(Distance(v_j, v_j) = d)$, $v_j, v_k \in V'_i$.

The construction of subgraphs plays an important role in determining the generalized information to be shared and the usefulness of the generalized information. Retaining the useful insensitive generalized information to increase the utility of the shared information is a major objective of subgraph generalization. By understanding the impact of the *n-neighborhood*, *k-connectivity*, and *edge-betweeness* techniques on the utility of the generalized information, we will devise other subgraph construction algorithms to optimize the utility.

In addition to the utility of the generalized information, the development of the subgraph construction algorithms must take privacy leakage into consideration. By taking the generalized subgraphs and the generalized information of each subgraph, attacks can be designed to discover identities and adjacencies of sensitive and insensitive nodes. We focus on the passive attacks first by assuming the organizations within the information-sharing coalition are honest parties that do not plan active attacks on each other. The subgraph construction algorithms must minimize the possibility of privacy leakage and ensure that the prescribed level of privacy leakage tolerance is satisfied.

Integrating generalized social network for SNAM task

Figure 3.2 presents an overview of the subgraph generalization approach. Taking the generalized social network from multiple organizations, we need to develop techniques to make use of the shared data with the existing social network to accomplish the intended SNAM task, as illustrated in Figure 3.3. For example, if the SNAM task computes the closeness centrality, we need to develop a technique to make use of the additional information from the generalized nodes to obtain accurate estimations of the distances between nodes in a social network.

The result of an SNAM task is denoted as $\mathfrak{J}(G)$, where G is a social network. The SNAM result of organization P is $\mathfrak{J}(G_P)$. If organization Q shares its social network, G_Q, with organization P, P can integrate G_P and G_Q to $\boldsymbol{G}$ and obtain an SNAM result $\mathfrak{J}(\boldsymbol{G})$. The accuracy of $\mathfrak{J}(\boldsymbol{G})$ is much higher than that of $\mathfrak{J}(G_P)$; however, Q cannot share G_Q with P due to privacy concerns, but only the generalized social network, G_Q'. The integration technique

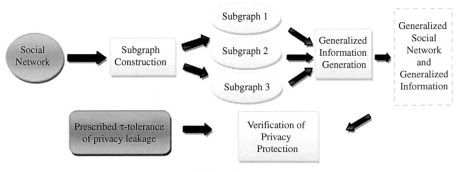

Figure 3.2:
Framework of subgraph generalization approach.

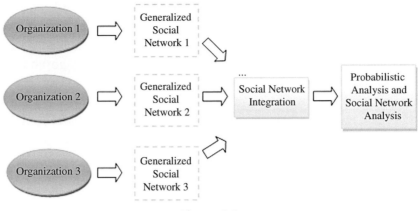

Figure 3.3:
Integration of generalized social networks for social network analysis.

we investigate here should be capable of utilizing the useful information in G'_Q and integrate with G_P, which is denoted as $I(G_P, G'_Q)$. The accuracy of $\Im(I(G_P, G'_Q))$ should be close to $\Im(G)$ and significantly better than $\Im(G_P)$.

Integration of probabilistic models from multiple generalized social networks

We integrate the probabilistic models of the generalized social networks from multiple organizations to obtain an integrated probabilistic model of **G**. Merugu and Ghosh [60] have investigated a distributed learning framework to obtain a global probabilistic model from the probabilistic models of local tabular data. In their framework, they combine the features of multiple local databases into a combined feature set. The local models are integrated to obtain the global model by entropy maximization. Their experimental results show that the learned global model is close to the centralized model and better than any local models. However, this work is limited to integrating local models of tabular data to a global model for data mining tasks. We investigate how to integrate the probabilistic models of the generalized social networks from multiple organizations to obtain an integrated probabilistic model to achieve better social network analysis and mining results. Our preliminary work [32,61,62] shows that we can achieve better centrality analysis of social networks by integrating simple generalized information such as maximum and minimum distances in subgraphs. By integrating sophisticated probabilistic models, it should be able to achieve better performance.

For instance, estimating the distance between two nodes A and B is important for many centrality measurements. Let d be the distance between a pair of nodes in a subgraph G_i. Let $P_{G'_i}(d)$ be the probability of the distance between any two nodes in the subgraph G'_i. Let A and B be the nodes in two different subgraphs and the shortest path between A and B (observed from the generalized graph) goes through a set of subgraphs $\mathbf{G'}$. Given $P_{G'_i}(d)$ of all subgraphs in G'_Q and the subgraphs on the shortest path between A and B in $\mathbf{G'}$, we can compute

$P(Distance(A, B) = d)$ by integrating $P_{G'_j}(Distance(A, B) = d)$, $\forall\ G'_j \in \mathbf{G'}$. This probabilistic analysis helps us in making better estimations of the distance between A and B. By using the probabilities of other measurements such as eccentricity and degree, and other values such as radius, diameter, and connecting nodes of subgraphs, we can develop algorithms to integrate this generalized information to obtain better social network analysis and mining results. The challenges are in determining what generalized information is useful for a particular social network analysis and mining task and how to make use of this generalized information to obtain the optimized results.

Given the probabilistic models from more than one generalized social network originating from more than one organization, the integration of these probabilistic models will help to improve the estimation of the properties between nodes in the integrated graph. It is assumed that the more information sharing from generalized graphs, the better the estimation. However, it also depends on how we can optimize the utility of the generalized information and yet minimize the sharing of unnecessary information and privacy leakage.

3.4 Conclusion

Social network data are important for discovering knowledge about a community, which is critical in criminology, terrorism, public health, and many other applications. At the same time, there is a great deal of private information about individuals in a social network, which makes it sensitive when social network data are shared across organizations. Without sharing social network data, each organization may only have part of a large global social network. For example, each local law enforcement unit may have a criminal social network. Without integrating the social networks of multiple law enforcement units, each unit may not be able to identify the relationship between suspects or groups precisely. In this chapter, we review the literature on privacy-preserving data publishing and sharing. We define the problems of social network integration, analysis, and mining. We define the τ-tolerance privacy leakage to ensure that a specified tolerance of privacy leakage must be satisfied. We develop the subgraph generalization technique for sharing insensitive information, which can be integrated for social network analysis and mining of the global social network. Our preliminary work has shown promising results of the proposed technique but there are more avenues to explore to enhance its performance.

References

[1] C.C. Yang, T.D. Ng, Terrorism and crime related weblog social network: Link, content analysis and information visualization, IEEE International Conference on Intelligence and Security Informatics, New Brunswick, NJ, 2007.
[2] L. Getoor, C.P. Diehl, Link mining: A survey, ACM SIGKDD Explor. 7 (2) (2005) 3−12.

[3] R. Bhatt, V. Chaoji, R. Parekh, Predicting product adoption in large-scale social networks, ACM CIKM, Toronto, Ontario, 2010.

[4] J. Kleinberg, Authoritative sources in a hyperlinked environment, J. ACM 46 (5) (1999) 604−632.

[5] L. Page, S. Brin, R. Motwani, T. Winograd, The PageRank citation ranking: Bringing order to the Web. Technical Report, Stanford University, 1998.

[6] R. Himmel, S. Zucker, On the foundations of relaxation labeling process, IEEE Trans. Pattern Anal. Mach. Intell. 5 (3) (1983) 267−287.

[7] L. Lafferty, A. McCallum, F. Pereira, Conditional random fields: Probabilistic models for segmenting and labeling sequence data, International Conference on Machine Learning, 2001.

[8] Q. Lu, L. Getoor, Link-based classification, International Conference on Machine Learning, 2003.

[9] J. Adibi, H. Chalupsky, E. Melz, A. Valente, The KOJAK group finder: Connecting the dots via integrated knowledge-based and statistical reasoning, Innovative Applications of Artificial Intelligence Conference, 2004, pp. 800−807.

[10] J. Kubica, A. Moore, J. Schneider, Y. Yang, Stochastic link and group detection, National Conference on Artificial Intelligence, American Association for Artificial Intelligence, 2002.

[11] J. Kubica, A. Moore, J. Schneider, Tractable group detection on large link data sets, IEEE International Conference on Data Mining, 2003.

[12] M.E.J. Newman, Detecting community structure in networks, Eur. Phys. J. B 38 (2) (2004) 321−330.

[13] J.R. Tyler, D.M. Wilkinson, B.A. Huberman, Email as Spectroscopy: Automated Discovery of Community Structure Within Organizations, The Netherlands, 2003.

[14] I. Bhattacharya, L. Getoor, Entity resolution in graphs. Technical Report 4758, Computer Science Department, University of Maryland, 2005.

[15] X. Dong, A. Halevy, J. Madhavan, Reference reconciliation in complex information spaces, ACM SIGMOD. International Conference on Management of Data, 2005.

[16] M. Craven, D. DiPasquo, D. Freitag, A. McCallum, T. Mitchell, K. Nigam, S. Slattery, Learning to construct knowledge bases from the world wide web, Artif. Intell. 118 (1−2) (2000) 69−114.

[17] V. Leroy, B.B. Cambazoglu, F. Bonchi, Cold start link prediction, ACM SIGKDD, Washington, DC, 2010.

[18] D. Liben-Nowell, J. Kleinberg, The link prediction problem for social networks, International Conference on Information and Knowledge Management. (CIKM'03), 2003.

[19] J. O'Madadhain, J. Hutchins, P. Smyth, Prediction and ranking algorithms for event-based network data, ACM SIGKDD Explor. 7 (2) (2005) 23−30.

[20] M. Kuramochi, G. Karypis, Frequent subgraph discovery, IEEE International Conference on Data Mining, 2001.

[21] X. Yan, J. Han, gSpan: Graph-based substructure pattern mining, International Conference on Data Mining, 2002.

[22] T. Frantz, K.M. Carley, A formal characterization of cellular networks. Technical Report CMU-ISRI-05-109, Carnegie Mellon University, 2005.

[23] J. Watts, S.H. Strogatz, Collective dynamics of "small-world" networks, Nature 339 (6684) (1998) 440−442.

[24] M. Morris, Network Epidemiology: A Handbook for Survey Design and Data Collection, Oxford University Press, London, 2004.

[25] M.A. Ahmad, J. Srivastava, An ant colony optimization approach to expert identification in social networks, in: H. Liu, J.J. Salerno, M.J. Young (Eds.), Social Computing, Behavioral Modeling, and Prediction, Springer, 2008.

[26] J. Xu, H. Chen, CrimeNet Explorer: A framework for criminal network knowledge discovery, ACM Trans. Inf. Syst. 23 (2) (2005) 201−226.

[27] C.C. Yang, N. Liu, M. Sageman, Analyzing the terrorist social networks with visualization tools, IEEE International Conference on Intelligence and Security Informatics, San Diego, CA, 2006.

[28] C.C. Yang, T.D. Ng, J. Wang, C. Wei, H. Chen, Analyzing and visualizing gray web forum structure, Pacific Asia Workshop on Intelligence and Security Informatics, 2007.

[29] J. Tang, J. Zhang, L. Yao, J. Li, L. Zhang, Z. Su, ArnetMiner: Extraction and Mining of Academic Social Networks, ACM KDD'08, ACM Press, Las Vegas, NV, 2008.

[30] Y.K. Chau, C.C. Yang, The shift towards multi-disciplinarily in information science, J. Am. Soc. Inf. Sci. Technol. 59 (13) (2008) 2156−2170.

[31] C.C. Yang, M. Sageman, Analysis of terrorist social networks with fractal views, J. Inf. Sci. 35 (3) (2009) 299−320.

[32] C.C. Yang, X. Tang, B. Thuraisingham, An analysis of user influence ranking algorithms on Dark Web forums. Proceedings of ACM SIGKDD Workshop on Intelligence and Security Informatics (ISI-KDD), Washington, DC, July 25, 2010.

[33] L. Sweeney, K-anonymity: A model for protecting privacy, Int. J. Uncertain. Fuzz. Knowl. Syst. 10 (5) (2002) 557−570.

[34] A. Machanavajjhala, J. Gehrke, D. Kifer, L-diversity: Privacy beyond k-anonymity, ICDE'06, 2006.

[35] N. Li, T. Li, t-Closeness: Privacy beyond k-anonymity and l-diversity, ICDE'07, 2007.

[36] X. Xiao, Y. Tao, m-Invariance: Towards privacy preserving re-publication of dynamic datasets. ACM SIGMOD'07, ACM Press, 2007.

[37] M.E. Nergiz, M. Atzori, C. Clifton, Hiding the presence of individuals from shared database, SIGMOD'07, 2007.

[38] C. Tai, P.S. Yu, M. Chen, k-Support anonymity based on pseudo taxonomy for outsourcing of frequent itemset mining, ACM SIGKDD, Washington, DC, 2010.

[39] X. Xiao, Y. Tao, Personalized privacy preservation, SIGMOD, Chicago, IL, 2006.

[40] R.C. Wong, J. Li, A. Fu, K. Wang, (alpha, k)-Anonymity: An enhanced k-anonymity model for privacy-preserving data publishing, SIGKDD, Philadelphia, PA, 2006.

[41] X. Jin, M. Zhang, N. Zhang, G. Das, Versatile publishing for privacy preservation, ACM KDD, Washington, DC, 2010.

[42] S.U. Nabar, B. Marthi, K. Kenthapadi, N. Mishra, R. Motwani, Towards robustness in query auditing, VLDB (2006) 151−162.

[43] A. Blum, C. Dwork, F. McSherry, K. Nissim, Practical privacy: the Sulq framework, ACM PODS'05, 2005.

[44] I. Dinur, K. Nissim, Revealing information while preserving privacy, ACM PODS'03 (2003).

[45] C. Dwork, F. McSherry, K. Nissim, A. Smith, Calibrating noise to sensitivity in private data analysis, TCC'06, 2006.

[46] R. Agrawal, R. Srikant, D. Thomas, Privacy preserving OLAP, ACM SIGMOD'05, Baltimore, MD, 2005, pp. 251−262.

[47] K. Muralidhar, R. Sarathy, Security of random data perturbation methods, ACM Trans. Database Syst. 24 (4) (1999) 487−493.

[48] R.J. Vaidya, C. Clifton, Privacy-preserving top-k queries, International Conference of Data Engineering, 2005.

[49] L. Backstrom, C. Dwork, J. Kleinberg, Wherefore art thou R3579X? Anonymized social networks, hidden patterns, and structural steganography. WWW'07 Banff, Alberta, Canada, 2007.

[50] M. Hay, G. Miklau, D. Jensen, P. Weis, S. Srivastava, Anonymizing social networks, Technical Report 07−19, University of Massachusetts, Amherst, 2007.

[51] K. Liu, E. Terzi, Towards Identity Anonymization on Graphs. ACM SIGMOD'08, ACM Press, Vancouver, BC, Canada, 2008.

[52] B. Zhou, J. Pei, Preserving privacy in social networks against neighborhood attacks, IEEE International Conference on Data Engineering, 2008.

[53] X. Ying, X. Wu, Randomizing social networks: A spectrum preserving approach, SIAM International Conference on Data Mining (SDM'08) Atlanta, GA, 2008.

[54] K.B. Frikken, P. Golle, Private social network analysis: How to assemble pieces of a graphy privately, 5th ACM Workshop on Privacy in Electronic Society (WPES'06), Alexandria, VA, 2006.

[55] A.C. Yao. Protocols for secure computations, Proceedings of the 23rd Annual IEEE Symposium on Foundations of Computer Science (1982) 160−164.

[56] Y. Lindell, B. Pinkas, Secure multiparty computation for privacy-preserving data mining, J. Priv. Confident. 1 (1) (2009) 59−98.

[57] J. Brickell, V. Shmatikov, Privacy-preserving graph algorithms in the semi-honest model, Proceedings of ASIACRYPT (2005) 236–252.

[58] F. Kerschbaum, A. Schaad, Privacy-preserving social network analysis for criminal investigations, Proceedings of the ACM Workshop on Privacy in Electronic Society (2008). Alexandria, VA.

[59] J. Sakuma, S. Kobayashi, Link analysis for private weighted graphs, Proceedings of ACM SIGIR'09, Boston, MA, 2009, pp. 235–242.

[60] S. Merugu, J. Ghosh, A distributed learning framework for heterogeneous data sources, ACM KDD'05 (2005). Chicago, IL.

[61] C.C. Yang, Information sharing and privacy protection of terrorist or criminal social networks, IEEE International Conference on Intelligence and Security Informatics, Taipei, Taiwan, 2008, pp. 40–45.

[62] C.C. Yang, X. Tang, Social networks integration and privacy preservation using subgraph generalization, Proceedings of AMC SIGKDD Workshop on CyberSecurity and Intelligence Informatics. Paris, France, June 28, 2009.

CHAPTER 4

A Digraph Model for Risk Identification and Management in SCADA Systems

Jian Guan[*], James H. Graham[†], Jeffrey L. Hieb[†]

[*] *Department of Computer Information Systems, University of Louisville, Louisville, Kentucky, USA*
[†] *Department of Electrical and Computer Engineering, University of Louisville, Louisville, Kentucky, USA*

Chapter Outline

4.1 Introduction

Supervisory control and data acquisition (SCADA) systems are critical to today's industrial facilities and infrastructures. SCADA systems have evolved into large and complex networks of information systems and are increasingly vulnerable to various types of security risks. SCADA systems play an important role in the daily operation of geographically distributed critical infrastructures such as gas, water and power distribution, and transportation systems such as railways. Early SCADA systems were isolated, proprietary, standalone systems in which cyber or electronic security was largely ignored [1]. However, these systems have undergone tremendous changes in the last few decades and have evolved into complex networks of heterogeneous information systems with highly sophisticated interconnections and interactions [2,3]. The growing dependence of critical infrastructures and industrial automation on these interconnected control systems has resulted in an increasing security threat to SCADA systems [4]. While a major disaster has thus far been averted, there have been incidents such as the 2003 slammer worm penetration of part of a network at a Davis-Besse nuclear power plant in Ohio [5], the release of raw sewage into parks and streams at an Australian sewage treatment plant [6], and the recent hacker penetration of a system used to operate part of a water treatment facility in Harrisburg, PA [7].

Intelligent Systems for Security Informatics.
http://dx.doi.org/10.1016/B978-0-12-404702-0.00004-5

Identifying and managing risks in SCADA systems has become critical in ensuring the safety and reliability of these facilities and infrastructure. Most of the existing research on SCADA risk modeling and management has focused on probability-based or quantitative approaches. While probabilistic approaches have proven to be useful, they also suffer from common problems such as simplifying assumptions, large implementation costs, and their inability to completely capture all the important aspects of risk. This chapter presents a digraph model for SCADA systems that allows formal, explicit representation of a SCADA system. A number of risk management methods are presented and discussed for a SCADA system based on the proposed model. In particular, this chapter presents methods for risk impact assessment and fault diagnosis using the proposed model. The approach differs from existing ones in that the proposed methods are mainly based on a model of the structural and functional features of a SCADA system rather than attack and/or vulnerability characteristics, which can be difficult to obtain and are prone to change.

The contributions of the chapter are twofold. First, the proposed model may serve as a conceptual basis for representing both the static and dynamic aspects of a SCADA system for purposes of design, synthesis, and integration. Second, the proposed model can be used for common risk management tasks such as risk assessment and fault diagnosis. The implications for management of SCADA systems are immediate. Managers of SCADA networks need precise and justifiable data about the consequences of specific types of security breaches, and precise and justifiable data about what possible attack consequences are eliminated by specific security measures. The approach proposed here provides managers with both types of data.

The rest of the chapter is organized as follows. The next section provides background and a brief literature review. This is followed by the presentation of the model for SCADA systems. After that two risk management algorithms are proposed for risk assessment and fault diagnosis. Throughout the chapter a SCADA system for a chemical distillation column is used to illustrate the proposed model and algorithms. Finally, in the last section the chapter discusses management implications for the proposed approach to SCADA modeling and risk management.

4.2 Background

SCADA systems have evolved in the last decade into highly complex, interconnected systems. For reasons such as efficiency, cost savings, and integration with enterprise-wide information systems, SCADA systems no longer have dedicated lines of communication. Instead, they share communication channels with the rest of the organization. This change has led to a very different risk profile for SCADA systems and exposed them to the common problems and threats of the Internet [8,9]. This increased level of security threat calls for more rigorous management of SCADA systems to ensure the safe and smooth operations of the underlying infrastructures. Most of the existing research on SCADA security focuses on quantitative/probabilistic risk modeling and analysis. The proposed methods include those based on Hidden Markov Models, statistically based models, and attack trees [4,10−12].

Madan et al. [10] applied a stochastic model to a computer network system to capture attacker behavior and analyze and quantify the security attributes. They determined steady-state availability of quality-of-service requirements and mean times to security failures based on probabilities of failure due to violations of different security attributes. Taylor et al. [12] merged probabilistic risk analysis with survivability system analysis with minor modification of what would be considered traditional probabilistic risk analysis, but it is still dependent on obtaining estimates of probabilities. The ability to determine whether or not risk reduction is achieved when modifications are made is important. Simple calculations for risk reduction have been published [13]. In Tolbert's paper, a risk metric was calculated that was simply the product of the frequency, likelihood of occurrence, and severity according to an arbitrarily selected scale of 1−5 for each of the three factors. The calculation is made before and after a system modification is made. More recently, McQueen et al. [11] published results of a promising method to calculate risk reduction estimates for a SCADA system and a set of control system remedial actions. The method employed a directed graph (compromise graph) where the nodes represent stages of a potential attack and the edges represent expected time-to-compromise for differing attacker skill levels. Probabilistic risk assessment provides for calculation of risk reduction when applied to SCADA security. If a lower event probability of a specific threat can be set to zero by the addition of a security enhancement, the effect on the top event probability of an overall attack can be computed. Patel et al. [14] have developed a risk modeling tool with two indices for quantifying risk associated with SCADA systems. Their work makes use of augmented vulnerability trees, which combine attack tree and vulnerability tree methods. Attack trees have been applied to a SCADA communication system [4]. The authors identified 11 attacker goals and associated security vulnerabilities in the specifications and development of typical SCADA systems. They were then used to suggest best practices for SCADA operators and improvements to the MODBUS standard. Their application was qualitative in that attack tree analysis was used only to identify paths and qualify the severity of impact, probability of detection, and level of difficulty. They did not calculate the probability of an actual attack being successful.

A common weakness of these methods is their reliability on prior statistical information and/ or attack patterns, which are often difficult to obtain. In addition, any solution for SCADA security cannot ignore the importance of the interoperability of these highly complex systems. Igure et al. point out that many proprietary protocols exist in today's SCADA market [9]. This can make both inter- and intra-company communication difficult, thus adding to the difficulty of risk management for SCADA systems.

4.3 A Digraph Model of SCADA Systems

This section presents a different approach to modeling SCADA systems using a directed graph representation of SCADA systems. First, a general description of SCADA systems is provided and that is followed by the presentation of the proposed digraph model. Finally, a risk impact algorithm and a fault diagnosis algorithm are provided to illustrate how the digraph model can facilitate the risk management task.

4.3.1 Structure of SCADA Systems

A typical SCADA system consists of one or more control centers, one or more field sites, and a communications infrastructure (see Figure 4.1). At the control center a master or master terminal unit (MTU) processes information received from field sites to create a digital representation of the physical process or infrastructure and sends control directives back out to field sites. Operators view the state of the system and issue control directives using various human machine interfaces (HMIs) in the form of operator displays. Field operation is carried out by field devices. Common types of field devices are remote telemetry units (RTUs), intelligent electronic devices (IEDs), and programmable logic controllers (PLCs). The remainder of this chapter will use the term RTU with the understanding that the cyber security-related discussion applies equally well to IEDs and PLCs. RTUs and MTUs are connected by a Wide Area Network (WAN). Possible types of networks include leased lines, Public Switched Telephone Networks (PSTNs), cellular networks, IP-based landlines, radio, microwave and even satellite. A single SCADA system may make use of more than one type

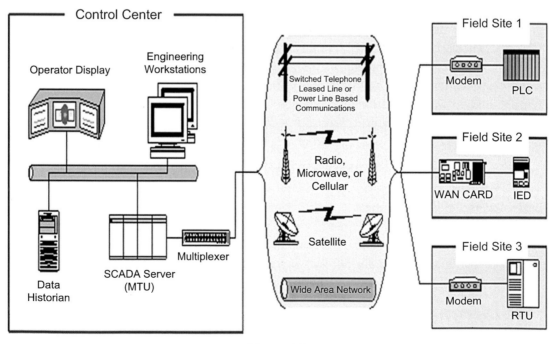

Figure 4.1:
Typical SCADA architecture. *Adapted from Ref. [15].*

of network and the connection between an MTU and RTU may even include more than one type of network technology.

4.3.2 A Digraph Model of SCADA Systems

Throughout the discussion in the rest of the chapter, a laboratory-scale distillation column is used as an example of a SCADA system. Figure 4.2 is a schematic diagram of the distillation column SCADA system and Figure 4.3 represents the SCADA system as a digraph.

Let $X = \{x_1, \ldots, x_n\}$ be a set of components in a SCADA system where x_i is a component, such as a master station, submaster station, or an RTU. Then a risk impact relation R can be defined on X such that $x_i R x_j$ means that components x_i and x_j are coupled. In others a fault at x_i can propagate to x_j. A risk impact digraph G is then used to represent this relation as

$$G = \{V, E\} \tag{4.1}$$

where

$$V = \{x_i | x_i \text{ is a component}\} \tag{4.2}$$

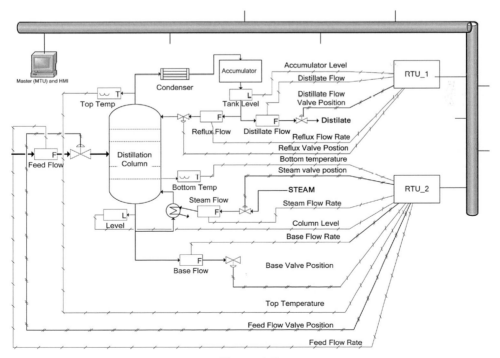

Figure 4.2:
Distillation column schematic.

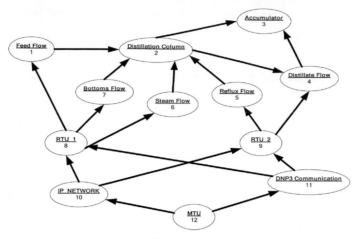

Figure 4.3:
Conceptualization of the distillation column as a digraph.

is the vertex set, and

$$E = \{(x_i, x_j) | x_i \text{ and } x_j \text{ are coupled and } i \neq j\} \quad (4.3)$$

is the edge set. Let $A = (a_{ij})$ be the adjacency matrix representing the risk management digraph such that $a_{ij} = 1$ if $(x_i, x_j) \in R$ and $a_{ij} = 0$ if $(x_i, x_j) \notin R$. If there is a path in G from x_i to x_j, x_j is said to be reachable from x_i. In the context of risk impact assessment or diagnosis this means that a security risk occurring at x_i may have a security impact on x_j. For completeness every vertex in G is defined to be reachable from itself by a path of 0. As defined above, reachability is transitive. For notational convenience the components in the distillation column example are numbered 1, 2, 3, etc., and the diagraph for the distillation column is as shown in Figure 4.3. The adjacency matrix for the example SCADA system is given as follows:

$$A = \begin{bmatrix} 1 & 1 & 0 & 0 & 0 & 0 & 0 & 0 & 0 & 0 & 0 & 0 \\ 0 & 1 & 1 & 1 & 0 & 0 & 0 & 0 & 0 & 0 & 0 & 0 \\ 0 & 0 & 1 & 0 & 0 & 0 & 0 & 0 & 0 & 0 & 0 & 0 \\ 0 & 0 & 1 & 1 & 0 & 0 & 0 & 0 & 0 & 0 & 0 & 0 \\ 0 & 1 & 0 & 0 & 1 & 0 & 0 & 0 & 0 & 0 & 0 & 0 \\ 0 & 1 & 0 & 0 & 0 & 1 & 0 & 0 & 0 & 0 & 0 & 0 \\ 0 & 1 & 0 & 0 & 0 & 0 & 1 & 0 & 0 & 0 & 0 & 0 \\ 1 & 0 & 0 & 0 & 0 & 1 & 1 & 1 & 0 & 0 & 0 & 0 \\ 0 & 0 & 0 & 1 & 1 & 0 & 0 & 0 & 1 & 0 & 0 & 0 \\ 0 & 0 & 0 & 0 & 0 & 0 & 0 & 1 & 1 & 1 & 0 & 0 \\ 0 & 0 & 0 & 0 & 0 & 0 & 0 & 1 & 1 & 0 & 1 & 0 \\ 0 & 0 & 0 & 0 & 0 & 0 & 0 & 0 & 0 & 1 & 1 & 1 \end{bmatrix} \quad (4.4)$$

The reachability matrix P may be defined as follows:

$$P = (A + I)^r = (A + I)^{r-1} \neq (A + I)^{r-2} \tag{4.5}$$

where I is the identity matrix and the operations are Boolean. The reachability matrix P for the digraph in Figure 4.3 is calculated as follows:

$$P = \begin{bmatrix}
1 & 1 & 1 & 1 & 0 & 0 & 0 & 0 & 0 & 0 & 0 & 0 \\
0 & 1 & 1 & 1 & 0 & 0 & 0 & 0 & 0 & 0 & 0 & 0 \\
0 & 0 & 1 & 0 & 0 & 0 & 0 & 0 & 0 & 0 & 0 & 0 \\
0 & 0 & 1 & 1 & 0 & 0 & 0 & 0 & 0 & 0 & 0 & 0 \\
0 & 1 & 1 & 1 & 1 & 0 & 0 & 0 & 0 & 0 & 0 & 0 \\
0 & 1 & 1 & 1 & 0 & 1 & 0 & 0 & 0 & 0 & 0 & 0 \\
0 & 1 & 1 & 1 & 0 & 0 & 1 & 0 & 0 & 0 & 0 & 0 \\
1 & 1 & 1 & 1 & 0 & 1 & 1 & 1 & 0 & 0 & 0 & 0 \\
0 & 1 & 1 & 1 & 1 & 0 & 0 & 0 & 1 & 0 & 0 & 0 \\
1 & 1 & 1 & 1 & 1 & 1 & 1 & 1 & 1 & 1 & 0 & 0 \\
1 & 1 & 1 & 1 & 1 & 1 & 1 & 1 & 1 & 0 & 1 & 0 \\
1 & 1 & 1 & 1 & 1 & 1 & 1 & 1 & 1 & 1 & 1 & 1
\end{bmatrix} \tag{4.6}$$

The reachability matrix can be used to derive several important properties describing a SCADA system [16–18]. Two partitions can be defined on the reachability matrix P, the level partition and the separate-parts partition. Let $R(x)$, the reachability set, be the set of vertices reachable from x_i and $A(x_i)$, the antecedent set, be the set of vertices which reach x_i. Then the level partition $L(P)$ is defined as

$$L(P) = [L_1, \; L_2, \; L_k] \tag{4.7}$$

where k is the number of levels. If the 0th level is defined as the empty set, $L_0 = \varnothing$, the level partition of P can be found iteratively as follows:

$$L_j = \{x_j \in P - L_0 - L_1 \ldots - L_{j-1} \big| R_j(x_j) = R_j(x_i) \cap A_j(x_i)\} \tag{4.8}$$

The levels so obtained have the following properties:

- $\cup L_i = V$, for $i = 1, \; k$
- $L_i \cap L_i = \varnothing$, for $i \neq j$
- Edges leaving vertices in level L_i can go only to vertices in levels L_j such that $i \leq j$. In other words, a security risk in components in one level can only impact or propagate to components in the same or lower levels.

Level partitioning can be obtained through tabulation [17]. The level partitions for the distillation column are as follows (shown in Figure 4.4):

$$L = \{(3,)(2, 4), (1, 5, 6, 7), (8, 9), (10, 11), (12)\} \tag{4.9}$$

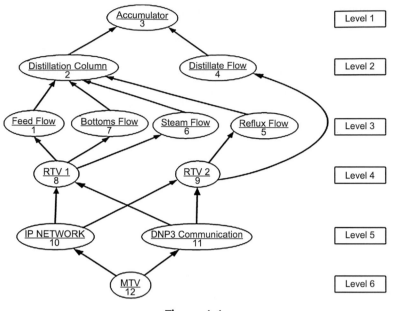

Figure 4.4:
The level partitions for the distillation column digraph.

It is possible that some of the components of P constitute a smaller digraph that is disjoint from the remainder of the digraph. The separate-parts partition is used to identify these disjoint parts of the SCADA system. To define the separate-parts partition, a set of bottom-level components must be defined. B is a set of bottom-level components, if and only if, for any $p_i \in B$:

$$A(x_i) = R(x_i) \cap A(x_i) \tag{4.10}$$

Given the reachability matrix P for a SCADA system, a separate-parts partition $S(P)$ can be defined as

$$S(P) = [D_1;\ D_2;\ ...;\ D_m] \tag{4.11}$$

where m is the number of disjoint digraphs that constitute the digraph represented by A. To find $S(P)$, the set of bottom-level components B must be found, where

$$B = \{x_i \in P | A(x_i) = R(x_i) \cap A(x_i)\} \tag{4.12}$$

Then, any two components $x_i,\ x_j \in B$ are placed in the same block if and only if:

$$[R(x_i) \cap R(x_j)] \neq [\varnothing] \tag{4.13}$$

Once the components of B have been assigned to blocks, the remaining components of the reachability sets for each block are appended to the block.

4.3.3 Risk Impact and Identification Algorithms

One of the main objectives of this chapter is to demonstrate the utility of this SCADA model in managing security risks in a SCADA system. Two such algorithms are presented in this section. The first algorithm allows the assessment of the impact of an at-risk component on a SCADA system. The second algorithm performs fault diagnosis to locate sources of errors.

The first algorithm locates those components that may be affected by a given set of at-risk components. The input to the algorithm are the adjacency matrix A representing the SCADA digraph G and the set of components F that are assumed/known to be at risk. The output of the algorithm is a set of components, $O = \{x_1, x_2, x_3, \dots, x_n\}$, that are likely to be affected by the identified security vulnerabilities.

1. Compute the reachability matrix P of G.
2. Compute the level-partition of G.
3. Compute the separate-parts partition of G.
4. For each separate part:
    a. Find the impact set $Q = \{\cup R(x_i) | x_i \subset F\}$.
    b. Find the leveled impact set $LQ = \{LQ_i | \cup LQ_i = Q\}$, for i $= 1, k$, where k is the number of level partitions.

Steps 1–3 preprocess the digraph representing the model by finding the reachability matrix, level partitions, and separate-parts partitions. Step 4a finds the impact set in each separate partition (disjoint digraph). An impact set is defined as the components that may be impacted by the at-risk component(s) in F. It follows that these impact sets represent components in the reachability set(s) of the at-risk components. Step 4b divides each impact set into levels using level partitions. Dividing the impact set components helps distinguish components that are more likely to be impacted from those that are less likely to be impacted. Components in a higher level partition are more likely to be or more immediately affected by the at-risk components because of their closer proximity to the at-risk components. The final output O is the union of all the leveled impact sets in all the partitions.

Again using the distillation column example, assume that the component at risk is $F = \{11\}$, then the leveled impact set would be

$$LQ = \{(8, 9), (1, 5, 6, 7), (2, 4), (3)\} \tag{4.14}$$

where

$$LQ_1 = \{(8, 9)\}, \quad LQ_2 = \{(1, 5, 6, 7)\}, \quad LQ_3 = \{(2, 4)\}, \quad \text{and } LQ_4 = \{(3)\} \tag{4.15}$$

In other words if component 11 is found/assumed to be at risk, then components (1,2,3,4,5,6,7,8,9) are likely to be affected. In addition, from the leveled partition impact sets, it is easy to see that the leveled impact set $LQ_1 = \{(8,9)\}$ is more likely to be immediately affected than the other components. Thus the impact set Q can be used to obtain an assessment of impacted components given a risk alert. Furthermore, the level partitioned impact set, LQ, ranks the set of impacted components in terms of immediacy of impact, so risk reduction methods/action can be directed at those components that are likely to be impacted first.

The model can also be used to support another risk management-related task, i.e. fault diagnosis. Fault diagnosis is a process of locating the components that have led to failure in a SCADA system or parts of a SCADA system. Often when a system fails, the components where failure are observed are not the true causes of failures, but the victims of faults that have propagated from other parts of the system [16,17]. This section presents an algorithm adapted from Ref. [16] for diagnosing faults in a SCADA system given observed symptoms.

Just as in the risk impact assessment algorithm, the diagnostic process starts with the computation of the reachability matrix and the partitions. These are referred to as the preprocessing steps.

Compute the reachability matrix P of G.
Compute the level partition of G.
Compute the separate-parts partition of G.

DIAGNOSIS

1. $\Sigma = \cap\ AS(x_i)$ for $x_i \in F$
2. $Q = \varnothing$
3. While $\Sigma <> \varnothing$
4. $T = \{x | x \in \Sigma \text{ and } \text{level}(x) = \min\{\text{level}(x_i) \text{ for all } x_i \in \Sigma\}\}^1$
5. *TESTCOMPONENTS(T)*
6. Return Q as the error source

where the *TESTCOMPONENTS* algorithm is as follows:

TESTCOMPONENTS(T)

1. If $|T| = 1$:
2. $v = T$
3. If $|T| > 1$:
4. $v \in T$ such that $p_{vz} = \max\{p_{xz} \text{ for all } x \in T \text{ and } z \text{ is the common descendant of all } x \in T\}$
5. If v has not been tested:
6. $\Sigma = \Sigma - \{v\}, T = T - \{v\}$

---

[1] If there is more than one node at the lowest level in Σ, one of them is chosen randomly to start the testing process.

7. Test the component v and mark v as tested
8. If the component is abnormal:
9. $Q = Q \cup \{v\}$
10. If the component is tested normal:
11. Remove in A all edges incident to and from v
12. Preprocess the digraph
13. Restart the diagnosis algorithm
14. If Ancestor$(v) <> \emptyset$:
15. $T = $ Immediate Ancestor(v)
16. If $|T| <> \emptyset$:
17. *TESTCONTROLS(T)*

The above algorithms are designed to assist in the identification of components for testing when a set of components has been observed to have failed/malfunctioned. The objective is to find the source(s) of the failures/malfunctions as it is likely that the observed failures/malfunctions are the result of error propagation originating from components/sources in the higher levels in the digraph. The algorithm starts by finding the common ancestors of the observed failures F and saves the result in Σ (see step 1). This set of common ancestors, Σ, is the set of candidate error sources and is defined as the intersection of the ancestors of the nodes in F ($\cap A(x_i)$ for $x_i \in F$ in step 1). The algorithm will next test the components in Σ and/or their ancestors to identify error sources in steps 3—5. The "while" loop (steps 3—5) examines each of the potential error sources starting with the one at the lowest level of the level-partitioned digraph. Once the component on the lowest level is identified (step 4), a modified depth-first search algorithm (*TESTCOMPONENTS*) guides the diagnostic process by backtracking along all possible error propagation paths (step 5). In the algorithm *TESTCOMPONENTS* the input T contains the set of components to examine next. Please note that the first time the algorithm *TESTCOMPONENTS* is invoked from *DIAGNOSIS*, T contains only one component. If T contains only one component, this component will be tested (step 7 in *TESTCOMPONENTS*). Once a component is tested, it is removed from the set of candidate error sources (step 6) and marked as tested (step 7). If the component is normal, the error is unlikely to have originated from its ancestor components further upstream so the related propagation paths are removed from the diagraph, the partitions are recomputed, and the diagnosis process is restarted (restart *DIAGNOSIS*) (steps 10—13). Otherwise the tested abnormal component is added to the set of error sources Q (step 9). At this point the human operator has the option of stopping the diagnostic process or continuing until all the potential error sources are tested. Steps 14 and 15 will move the search forward by examining the parents of the abnormal node v. If the abnormal node v does not have any parent, the diagnostic process continues with the candidate error source(s) in the next lowest level in the algorithm *DIAGNOSIS* (step 4 in *DIAGNOSIS*). If the abnormal node v has parents, they are examined by calling the algorithm *TESTCOMPONENTS* recursively (step 17 in *TESTCOMPONENTS*).

There are two possible cases. In the first case there is only a single parent and this parent will be tested (condition in step 1 in *TESTCOMPONENTS*). In the second case there is more than one parent and the parent from which the error is most likely to have propagated can be determined according to the propagation probabilities. This is to allow the search to stay as closely as possible on the most probable path to the source (step 4). For any component x the error may have propagated from any of the ancestor components upstream. In some cases there may be several immediate ancestors of x and the fault could have propagated from any of these ancestors or any of the error propagation paths headed by these ancestors. Obviously for x a fault may be more likely to propagate from some of the components rather than others. This information can be captured through a propagation probability. Associated with each edge then is p_{ij}, the probability that a fault will propagate from x_i to x_j, $0 < p_{ij} \leq 1$. It is assumed that this information is available from users experienced with the SCADA system. In case such information is not available, equal probability can be assigned to each p_{ij} and the true probability for p_{ij} can be gradually acquired through use of the system [19]. So for each component x_j, p_{ij} is defined such that $\Sigma_{i=1}^{n} p_{ij} = 1$, where n is the in-degree of the vertex representing the component x_j. For example, Figure 4.5 shows a component that has three ancestor components that could propagate a fault to it.

Step 4 in the *TESTCOMPONENTS* algorithm directs the search in the most probable path according to the fault propagation probabilities and helps ensure that the search will stay as closely as possible on the most probable path to the fault source. In general, a component is chosen for testing so that the test result can prune away at least one path of components from further consideration.

Thus, the algorithm backtracks along the path until the path branches off into two or more paths. If the component just tested does not have any parent, then the recursive algorithm will

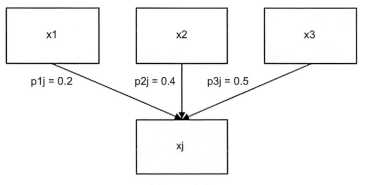

Figure 4.5:
Fault propagation probability.

allow all other possible error paths to be tested (step 17). Once all possible paths originating from the chosen component in the main algorithm have been examined, the potential error source at the next lowest level will be used to guide the next round of testing (step 4 in the main algorithm). This process continues until all potential error sources in Σ are exhausted.

As an example of a fault diagnosis scenario, assume that a hacker is able to penetrate the corporate network and inject SCADA traffic onto the control network. The hacker may not have any knowledge of the distillation column set up but finds the DNP3 traffic flow on the network. A malicious code injected into the DNP3 (node 11 in Figure 4.4) traffic can result in harm to the distillation column. The injected code/command can tell the devices to directly operate Feed Flow (node 1 in Figure 4.4), Distillation Column (node 2 in Figure 4.4), and/or Reflux Flow (node 5 in Figure 4.4). As a result, for example, the Reflux Flow valve starts to oscillate between 100% open and the target valve steam valve position setting. The other two components may exhibit similar problems. Hence the components $F = \{1,2,5\}$ may exhibit fault symptoms. The human operator, upon detecting the faulty readings in components 1, 2, and 5, can use the *DIAGNOSIS* algorithm to locate the source of the faults, i.e. malicious code injected into the DNP3 (node 11 in Figure 4.4). According to the algorithm the only common ancestor to the faulty components is DNP3 (11). As a result $\{11\}$ will be returned as a probable source of faults. This will alert the operators to take specific and immediate action,

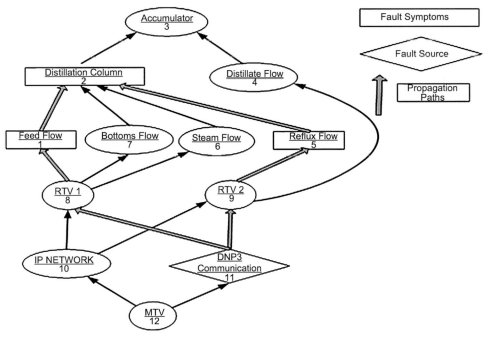

Figure 4.6:
Example fault scenario.

such as temporarily raising the security at the control gateway, stopping traffic from the corporate network, etc. See Figure 4.6 for a depiction of the fault scenario. As an example of propagation probabilities guiding the diagnosis process, the distillation column in Figure 4.6 could be part of a larger SCADA system and in a fault diagnosis process component 2 (see Figure 4.4) may have been found to be abnormal. In this scenario the fault could have propagated from one of the four immediate ancestor components {1,5,6,7}. In that case fault propagation probabilities would direct the diagnostic process to search along the most likely path in step 4 of the *TESTCOMPONENTS* algorithm. This fault diagnosis algorithm can be particularly useful in a large SCADA system that contains hundreds or thousands of components and a timely identification of fault sources is critical.

4.4 Conclusions

This chapter presents a digraph model for SCADA systems. A SCADA system, a laboratory-scale distillation column, is used as an example to illustrate the proposed model. The proposed SCADA model offers a simple and easy-to-implement approach for representation of both static and dynamic aspects of a SCADA system. The approach differs from most existing research where the prevalent approach is modeling of risk probabilities or attack patterns. Instead, this model is designed to capture the more fundamental aspects of a SCADA system (i.e. its structure and behavior), and build risk assessment and diagnostic operations from such a model of fundamental aspects. Each component in a SCADA system is represented as a node in a digraph and possible error propagation paths constitute the edges of the digraph. Several important partitions of the digraph can help operators quickly assess impact of possible vulnerabilities and locate error sources. These features of the proposed model are demonstrated through two algorithms. The first algorithm allows an operator to assess the possible impact of security risk in any component or combination of components. The second algorithm assists an operator in locating sources of faults that have been propagated through the system. Such an approach has important advantages. Firstly, the proposed model's simple structure is easy to implement. In addition to its simplicity most of the information needed for the construction of the model is readily available from system documentation, i.e. structure and function of the system. Secondly, the proposed model may serve as a conceptual basis for representing both the static and dynamic aspects of a SCADA system for purposes of design, synthesis, and integration. Thirdly, the proposed model can be used for common risk management tasks such as risk assessment and fault diagnosis. The implications for management of SCADA systems are immediate. Managers of SCADA networks need precise and justifiable data about the consequences of specific types of security breaches, and precise and justifiable data about what possible attack consequences are eliminated by specific security measures. The approach proposed here provides managers with both types of data.

References

[1] R.H. McClanahan, SCADA and IP: Is network convergence really here? Ind. Appl. Mag. IEEE 9 (2) (2003) 29–36.

[2] D.C. McFarlane, Developments in holonic production planning and control, Prod. Plan. Control 11 (6) (2000) 522–536.

[3] R.M. Murray, K.J. Astrom, S.P. Boyd, R.W. Brockett, G. Stein, Future directions in control in an information-rich world, IEEE Control Syst. Mag. 23 (2) (2003) 20–33.

[4] E.J. Byres, M. Franz, D. Miller, The use of attack trees in assessing vulnerabilities in SCADA Systems, International Infrastructure Survivability Workshop (IISW'04), IEEE, Lisbon, Portugal, December 2004.

[5] K. Poulsen, Slammer worm crashed Ohio nuke plant net, <http://www.securityfocus.com/news/6767> 2003.

[6] T. Smith, Hacker iailed for revenge sewage attacks, <http://www.theregister.co.uk/2001/10/31/hacker_jailed_for_revenge_sewage/> 2001.

[7] R. Esposito, Hackers hit Pennsylvania water system, <http://www.isa.org/InTechTemplate.cfm?Section=NewHome&template=/ContentManagement/ContentDisplay.cfm&ContentID=57151> 2006.

[8] T. Brown, Security in SCADA systems: How to handle the growing menace to process automation, Comput. Control Eng. 16 (3) (2005) 42–47.

[9] V.M. Igure, S.A. Laughter, R.D. Williams, Security issues in SCADA networks, Comput. Secur. 25 (7) (2006) 498–506.

[10] B.B. Madan, K. Gogeva-Popstojanova, K. Vaidyanathan, K.S. Trivedi, Modeling and quantification of security attributes of software systems, International Conference on Dependable Systems and Networks, DSN (2002) 505–514.

[11] M.A. McQueen, W.F. Boyer, M.A. Flynn, G.A. Beitel, Quantitative Cyber Risk Reduction Estimation Methodology for a Small SCADA Control System, IEEE Computer Society, Washington, DC, USA, 2006.

[12] C. Taylor, A. Krings, J. Alves-Foss, Risk analysis and probabilistic survivability assessment (RAPSA): An assessment approach for power substation hardening, Proc. ACM Workshop on Scientific Aspects of Cyber Terrorism (SACT), Washington, DC, 2002.

[13] G.D. Tolbert, Residual risk reduction: systematically deciding what is "safe", Prof. Saf. 50 (2005) 25–33.

[14] S.C. Patel, J.H. Graham, P.A.S. Ralston, Security enhancement for SCADA communication protocols using augmented vulnerability trees, Proceedings of the 19th International Conference on Computer Applications in Industry and Engineering, 2006, pp. 244–251.

[15] K. Stouffer, NIST industrial control system security activities, Proceedings of the ISA Expo, Chicago, IL, 2005.

[16] J. Guan, J.H. Graham, Diagnostic reasoning with fault propagation digraph and sequential testing, IEEE Trans. Syst. Man. Cybern. 24 (10) (1994) 1552–1558.

[17] N.H. Narayanan, N. Viswanhadam, A methodology for knowledge acquisition and reasoning in failure analysis, IEEE Trans. Syst. Man. Cybern. 17 (2) (1987) 274–288.

[18] J.N. Warfield, Structuring Complex Systems, Battelle Memorial Institute (1974).

[19] J. Guan, J.H. Graham, An integrated approach for fault diagnosis with learning, Comput. Indus. 32 (1) (1996) 33–51.

CHAPTER 5

High-Level Architecture and Design of a Decision Engine for Marine Safety and Security[1]

Piper Jackson[*], Uwe Glässer[*], Hamed Yaghoubi Shahir[*], Hans Wehn[†]

[*] Software Technology Lab, School of Computing Science, Simon Fraser University, Burnaby, British Columbia, Canada [†] Research & Development, MDA Corporation, Richmond, British Columbia, Canada

Chapter Outline

---

[1] Based on: P. Jackson, U. Glässer, H. Yaghoubi Shahir, and H. Wehn. An Extensible Decision Engine for Marine Safety and Security. IEEE Int. Conf. on Intelligence and Security Informatics (ISI), 2011: 54–59, with permission.

   This work has been supported in part by MDA Corporation and MITACS through the MITACS-Accelerate internship program.

5.1 Introduction

By their very nature, some application domains are unpredictable. While we strive to develop the best technologies and practices in order to solve the problems we face, we are unable to assume that our actions will proceed without interruption. Equipment can fail and people can make mistakes. Despite the best planning, wrong decisions can be made. This is especially true in critical situations, when time is limited and the penalties for failure are severe. When we face the possibility of interference by neutral or adversarial actors, things become even more difficult. However, we are able to deal with this reality in everyday life because we are able to dynamically react to the world around us. We learn from failure and avoid problems when they become apparent. For an automated system to perform well in real-world situations, it must also be capable of doing these things.

Planning is the process of generating a series of actions that accomplish a goal. In computing, classical approaches to planning focus on theoretical properties and general algorithms. Over the last several decades, classical planning has been well studied [1]. However, a number of simplifying assumptions are made for this kind of research. Most commonly, only systems that are static, finite, deterministic, and fully observable are considered. These assumptions are appropriate only for some real-world applications, such as manufacturing, but for others they do not apply. Marine safety and security is a domain for which automated planning would be highly useful. Related operations include a mixture of routine and emergency activities, rapidly changing conditions, and complex resource requirements. Canada, with the longest coastline in the world [2], has a particular interest in innovations in this field. For automated planning to be able to perform in such a domain, it must be more flexible than a classical model allows. There are uncontrollable events and entities, imperfect knowledge and nondeterminism, i.e. actions may have unexpected results. Replanning, the dynamic generation of new plans, is a strategy that can help to address these issues.

Consider this example: A 911 call comes into a maritime services command center, initiating a search and rescue mission. A plan is put together that has the best chance of finding the capsized ship as well as any survivors within the given time window. Since we are dealing with unknowns, this plan cannot account for all eventualities. Several things can happen that could require rapid alteration of the plan. For example, new information (such as eyewitness reports) could add or remove areas of interest from the search. Another possibility is resource failure, either in the form of actual resource loss or due to situational reduction of capabilities. Bad weather is a prime cause of this, either by directly causing damage to equipment, or by interfering with movement or sensors (including vision). Finally, it is possible that a decision outlined in the plan may fail. In this case, it is a critical decision whether or not to repeat the failed action, try something else, or abort the current mission. Searching for survivors in open water during bad weather may not proceed in a textbook manner. It may be necessary to try a variety of sensing technologies or solutions, and it is possible the search attempt may become too dangerous to continue.

We propose here a comprehensive architectural model and algorithmic framework of continual planning using formal methods to represent the model at an abstract operational level, capturing the behavior of the system as a whole. Specifically, we use the Abstract State Machine (ASM) method [3] to express and delineate the responsibilities of the system components. The Decision Engine is designed to have a plug-in architecture, allowing various planning paradigms to be used within its components. For example, the set of available planning algorithms should match the needs of the domain model as represented by INFORM Lab [4], an industrial simulation platform for developing decision support systems in the marine safety and security domain (see Section 5.2.4 for more details). We also present a planning paradigm appropriate to the application domain. This design is built so that as new techniques and relevant technology are developed, they can be swapped in without difficulty. When complete, it is meant to act as a guide for future implementations of a continual planning layer.

The rest of this chapter is organized as follows: Section 5.2 discusses background knowledge and concepts related to the project; Section 5.3 presents Decision Engine design; Section 5.4 proposes a formal representation approach for the Decision Engine based on the Abstract State Machine method with some examples; Section 5.5 describes the application context in which the Decision Engine was developed; finally, Section 5.6 concludes the chapter with a discussion of future work and other possible applications of this research.

5.2 Background

In this section, we discuss several topics that are fundamental to our research. The OODA loop is the operational framework within which the system exists. Automated planning is the academic discipline that governs this research topic. In the Fundamental Planning Elements subsection, we discuss several ideas and entities of importance to the focus of our research. Next is a general explanation of Hierarchical Task Networks, since they are of particular interest to this project. Finally a short description of other related research is given.

5.2.1 The OODA Loop

The OODA loop (Figure 5.1), developed by the United States Air Force Colonel John Boyd, is a model of how an intelligent, sensing agent interacts with a dynamic environment, well

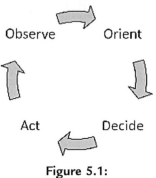

Figure 5.1:
John Boyd's OODA loop.

established in both business and military contexts. It consists of four main steps: *Observe* the environment to discover what is happening; *Orient* the evidence observed, to establish its meaning in terms of one's own situation and interests; *Decide* what to do based on what was understood during orientation; and, finally, *Act* on that decision. This is an iterative loop, with the results of the *Act* phase feeding into the next *Observe* phase. By continually following the OODA loop, an individual agent or group of agents are able to act in accordance to the situation they are in. Here, the OODA loop is employed as a definitive model of how both directed and reactive behavior can be broken down into their constituent elements, and how those elements interact with each other. For this reason, the four steps will be used throughout this text to refer to any process or algorithm that achieves their purpose within the context of a real-time adaptive system.

5.2.2 Automated Planning

Planning is the process of finding a set of actions that accomplish one or more goals. Automated planning is performed computationally in order to control automated systems or aid human operators in their decision making. Automated planning has great potential in dealing with the complexity of managing systems that use many resources. As a field, automated planning has provided multiple methods that can be used to decide on how to act when given goals and an environment in which to act. However, planning algorithms are brittle on their own, since conditions can change after a plan is constructed. Most have been formulated assuming a closed and predictable environment [1]. There is even greater complexity for domains that interact with the world at large, since this means that there will be many factors that are difficult or impossible to control. Classical approaches to planning are well understood, but do not deal well with incomplete knowledge or the unexpected. Continual planning systems adapt dynamically in order to handle challenges encountered during execution. Continual planning deals with the challenges of complex conditions by allowing the planning system to react to feedback from the environment and replan when necessary. Characteristics that enable effective continual planning are outlined in Refs [5,6]. These include: the ability to monitor changes in the environment and in execution of a plan; being able to maintain multiple plans and choose which to commit to; elaboration of a plan as appropriate to current knowledge and available resources; and the capacity for auditing plans and altering them as necessary. The design proposed in this chapter aims to embody these characteristics.

5.2.3 Fundamental Planning Elements

There are four classes of objects that are fundamental to planning. These are: goals, plans, decisions, and actions. Goals are high-level statements that the system aims to fulfill. A mission, such as search and rescue, is a prime example of a goal. Solving a problem that is interfering with system activities is also a goal, although in this case it would be generated dynamically rather than being introduced by system operators. Goals are achieved through the performance of appropriate actions.

Actions are straightforward: they are the external actions performed by a system as it interacts with its environment during execution. They are closely linked to decisions, which are their logical counterpart. In this way, it is possible to represent both the *intention* to do something (the decision) and the *act* of doing it (the action). This distinction is vital when the results of an action are not completely predictable. Actions can fail or never have an opportunity to begin. They may succeed partially or have unintended consequences. In fact, it is precisely the difference between decision and action that a system must evaluate in order to determine an appropriate reaction to an unforeseen result. This distinction enables robust planning behavior in a dynamic environment with uncertainty.

Plans are the intermediary objects necessary to generate decisions appropriate for a given goal. They are used to construct and organize a set of decisions that are likely to result in the fulfillment of that goal. A plan may contain decision points (conditionals) and constraints that limit when the plan can be enacted, such as preconditions that must be fulfilled before beginning (including which other decisions must precede it in terms of execution).

5.2.4 Hierarchical Task Networks

The Hierarchical Task Network (HTN) paradigm is an approach to automated planning that takes advantage of domain knowledge to reduce the search space when developing a solution to a planning problem. Traditional approaches to planning attempt to transform an initial state to a goal state by applying available actions in a specific order. This requires considering many possible actions at every decision point when building a solution, so the search space for such a planner is immense: without severe restrictions in representation or syntax, it is of exponential computational complexity [1]. Instead of looking at every possible action, HTNs use methods to incrementally break down an initial abstract goal task into progressively more specific tasks (referred to as decisions in the context of our project). For example, a rescue mission to save a capsized boat would be broken down into three high-level tasks: Search, Extract (personnel), and Secure (the boat). In turn, each of these would need to be further refined into specific tasks related to moving resources, using equipment, etc. The methods are developed using expert knowledge specific to the domain that the planner will be used for. This requires more effort in construction than a general planner, but this effort results in a quicker and more useful planner at execution time.

HTN methods express domain knowledge in a structured and formal manner. Since HTN methods are created by human experts from the field that the planner is used in, this makes the resulting plans more useful for human users in a number of ways. First of all, the plans are easier to understand, since they are similar to a plan formulated by a human. Secondly, since the overall structure of a plan matches one that a human expert would come up with, this means that a system user will be able to use a generated plan as part of their planning process without needing to rely on it completely. They can be confident in their ability to alter or correct parts of the plan based on their own expertise or knowledge of things not represented in the simulation environment. Since every computer simulation is necessarily an approximation of the real world, this situation is unavoidable. It is important to recognize the role of a Decision Support System (DSS) like INFORM Lab. It is able to perform difficult calculations and consider a vast number of items much more effectively than a human being is able to. However, it is limited to the knowledge represented in it, and is unable to innovate. Thus, the output of a DSS must be in a form that a human user is still able to work with. A planning system that produces plans in an unexplainable or arcane form will not be as useful, because it will be very difficult for human operators to verify that the plans are indeed worth implementing. These are the two big advantages of HTNs: a search space tractable under normal execution conditions, and an approach that mimics human experts and can therefore be understood and managed by them.

The HTN approach has been implemented in numerous programming languages, including C, Java, Prolog, and Golog [7—10]. HTNs are also appropriate for planning problems that are dynamic in nature, and studies have shown how they can be used in conjunction with replanning and plan repair [11]. One group at Toshiba Research have produced a number of articles looking at using HTNs in systems with replanning [9,12,13]. Their research is particularly interested in identifying which actions may be canceled, and what effects a cancellation has. HTNs are considered to be a general and useful approach to planning by many researchers, including planning for dynamic environments with uncertainty.

5.2.5 Other Related Research

A comprehensive overview of the field of automated planning is found in the eponymous text by Ghallab, Nau, and Traverso [1]. The bulk of the text focuses on well-established classical planning techniques that must be done offline. However, even in the introduction, the issues related to real-world planning applications, including continual planning, are outlined clearly. A more expansive description of the difficulties and potential of distributed, continual planning is found in Ref. [14]. One of the authors of that article, Edmund Durfee, thoroughly outlines distributed planning in his canonical article, which has been updated several times, the most recent of which is Ref. [15]. One issue in general with distributed planning is the reliability of other agents. If agents working together on a plan are unable to trust each other completely, a great deal of effort must be spent on tracking the behavior and reputations of other agents in order to determine who can be trusted. This is not an issue for multi-agent systems aimed at fulfilling the goals of a single organization, such as in safety and security operations. All agents can safely be assumed to be willing to cooperate in order to achieve system-wide goals. While this may seem obvious, it significantly reduces the complexity of distributed planning when compared to the more general case.

Several examples of systems similar in scope to INFORM Lab that integrate both planning and simulation exist. They highlight the benefits of planning for safety and security scenarios. I-GLOBE simulates emergency responses; in particular, it simulates the construction of temporary medical facilities in response to an island-based disaster. It illustrates how distributed planning can be implemented in a continual manner [16]. EKEMAS is a continual planning simulation with an emphasis on geographical considerations. It employs both spatial reasoning and geo-simulation for natural disaster response [17]. It uses forest fire response as the example domain of application. MADGS is a US Air Force project that is a comprehensive simulation system incorporating several legacy components. It puts particular emphasis on satisfying resource requirements [18]. These examples illustrate different solutions for these kinds of challenges. A goal of our project is the development of a general approach that draws upon existing techniques and may be more widely applied.

5.3 Conceptual Design

In this section we outline the requirements of a comprehensive decision-making component of an OODA-based system operating in a complex, dynamic environment. We describe the design of the Decision Engine and explain how it satisfies these fundamental concerns.

5.3.1 Requirements

Eliciting and capturing the requirements of a software system is one of the first fundamental steps in software and systems engineering. Since designing and implementing an extensible system is complex, it is important to clearly establish the requirements. Here we list the high-level and high-priority requirements of the Decision Engine:

- *Appropriate output*: Produce a set of *decisions* when provided with a *goal*. These decisions must be likely to accomplish that goal.
- *Continuous updating*: Update ongoing goals, plans, and decisions based on situation evidence provided by an orienting process.
- *Flexible scheduling*: Be able to do scheduling as appropriate to the current state of the system. When time is available, scheduling should be done as part of the planning process. In this situation, the system should take advantage of any optimizing scheduling algorithms that are available to it. When time is limited, scheduling should simply consist of finding appropriate resources that are available with regards to goal priority, and assigning the resources in a first-come, first-served manner.
- *Robustness*: The Decision Engine should be able to repair a problematic plan (see Section 5.3.4 for a detailed explanation), and be able to retry, reassign or replan a failed decision, as appropriate.
- *Extensibility*: The system must be able to include other algorithms as subplanners and schedulers within the Plan Management component.
- *Generality*: The system needs to be a general model of decision making for two reasons. Firstly, since it is part of a research simulation environment, it should be readily comprehensible so that other research groups can use it and modify it as part of their own work. Secondly, it should be able to integrate new technologies as they mature and become a growing consideration within the domain of study.

5.3.2 System Architecture and Design

The Decision Engine is a state machine model, consisting of four active entities: Evaluation, Goal Management, Plan Management, and Decision Management (see Figure 5.2). Each behaves as a concurrently operating autonomous entity, interacting with each other asynchronously within their operational environment (the Decision Engine). The management components are responsible for maintaining and updating their respective pools of objects (goals for Goal Management, etc.). The Evaluation component monitors progress and current conditions in order to recognize when replanning is necessary. The process of generating decisions begins when the Decision Engine is sent goals and/or evidence from the parent system (in our case, INFORM Lab, see Section 5.5). Plans are constructed to address goals; decisions are then derived from plans to provide concrete means of achieving those goals. In order to support these efforts, the Decision Engine is capable of querying the parent system for relevant information, such as resource status or current weather conditions. This information is used to track the progress and results of activities under way, and corrective action is taken if corresponding expectations are not met. In this way, the Decision Engine as a whole aims to provide decisions for the parent system to use in assigning resources to various activities. We now describe the four main components in more detail, as well as technological considerations and requirements relevant to our design.

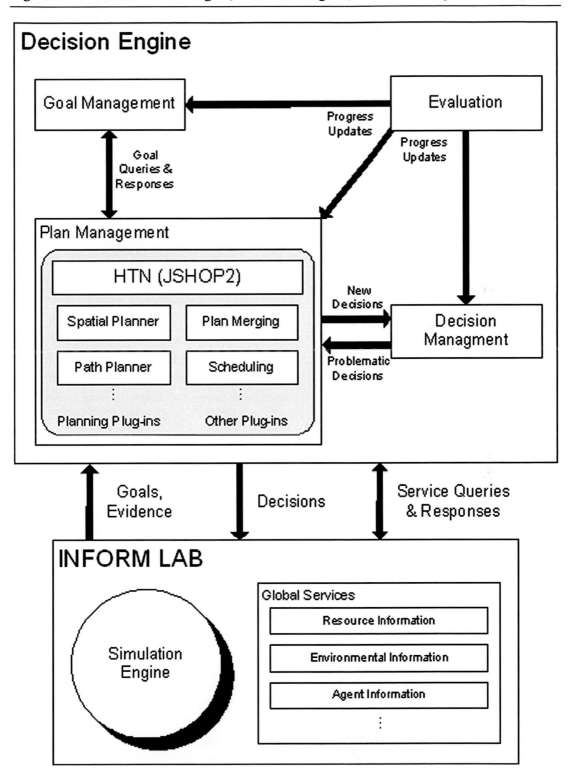

Figure 5.2:
Conceptual design of the Decision Engine.

Goal management

The Goal Management component is responsible for updating and processing the goals held in the goal pool, which is the set of active goals in the system. Like the other management components, it regularly checks the progress of the objects in its pool, performing management tasks when necessary and reacting to problems when they arise. The Goal Management component accepts new goals when they are inserted into the Decision Engine and maintains the list of plans associated with that goal. The potential for having multiple plans for a single goal provides greater robustness since the criteria for selecting which plan to act upon can change depending on current priorities and/or environmental conditions. Hierarchical goal analysis is used whenever possible to break down goals into independent subgoals in order to simplify planning.

Plan management

The Plan Management component creates, builds, and maintains plans within the system. For each goal, one or more plans are created, depending on the number of viable options available. If there is more than one plan, the relative cost of each will determine which is chosen to be the active plan for a goal and set into motion. Plans are completed when possible: a lack of information may prevent a plan from being completed before starting. Placeholder decisions can be used as a method of dealing with this challenge, as outlined in Ref. [19]. The history of choices made when developing a plan is also maintained, in order to allow backtracking when repairing a plan. The planning component turns the high-level requirements of a goal into decisions of a level practical enough that they can be acted upon. A variety of algorithms can be used to accomplish this process. This can be done as a single atomic process or incrementally, gradually refining an incomplete plan as required information becomes available. A plan must maintain the history of its construction process so that it may backtrack and look through alternate courses of action. This may occur during initial plan construction or as part of a replanning attempt to repair a plan that has become problematic during execution.

It is important to note that planning and scheduling are not modeled as separate processes at the highest level. This is due to the fact that the division between the two is not clear, and perhaps even arbitrary. They exist along a continuum of searching through the decision space. In general, planning can be considered to be the aspect of decision making related to choosing the actions to perform, while scheduling deals with the assignment of resources to be used. The two aspects are rarely independent, since the availability of resources can affect which actions can be performed. A given planning implementation may choose to optimize resource assignments by integrating planning and scheduling at each step, or it may largely disregard scheduling so that performance is optimized for timely reaction to critical situations. The current INFORM Lab implementation of planning is separated into three phases: Capability Planning (choosing actions), Mode Planning (choosing type of platforms), and Scheduling (deciding on specific platforms to assign). Any of these configurations of planning and scheduling are valid, and a high-level design of the decision process should be able to encompass them all. Indeed, considering the mixture of routine and emergency activity experienced in marine operations, it is beneficial to be able to do quick planning with simple scheduling when necessary and optimization when time is available. The Decision Engine accomplishes this by allowing either the Plan Management process (optimizing) or the Decision Management process (quick) to make resource assignments. Furthermore, an interim plan can be quickly proposed and begun while the Planning process continues to look for an improved alternate plan. If time is available and the change is worthwhile, the system can switch over to the alternate plan. By modeling the internal steps of the Decision Engine as processes and supporting alternate plans, this kind of robust, flexible behavior is possible.

Decision management

The Decision Management component handles the decisions that are currently active in the system. This includes both decisions that are executing, and thus are paired to an action being undertaken by the system, and decisions that are waiting for execution. Management of these decisions includes ensuring that decisions have resources assigned to them, recognizing when a decision should begin execution, as well as monitoring and reacting to status updates. For example, it may be necessary to interrupt the execution of a decision due to a failed execution, or a change in weather conditions, or because it was forced to release its current resource to a higher priority decision. Thus, it is necessary for Decision Management to monitor changes in the current status of a decision. This is in order to recognize information that relates to the progress of decisions under execution. Primarily, this is with regard to deviation from expected behavior. For example, a resource may not be moving as quickly as expected towards a target location, or a necessary sensory capability may be compromised, either due to weather or equipment failure. If possible, such problems should be solved at the decision management or scheduling level before resorting to replanning. In this way, the Decision Management component handles waiting decisions as well as those whose corresponding action is currently under execution.

Evaluation

The remaining part of the Decision Engine is the Evaluation component. It is responsible for deciding whether the current state of the world necessitates replanning. Evaluation receives the input to the Decision Engine, in the form of goals and situation evidence. Goals are passed along to the Goal Management component to be added to the goal pool. Situation Evidence is the information generated through an Orientation process that relates specifically to the goals, plans, and decisions that are currently active in the system. This includes things such as estimation of time or resources required to complete a decision, and forecasting the results of current activity. Evaluation is necessary for continual planning since it is the process that identifies when the current plan needs to change. Comparison of original expectations or requirements against current conditions or forecasts helps to identify when a problem has appeared, such as when a vehicle is moving too slowly to get to its destination by the time it is expected there. This could result in the adjustment of dependent decisions, or even the abandonment of the current mission in the extreme case. This can result in a change of status for a goal, plan, or decision, which can include cancellation. In many cases, no change would be required. It may also be necessary to create a new goal to handle some new set of conditions. The ability to reason about and react to change, provided here by the Evaluation component, is necessary for success in a dynamic environment [6].

Communication mechanism

The Decision Engine employs a message-passing paradigm as part of its foundation. The information being considered includes anything that is related to currently executing decisions. Such information needs to be modeled as coming from sensor data, like the other data already being collected in the simulation. Sensors that monitor those factors that affect decision execution, such as engine status, sensory capabilities, etc., are considered to be *internal* sensors. This is in contrast to *external* sensors, such as visibility and radar, which monitor the state of the world as encountered by a resource.

The first benefit of this is that status updates to goals, plans, decisions, and actions are all processed first as situation evidence by the Evaluation component. There is no direct, automatic updating done when an action completes, for example. The reasoning behind this is that the results of an action must be observed by sensors (internal or external) in order to be accepted as true. In other words, since we cannot fully predict the results of any action taken, we can only know for sure what has happened through observation. Another aspect of a message-based system is that we are able to model each of the components within the planning system as a software service agent, allowing the flexible use of resources to match current priorities. Similarly, multiple plans can be supported for a single goal, with the decision of which to use based on current conditions. Since each service agent acts upon shared data in a different manner, synchronization is not an issue. Furthermore, as a continual planning system, its fundamental purpose is to recognize and fix problematic situations.

The second benefit of employing message passing is that it allows the components to operate as asynchronous services. The model is more general since even a synchronous implementation will be a valid expression of the model. Also, it can improve flexibility during execution as, for example, the various processes could be running simultaneously but only use computing power proportional to their current needs. This could mean that the Planning process may be busy when first coming up with plans, and less busy afterwards. It may become busy again when it is feasible to spend resources on improving the existing set of plans. We can envision this kind of behavior as an OODA loop with multiple concentric rings. The results of some actions are immediately observable, and the Decision Engine has the potential to react to them swiftly, allowing for agile behavior in the system. Other processes take place over a long period of time, and the corresponding interactions between components, and thus their underlying OODA loop, are of a greater scale. By employing the message-passing paradigm to model the system, we are able to support this natural spectrum of dynamic behavior.

5.3.3 Hybrid HTN Framework

The Decision Engine model is designed to incorporate both current and upcoming technologies for managing plans. This is achieved in part by using an HTN planner as a general approach to planning that can call upon more specialized planners where appropriate. For example, an HTN planner may identify that a Move decision is necessary to get a resource into the right place. In this case, it is more appropriate and efficient to have a Path Planner to calculate the actual trajectories and spatial issues (such as collision detection and avoidance). Since HTNs only consider decisions as operators that change the world state, it would be difficult and inefficient to try to represent all decisions related to movement through space as HTN decisions. In this way, the HTN planner acts as the central mechanism in an automated planner, binding together a family of more specialized planners. This allows a varied group of decisions that require different algorithms for computing their plans to be used together to achieve a goal. For example, a search and rescue mission will require the coordination of sensing, communication, and movement of appropriate resources (such as rescue vehicles) just to set up the actual rescue attempt. Each of these activities involves different algorithms to compute, such as Path Finding for movement. Since HTNs break down abstract, high-level goals, an HTN planner can act as a framework, distributing more specific decisions to the appropriate subplanners when applicable. This use of HTNs as a framework can be considered to be the logical extension of the concept of critics within HTNs [20].

Figure 5.3 illustrates an example of how the Hybrid HTN planning architecture works. Given a goal to detect smuggling operations in a given area, the HTN planner begins with a high-level abstract decision that directly corresponds with this goal: Detect Smuggling. This decision possesses parameters that detail the specifics of this particular mission, e.g. the area that should be observed. The HTN planner then iteratively uses methods to break down the highest level decision into more specific ones. For example, Move to Area of Interest is refined with Fly because this is the best method for reaching the area under consideration. However, the next level of refinement uses a geographical navigation subplanner in order to generate a Flight Plan for this flight. The subplanner in question is specialized for dealing with geographical objects and issues. Other subplanners are used to refine other decisions. For example, a subplanner which can calculate search patterns and consider sensor capabilities is

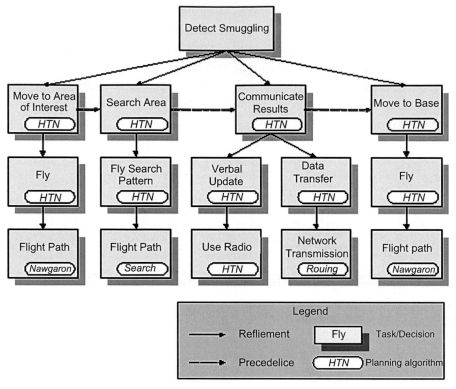

Figure 5.3:
Example plan generated by the proposed Hybrid HTN approach.

used to generate the Flight Plan for the Fly Search Pattern decision. HTN methods are used to select which subplanners to use. In this simplified example, the lowest level of decisions (the "leaves") would be the output of the entire planning process, being passed along as decisions to the Decision Manager in the case where this plan is chosen for activation.

5.3.4 Plan Robustness

Fundamentally, the model of planning employed here accepts the existence of failure and surprises, and deals with them in a proactive manner when able. An Evaluation component is used to analyze situation evidence generated both through agent activity as well as sensing of the environment. In this way, immediate problems are recognized as conflicts with constraints of decisions in the decision pool. Potential future problems are highlighted by comparing what is expected with current progress, e.g. expected time of arrival against current velocity. Success, problems, and failure are noted as status changes in decisions, plans, and goals. Failure is not an absolute state: it may allow for the retrying of an action as is, or with alternative methods or resources; it could also mean the need for replanning, and only result in the abandonment of a mission in a worst-case scenario. All planning is done in a manner such that relevant costs are minimized, including time and monetary expense. Replanning also considers the costs associated with changing a course of action, and the current plan is maintained as much as possible in order to support this. Scheduling of resources is done according to availability and the priority of a given decision. The continual planning model proposed in this project includes these current planning strategies in order to allow intelligent and dynamic behavior for automated agents in a complex environment.

The proposed system allows us to employ the most efficient approach when it comes to plan repair, in this order of preference:

1. *Retry*: If the planned action has failed but the plan as a whole is still valid, i.e. there are still resources and time available to perform it and its operational constraints still hold, then the most straightforward choice is to continue with the existing decision. This is undertaken in Decision Management.
2. *Reassign*: If resources assigned to the decision have become lost or ineffective, assign new resources to the decision. This is the obvious reaction to the failure of an action due to a resource problem (e.g. engine failure) or changes in the environment that interfere with capabilities of the current resources (e.g. severe weather). This option is also undertaken in Decision Management.
3. *Replan*: Employ a replanning algorithm to repair the plan. If possible, alterations to the plan should be minimal, in order to avoid difficulty in adjusting to the newly repaired plan. In this case, the response to the issue is taken care of in Plan Management.

Since the solution to the problem is taken care of in Decision Management when possible, this approach is the online analog to using a backtracking algorithm to fix a generated plan.

5.3.5 Emerging Technologies

Automated planning is an active area of research, and several new technologies and paradigms have become prominent recently. One example is plan merging, which is concerned with merging the actions of plans together in order to limit redundancy. For example, rather than sending two packages by separate couriers, it makes more sense to use one courier for both packages, if time and capacity constraints can still be met. It is important that any general design for a system that includes planning is able to integrate these new technologies as they start to mature. Plan merging is still a developing research topic, and as such it is not mature enough to include a plan merging algorithm within the Decision Engine yet. However, the general concepts of plan merging have been considered in this design so that it may more easily be integrated at a later date.

We do not outline the manner of performing planning in a distributed manner here, since the focus of this phase of our research is the complex dynamic behavior of a single agent.

However, a method for dealing with this that is directly applicable to the proposed system is described in Ref. [21].

5.4 Formal Representation

A primary goal of this research is to capture the central issues of continual planning in a manner that is fundamentally mathematical in nature. The comprehensive high-level design presented here uses formal methods to express the model at an operational level, capturing the behavior of the system as a whole. By using formal methods to analyze and design the proposed model, later development and implementation should be straightforward. Specifically, we use the Abstract State Machine (ASM) method to delineate the responsibilities of the system components.

5.4.1 Abstract State Machines

The ASM method is a formalism that is particularly suited to applied systems engineering. ASMs combine *first-order structures*, in order to represent states as arbitrary data structures, with *state transition systems*, in order to capture the dynamic behavior of a target system. They are capable of capturing concepts naturally and formally, such that the essential characteristics of the target system are expressed clearly. This clarity is useful when working in conjunction with domain experts, since it is easier for them to participate in the construction and validation of a system model. The ASM method includes a *stepwise refinement* process, allowing any part of the model to be defined at an appropriate level of detail or abstraction. ASMs are executable in principle, so may also be used in an empirical manner, such as by testing a model experimentally. In this way, they act as a bridge between specification methods and computational modeling. An authoritative explanation of ASMs is contained in Ref. [3].

5.4.2 CoreASM Environment

CoreASM is an executable specification language and tool environment that allows experimental analysis of ASM specifications. Its plug-in based architecture provides an extensible framework that can be augmented in a modular manner in order to meet the needs of the current application [22]. In our research, CoreASM is employed to test the Decision Engine ASM specifications through execution on example scenarios. A secondary outcome of pursuing this line of development with the Decision Engine is a method for using CoreASM in conjunction with existing Java code. Previously, only one-way communication from CoreASM to Java was possible. Now, CoreASM can be accessed from Java, allowing two-way interaction. This in turn makes it possible to run the Decision Engine as an ASM specification in conjunction with an existing system (in this case INFORM Lab, running in

```
domain GOAL
domain PLAN
domain DECISION
domain COST
domain RESOURCE
domain PROCESSES = { GoalManagement, PlanManagement,
              DecisionManagement, Evaluation }
domain PROGRESS_STATUS = { incomplete, success, failure }
domain DECISION_MODE = { waiting, executing, interrupted }
```

Figure 5.4:
ASM specification of the system domains.

Java). This enables a "hardware-in-the-loop" type of development process, where high-level design decisions can be immediately tested through interaction with previously existing code.

5.4.3 Decision Engine ASM Specifications

An Abstract State Machine specification of the Decision Engine has been developed at a high level of abstraction. First, the domains, or central element types and sets, are listed in Figure 5.4.

Next, the rules that govern Goal Management are shown in Figure 5.5.

In Figure 5.6, the primary rules related to the Plan Management component are presented. Note that the main Plan Management rule considers all of the goals in the *goalPool* (the currently active set of goals) in order to act upon (or create) the plans related to those goals; it also considers all of the plans in the *planPool* (the currently active set of plans) individually for appropriate updates.

The Decision Management component in Figure 5.7 largely follows the rule for task management presented in Ref. [23]. Finally, a general description of the Evaluation component is contained in Figure 5.8. This component is the newest conceptually, and further development would be beneficial. While specific criteria for evaluating progress are not difficult to establish, such as comparing current location against the target destination in the

```
GoalManagement =
  forall g in goalPool do
    if progress(g) = success then
      CompleteGoal(g)
    else if progress(g) = failure then
      CancelGoal(g)
    else if CanDecompose(g) then
      DecomposeGoal(g)
```

Figure 5.5:
ASM specification of the Goal Management component.

PlanManagement =
    forall g **in** *goalPool* **do**
      if *canMakeNewPlan(g)* **then**
        CreatePlan(g)
      else if *activePlan(g)* = **undef then**
        choose p **in** *plans(g)* **with** *ready(p)* **and** *minCost(p)* **do**
          ActivatePlan(g,p)
      else choose p **in** *plans(g)* **with** *superiorPlan(p)* **do**
        ChangePlans(g,p)
    forall p **in** *planPool* **do**
      case *progress(p)* **of**
        success: FinishSuccessfulPlan(p)
        failure: CancelPlan(p)
        incomplete: UpdatePlan(p)

UpdatePlan(p : PLAN) =
    if *isProblematic(p)* **then**
      RepairPlan(p)
    else if *isBuilding(p)* **then**
      BuildPlan(p)
    if *planReady(p)* **and** *active(p)* **then**
      InitiateDecisions(p)
    EstimateCost(p)

Figure 5.6:
ASM specification of the Plan Management component.

DecisionManagement =
    forall t **in** *decisionPool* **do**
      case *progress(t)* **of**
        success: FinalizeDecision(t)
        failure: CancelDecision(t)
        incomplete: UpdateDecision(t)

UpdateDecision(t) =
    if *mode(t)* = *interrupted* **then**
      StopDecision(t)
      mode(t) := *waiting*
    else if *mode(t)* = *waiting* **then**
      if *pastDeadline(t)* **or** *impossible(t)* **then**
        progress(t) := *failure*
      else if *resource(t)* = **undef then**
        FindResource(t)
      else if *constraintsSatisfied(t)* **and** *ready(resource(t),t)* **then**
        ExecutionInitialization(t)

Figure 5.7:
ASM specification of the Decision Management component.

EvaluationManagement=
CheckforNewGoal
CheckforGoalProgressChange
CheckforPlanProgressChange
CheckforDecisionProgressChange
CheckforDecisionModeChange

Figure 5.8:
ASM specification of the Evaluation component.

case of movement, a general algorithm for evaluating progress and reacting to unexpected developments is still an open problem. In particular, it is challenging to determine which reaction to a partial failure is best for a specific situation, such as whether replanning is necessary or simply waiting will be sufficient to deal with the problem. Thus, the current specification for this component outlines the requirements for this component, and we consider a further refinement as an open (and interesting) problem.

5.5 Application

The target system for implementation, INFORM Lab, combines higher-level distributed dynamic information fusion, distributed dynamic resource management, communication strategies, and configuration management in a marine safety and security simulation environment. In particular, INFORM Lab simulates the directed actions of assets allocated to the Marine Security Operations Centre based at Esquimalt, British Columbia. For example, the system is capable of investigating and identifying suspicious behavior that may be smuggling in the environs of the Strait of Georgia, including Vancouver Island and the British Columbia mainland coast. It was designed and developed at MDA Corporation, Richmond, B.C., Canada. It has served as a source for establishing the requirements of a continual planning layer, and has shown such a layer could fit into a larger simulation engine or decision support system. In the future, INFORM Lab can act as a test bed for testing the implementation of the continual planning layer in its role as a Decision Engine. This will be accomplished through an interface that bridges the two systems and allows for the interchange of information. The eventual goal of this project is for a well-tested implementation of the Decision Engine to act as an improved decision processor for INFORM Lab. Our research is also motivated by the potential future use of an application like INFORM Lab being used by human operators in a decision support role for real-world activities.

5.6 Conclusions and Future Work

This chapter has presented a conceptual design for a Decision Engine that can work within the context of an OODA-based control loop. Such an engine can be used for determining and controlling agent actions in any application for which making decisions is complex and must be done in an online manner. This fulfills the requirements of a continual planning system for marine safety and security operations, where critical decisions must be made quickly in a complex environment and with imperfect knowledge. However, many other activities that do not take place in an isolated environment (e.g. a factory) fall into the same category. Thus, we argue that it is appropriate for numerous real-world operations, including situations with autonomous agents (as a controller for robots or in simulations) and/or human beings (when used in a decision support role). Currently, this Decision Engine is being used in conjunction with INFORM Lab for research purposes, and we expect that it will widen the range of possible situations that can be represented and handled within that simulation environment.

One of the main benefits of the approach presented in this chapter is the use of the *Hybrid HTN framework* to deal with online and real-time situations. By developing a framework in CoreASM that can handle different planners, subplanners, and schedulers, it will be possible to integrate different implemented planners (including JSHOP2 for HTN) and INFORM Lab. In this way, a varied group of decisions that require different algorithms for computing their plans can be processed together in order to satisfy a goal. The system proposed here explicitly captures, at a high level, the qualities that a continual planner needs to possess in order to succeed in real-world operations in a dynamic environment with the presence of uncertainty, and it is meant to be suitable as a blueprint in the future for applications in similar simulation environments.

Acknowledgments

The work presented here has been funded by MDA Corporation and MITACS through the MITACS-Accelerate internship program.

References

[1] M. Ghallab, D. Nau, P. Traverso, Automated Planning: Theory and Practice, first ed., Morgan Kaufmann, 2004.

[2] Natural Resources Canada, The Atlas of Canada: Coastline and Shoreline (online). <http://atlas.nrcan.gc.ca/site/english/learningresources/facts/coastline.html> (accessed 01.09.11)

[3] E. Börger, R. Stärk, Abstract State Machines: A Method for High-Level System Design and Analysis, Springer, 2003.

[4] Z. Li, H. Leung, P. Valin, H. Wehn, High level data fusion system for CanCoastWatch, Proc. 10th Int. Conf. on Information Fusion, Quebec City, Canada, 2007.

[5] M. Pollack, J. Horty, There's more to life than making plans: Plan management in dynamic, multiagent environments, AI Mag. 20 (4) (19990 71−83.

[6] A. Hunter, J. Happe, W. Wei, M. Lau, C. Gagné, S. Peters, D. Shubaly, S. Jovanovic, S. Mitrovic-Minic, Execution Management and Plan Adaptation, Final Report, DRDC Toronto, CR 2008-123, 2008.

[7] D. Nau, O. Ilghami, U. Kuter, J. Murdock, D. Wu, F. Yaman, SHOP2: An HTN planning system, J. Artif. Intell. Res. 20 (2003) 379−404.

[8] O. Ilghami, Documentation for JSHOP2, Department of Computer Science, University of Maryland, CS-TR-4694, 2005.

[9] H. Hayashi, S. Tokura, F. Ozaki, Towards real-world HTN planning agents, Knowl. Process. Decis. Mak. Agent Syst. 170 (2009) 13−41.

[10] R. Goldman, A semantics for HTN methods, Proc. 19th Int. Conf. on Automated Planning and Scheduling, Thessaloniki, Greece, 2009.

[11] N. Ayan, U. Kuter, F. Yaman, R. Goldman, HOTRiDE: Hierarchical Ordered Task Replanning in Dynamic Environments, Proc. of the ICAPS Workshop on Planning and Plan Execution for Real-World Systems: Principles and Practices for Planning in Execution, 2007.

[12] H. Hayashi, K. Cho, A. Ohsuga, Speculative computation and action execution in multi-agent systems, Electron. Notes Theor. Comput. Sci. 70 (5) (2002) 153−166.

[13] H. Hayashi, K. Cho, A. Ohsuga, A new HTN planning framework for agents in dynamic environments, Comput. Log. Multi Agent Syst. 3259 (2005) 55−56.

[14] M. desJardins, E. Durfee, C. Ortiz, M. Wolverton, A survey of research in distributed, continual planning, AI Magaz. 20 (4) (1999) 13−22.

[15] E. Durfee, Distributed problem solving and planning, Multi Agent Syst. Appl. 2086 (2006) 118−149.

[16] A. Komenda, J. Vokřínek, M. Pěchouček, G. Wickler, J. Dalton, A. Tate, Distributed planning and coordination in non-deterministic environments, Proc. 8th Int. Conf. on Autonomous Agents and Multiagent Systems (AAMAS), Budapest, Hungary, 2009.

[17] N. Sahli, B. Moulin, EKEMAS, an agent-based geo-simulation framework to support continual planning in the real-word, Appl. Intell. 31 (2) (2009) 188−209.

[18] E. Santos, S. DeLoach, M. Cox, Achieving dynamic, multi-commander, multi-mission planning and execution, Appl. Intell. 25 (3) (2006) 335−357.

[19] M. Brenner, B. Nebel, Continual planning and acting in dynamic multiagent environments, Auton. Agents Multi Agent Syst. 19 (3) (2009) 297−331.

[20] K. Erol, J. Hendler, D. Nau, Semantics for hierarchical task-network planning, University of Maryland Computer Science Technical Report, CS-TR-3239, 1994.

[21] U. Glässer, P. Jackson, A. Khalili Araghi, H. Yaghoubi Shahir, H. Wehn, A collaborative decision support model for marine safety and security operations, Proc. 3rd IFIP TC 10 Int. Conf. on Biologically-Inspired Collaborative Computing (BICC), Brisbane, Australia, 2010.

[22] R. Farahbod, U. Glässer, The CoreASM modeling framework, Software: Practice and Experience, Special Issue: Tool Building in Formal Methods 41 (2) (2011) 167−178.

[23] U. Glässer, P. Jackson, A. Khalili Araghi, H. Yaghoubi Shahir, Intelligent decision support for marine safety and security operations, Proc. IEEE Int. Conf. on Intelligence and Security Informatics (ISI), Vancouver, Canada, 2010.

CHAPTER 6

Criminal Identity Resolution Using Personal and Social Identity Attributes: A Collective Resolution Approach

Jiexun Li[*], Alan Wang G[†]

*College of Information Science and Technology, Drexel University, Philadelphia, Pennsylvania, USA
† Department of Business Information Technology, Virginia Tech, Blacksburg, Virginia, USA

Chapter Outline

6.1 Introduction

Identity resolution is a semantic reconciliation process that determines if a single identity is the same when being described differently [1]. An effective resolution technique is especially important in fighting criminals and terrorists and ensuring national security. The Assistant Director of the FBI Counterterrorism Division testified in a congressional testimony, "We must

Intelligent Systems for Security Informatics.
http://dx.doi.org/10.1016/B978-0-12-404702-0.00006-9

be able to determine whether an individual is who they purport to be. This is essential in our mission to identify potential terrorists, locate their means of financial support, and prevent acts of terrorism from occurring" [2]. However, this is not a trivial task because a criminal may assume multiple identities using either fraudulent or legitimate means. Terrorists are known to commit identity crimes, namely identity fraud, identity theft, and identity deception, in order to enhance the chances of success in their missions. A report released by the Office of the Coordinator for Counterterrorism describes many cases where terrorists in different countries use false passports and other identifications to facilitate their financial operations and the execution of attacks [3]. The 9/11 Commission Report also describes in detail how terrorists fraudulently acquire travel documents using, for example, photo-substituted passports or blank baptismal certificates. In record management systems that manage massive amounts of identities, duplicated identity references for an individual may also be introduced due to data entry errors. The problem of an individual having multiple identities can easily mislead intelligence and law enforcement investigations and diminish their efforts.

In database and data-mining communities many identity resolution techniques have been developed to tackle this issue. Most traditional techniques of identity resolution only use personal identity attributes such as name and identification numbers to find matching identities because those attributes are often used to describe a person in most record management systems [4,5]. However, personal identity attributes are subject to problems such as deception, fraud, and data quality issues. Their availability and reliability vary across different record management systems. Recent development in generic entity resolution techniques, such as the Probabilistic Relational Model [2] and the Collective Entity Resolution model [6], has prompted the use of contextual information in addition to descriptive attributes of entities. In the context of identity resolution contextual information may refer to one's social acquaintance and relationships such as one's roommates and coworkers. Compared to personal identity attributes, social characteristics are difficult to falsify because they may require extraordinary efforts for collaborative deceit [7].

In this chapter we introduce a novel identity resolution technique that takes into account both personal identity and social identity attributes in a collective fashion. Compared to other identity resolution proposals, this technique has the following advantages. Firstly, it can utilize current record management systems without introducing an infrastructure overhaul and costly hardware. Secondly, by linking known identities that supposedly co-refer to one individual, it provides stronger evidence to intelligence and law enforcement investigators and improves the efficacy and efficiency of investigations. Thirdly, it reduces the search load by deduplicating records in a database. Lastly, it will enable new identity resolution techniques by exploring the rich information behind one's *de facto* identity.

This chapter is organized as follows. We first review identity theories and existing entity resolution techniques, followed by an introduction to our proposed collective identity resolution technique. We report an empirical evaluation of the performance of our proposed technique that combines both personal and social identity attributes.

6.2 Related Work

In this section we review identity theories from the social science literature and review identity attributes and analytical techniques used in existing identity resolution studies.

6.2.1 Identity Theories

The concept of identity has long been studied in philosophy, psychology, and sociology. It has a complex and changing subjective notion [8]. We consider an individual's identity to have two basic components, namely a personal identity and a social identity.

A personal identity is one's self-perception as an individual [9]. It deals with those necessary and sufficient conditions under which self persists over time. For example, people often ask common questions about their personal identities such as "Who am I" and "Where did I come from." A personal identity may include personal information given at birth (e.g. name, date and place of birth), personal identifiers (e.g. social security number, passport number), physical descriptions (e.g. height, weight), and biometric information (e.g. fingerprint, DNA). A study conducted by the United Kingdom Home Office [10] suggests that identity crimes usually involve the illegal use or alteration of those personal identity components.

A social identity is one's biographical history that builds up over time. It reflects how a person interacts with the society that he or she belongs to. Social identity theories consist of psychological and sociological views. The psychological view defines a social identity as one's self-perception as a member of certain social groups such as nation, culture, gender, and employment [11,12]. Based on the psychological view, people within a social group may share some common characteristics that can distinguish themselves from people in other groups. On the other hand, the sociological view focuses on "the relationships between social actors who perform mutually complementary roles (e.g. employer—employee, doctor—patient)" [13]. The emphasis is on the interpersonal relationships among people and the social structure formed based on the relationships [14]. In addition, one's social context determines the specific roles that the individual takes. For example, a man can have different roles in his family: the father of his children, the son of his parents, and the husband of his wife. An individual's social identity, in this sense, is defined as the role-based interactions between the individual and people in his or her surrounding social networks. Deaux and Martin [13] integrated the psychological view and sociological view into one framework by regarding them as different levels of social context. The psychological view deals with large-scale social groups, whereas the sociological view deals with the proximate social groups in which members interact with each other. In this framework, a social identity becomes a multi-level concept that involves understanding one's social groups at various scales.

6.2.2 Identity Attributes Used in Identity Resolution

For identity resolution, we are interested in determining features that can reliably identify an individual. Personal identity attributes such as names are often subject to data quality problems such as deception and data entry errors [5]. The use of identification cards and biometrics has been touted to be reliable identifiers by their proponents [15,16]. However, not only are there public concerns over its privacy implications, but a study also suggests that the connection between the use of national identity cards and antiterrorism is largely intuitive [17]. They investigated 25 countries that had been most adversely affected by terrorism since 1986. Those countries that employed an identity card system and biometric techniques did not show lessened terrorist activities in terms of number of attacks and deaths. O'Neil [18] discussed the shortcomings in biometrics as a counter-terrorist tool. He found that biometrics were not as reliable and fraud-proof as people expected. The lack of a reliable personal identifier prompts us to look for a good set of attributes for more accurate identity resolution than any single identifier.

The identity theories reviewed in the previous section suggest that personal and social identity attributes may complement each other for the purpose of identity resolution. Social identity attributes are derived from people's social activities and relationships with other individuals. Such attributes exist implicitly in identity management databases and can be extracted for identity resolution. For example, we may infer relationships among identities based on the facts that some identities share the same address or get involved in the same incident. These inferred social attributes might be more reliable that personal identity attributes in that they cannot be easily altered or falsified by an individual. Taking into account social identity features can provide additional evidence when distinguishing one individual from others.

6.2.3 Existing Resolution Techniques

Identity resolution techniques are one type of entity resolution technique specializing in identity management. Entity resolution is also known as record linkage and deduplication in the areas of statistics and database management respectively. Record linkage, originated in the statistics community, identifies records in the same or different databases that refer to the same real-world entity [19]. The very same task is studied as record deduplication in database and artificial intelligence communities [20–22]. These techniques consider records comprised of multiple fields. To determine whether or not two records match, they first compare corresponding individual fields between two records. A decision model determines whether or not the two records refer to the same real-world entity by combining all comparison results. Elmagarmid et al. [23] provide a survey on individual field-matching techniques and models that detect duplicate records.

Compared to general entity resolution, identity resolution has its own challenges. Firstly, identity resolution needs to be efficient, especially for security-related tasks. Secondly, the evaluation of an identity resolution technique may be subject to different criteria under different circumstances. For example, the false-positive rate may be less tolerable than the false-negative rate for identity authentication that grants access to a critical infrastructure facility. However, a high false-positive rate may not be of much concern when a detective searches for a suspect with limited information. Lastly, identity matching in intelligence and law enforcement communities suffers greatly from the missing data problem [4]. Those record linkage and deduplication techniques tend to work poorly if many fields are missing from a record. In the following we briefly review existing techniques most appropriate for identity resolution. We categorize them into rule-based and machine learning approaches.

In the literature there have been several rule-based approaches for identity resolution by encoding matching rules specified by human experts. For instance, in a study on cross-jurisdictional data integration, Marshall et al. [24] encode experts' heuristics into a simple rule: two identity records match only if their first name, last name, and date-of-birth (DOB) values are all identical. Obviously, in the case of data quality problems including missing values, such exact-match heuristics will cause many false-negative decisions and cannot effectively identify matching identity records. Some other approaches allow partial matching to reduce false negatives. The IBM DB2 Identity Resolution included in the Entity Analytic Solutions (EAS) is a leading commercial product designed to manage identity records [1]. It provides a rule-based identity-matching system that associates identity records representing the same person. For a pair of identity records, a matching score is calculated by following a set of rules predefined by human experts. For example, given two identity records with identical dates of birth and last names, the system will resolve them into one if the matching score of their first names is above 70%. The score can be calculated using any of the string comparison techniques reviewed in Ref. [23]. For these rule-based approaches, the rule creation process can be quite time-consuming, and the rules tend to be domain dependent and not portable across different contexts.

An alternative to manual rule coding is machine learning, which can automatically build identity resolution models by learning from a training dataset with annotated matching pairs. Identity resolution techniques based on machine learning can be further categorized into distance-based and probabilistic methods. Distance-based methods define distance/similarity measures for different types of descriptive attributes and combine them into a weighted average distance score. Two identity records whose overall distance is below a predefined threshold will be regarded as a match. Brown and Hagen [25] proposed a data association method for linking criminal records that possibly refer to the same suspect. This method compares two records and calculates a total similarity measure as a weighted sum of the similarity measures of all corresponding feature values. The features used by their method include suspect and *modus operandi* (MO) descriptions. The method lacks a matching decision model and only provides a list of matching candidates. Wang et al. [5] proposed a record comparison algorithm for detecting deceptive identities by comparing four personal features (name, DOB, social security number (SSN), and address) and combining them into an overall similarity score. A supervised learning process determines a threshold for match decisions using a set of identity pairs labeled by an expert. However, missing values could significantly affect the performance of the record comparison algorithm [4]. Probabilistic methods for identity matching are rooted in the seminal work of Ref. [19]. By posing record linkage as a probabilistic classification problem, they propose a formal framework to label pairs of identities from two different datasets as "match" or "non-match" based on the agreement among different features. Assuming conditional independence among features given the match class, the framework estimates the probabilistic parameters of the record linkage model in an unsupervised fashion. Many later studies were built based upon this work to enrich the probabilistic model [26–29]. These studies have shown that the probabilistic models achieve good performance for identity matching. However, the parameters of the probabilistic models may not be accurately estimated in the absence of sufficient training data [30].

Most identity resolution techniques reviewed above rely on personal identity attributes. Although these attributes provide a good basis for match decisions, they are prone to various issues, including entry errors, identity fraud and deception, and missing values. Identity resolution, especially in the crime/terrorist fighting context, is not simply a data quality problem as existing resolution techniques suggest. Solving such a complex problem requires a combination of multiple techniques and needs to be viewed from a network perspective [2]. Individuals are not isolated but interrelated to each other in a society. The social contexts associated with an individual can provide evidence that reveals his/her undeniable identity. Therefore, there is a need to develop identity resolution techniques that also incorporate the social perspective of identities.

6.2.4 Resolution Techniques Enabled by Social Contexts

Many recent studies have started to take into account linkage and contextual information for identity resolution. Köpcke and Rahm [31] categorized entity resolution approaches into attribute value matchers and context matchers. Unlike attribute value matchers, which solely consider descriptive attribute values, context matchers rely on information inferred through social interactions represented in a graph structure. Distance-based methods can combine the attribute similarity and relational similarity into one aggregated score for more reliable matching performance. Ananthakrishna et al. [32] introduced a deduplication method using a dimensional hierarchy (e.g. city—state—country) over the link relations in a customer data warehouse. This method enhances the personal feature comparison technique by only comparing feature values that have the same foreign key dependency. For example, the similarity of two people's names will be assessed only when both live in the same city. However, that method requires a hierarchy among attribute relationships. In addition, it does not address the impact of the existence of missing values in a database. In a study on reference disambiguation, Kalashnikov et al. [33] incorporated inter-object relationships such as co-affiliation and co-authorship to disambiguate references using a nonlinear optimization model. However, their method cannot easily work as a plug-and-play solution in other entity resolution applications. In addition, probabilistic models that capture social contexts have been proposed for entity resolution. Culotta and McCallum [34] constructed a conditional random field model (CRF) for record deduplication that captures interdependencies between different types of entities. This method, however, fails to model the explicit links among the same type of entities. Pasula et al. [35] proposed a generic probabilistic relational model (PRM) for citation matching. It captures the dependences among entities over a relational database structure through foreign key relationships. This model is built upon the existing relational database structure and can be used as a plug-and-play solution because most current record management systems store records in relational databases. This approach, however, suffers from computational intractability. Bhattacharya and Getoor [36] proposed a graph-based method for entity resolution. It defines a similarity measure that combines corresponding attribute similarities with graph-based relational similarity between each entity reference pair. Their experiments show that the new similarity measure improves performance over the resolution methods that consider only attribute similarities. Furthermore, Bhattacharya and Getoor [6] extended their relational resolution approach to match entities in a collective fashion. Rather than making pairwise entity comparisons, their method collectively merges records into clusters. Through this process, new relational information can be derived and help to support further matching decisions.

The recent developments in entity resolution techniques shows that the relationships among entities can be used to improve resolution performance in addition to attribute distances/ similarities. As we reviewed earlier, social relationships play an even more important role in personal identities than other types of entities because they affect one's psychological and sociological perception of one's own identity. It is our intention, based on the identity theories, to define social identity attributes that can be used to effectively enhance the performance of identity resolution.

6.3 A Collective Identity Resolution Approach

In this section we introduce an identity resolution technique that utilizes both personal identity attributes and social identity attributes. We define two types of social identity attributes, namely social behavior attributes and social relationship attributes. We will explore different matching strategies when combining personal identity attributes and social attributes. We will determine the optimal matching strategy using an empirical evaluation.

6.3.1 Problem Formulation

We formulate the identity resolution problem as follows. Given a set of identity references, $R = \{r_i\}$, where each reference r is described by a set of personal identity attributes $r{\bullet}A_1$, $r{\bullet}A_2$, ..., $r{\bullet}A_k$. These references correspond to a set of unknown entities $E = \{e_i\}$. Due to duplicates and deception, multiple references $\{r_{e_1}, ..., r_{e_n}\}$ may be co-referent to the same underlying entity e. We use $r{\bullet}E$ to refer to the entity to which reference r refers to. Also, each reference is involved with at least one incident and each incident may involve one or multiple references. We represent each incident as a hyper-edge in which multiple references may co-occur. We describe the co-occurrence with a set of hyper-edges $H = \{h_i\}$. Each hyper-edge h can also be described by a set of attributes $h{\bullet}B_1$, $h{\bullet}B_2$, ..., $h{\bullet}B_l$, and we use $h{\bullet}R$ to denote the set of references involved. A reference r can belong to zero or any number of hyper-edges and we use $r{\bullet}H$ to denote the set of hyper-edges in which r participates. The problem is to recover the hidden set of entities $E = \{e_i\}$ and the entity labels $r{\bullet}E$ for individual references given the observed attributes of the references and their involved hyper-edges. Figure 6.1 illustrates the problem of identity resolution in a graph of five reference nodes connected by three hyper-edges.

6.3.2 Identity Resolution Approaches

Each identity resolution approach includes two major components: an attribute similarity measure and a matching strategy. A similarity function measures how similar two references

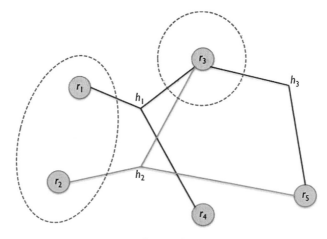

Figure 6.1:
A graphical view of the identity resolution problem.

are to each other based on certain attributes. A matching strategy specifies the algorithmic procedure of recovering the underlying entities from the given set of references. In this section we first define the identity attributes that can be used in identity resolution. We also discuss how we measure the similarity for each type of identity attribute. Lastly, we introduce matching strategies that make matching decisions based on the identity attribute similarities.

Identity attributes and similarity measures

To determine whether two references are co-referent, we need to measure their similarity. A greater similarity score implies a higher probability of co-reference or matching, and *vice versa*. We describe each type of identity attributes and their similarity measures as follows.

Personal identity attributes

Personal identity attributes are personal identifiers that are commonly used to distinguish one person from others. Examples include, but are not limited to, name, date of birth, social security number (SSN), and address. The similarity between these textual attributes can be calculated by editing distance measures such as the Levenstein Distance [37]. We use A to refer to the identity attribute-based approach. If the similarity score $sim_A(r_i, r_j)$ is above a threshold, references r_i and r_j are considered as co-referent. These approaches tend to perform well for references with duplicates and typos, but may not be able to detect intentional deceptions.

Social behavior attributes

Social behavior attributes represent the common characteristics of the social group that one belongs to. They reflect the psychological view of personal identities. Most identity management systems involve a certain type of transaction (e.g. crime incidents, credit card transactions). Therefore, we choose to use transaction-based behavioral patterns to describe the common characteristics of a social group. We denote the set of hyper-edges involving reference r as $r{\bullet}H$. Then, each hyper-edge $r_i{\bullet}h$ involving r_i is compared with each hyper-edge $r_j{\bullet}h'$ of r_j. The overall behavioral similarity between r_i and r_j is computed by the average of all the hyper-edge pairs' similarity scores. Thus, the behavioral similarity between two references r_i and r_j can be defined as:

$$sim_b(r_i, r_j) = sim_b(r_i{\bullet}H, r_j{\bullet}H) = \cfrac{1}{\left|r_i{\bullet}H\right| \times \left|r_j{\bullet}H\right|} \sum_{h \in r_i{\bullet}H,\ h' \in r_j{\bullet}H} sim_b(r_i{\bullet}h, r_j{\bullet}h') \tag{6.1}$$

where $|r{\bullet}H|$ denotes the number of hyper-edges involving r.

Taking into account both the personal identity similarity and social behavioral similarity, we use B to refer to this particular resolution approach. The overall similarity between two references r_i and r_j is defined as:

$$sim_B(r_i, r_j) = \alpha \times sim_A(r_i, r_j) + (1 - \alpha) \times sim_b(r_i, r_j) \tag{6.2}$$

where $0 \leq \alpha \leq 1$ and it can be changed to control the weights of the two similarity scores.

Social relationship attributes

Social relationship attributes capture the social contacts that one often interacts with. These attributes reflect the sociological view of personal identities. If two references r_i and r_j are both related to the same reference r_k (e.g. r_i and r_j co-occur with r_k in different hyper-edges), this can be regarded as evidence that these two references are co-referent. We denote the neighborhood of a reference r as $Nbr(r)$. Then, the neighborhood similarity between two references r_i and r_j can be defined as:

$$sim_N(r_i, r_j) = sim_N(Nbr(r_i), Nbr(r_j)) = sim_N(r_i{\bullet}H, r_j{\bullet}H) \tag{6.3}$$

To compute the neighborhood similarity between references r_i and r_j, we define hyper-edge neighborhood similarity $sim_N(h_i, h_j)$ between two hyper-edges h_i and h_j as a pairwise match between their references.

For each $r \in h_i$, the best match to h_j is defined as:

$$sim_N(r, h_j) = max_{r'\hat{I}h_j} sim_N(r, r') \tag{6.4}$$

Similarly, for each r' in h_j, the best match to h_i is defined as:

$$sim_N(h_i, r') = \max_{r \in h_i} sim_N(r, r') \tag{6.5}$$

Here, the relational similarity between two hyper-edges h_i and h_j is computed as the maximum of the similarity score between a reference $r \in h_i$ and a reference $r' \in h_j$. Furthermore, the neighborhood similarity between two references r_i and r_j is defined as:

$$sim_N(r_i, r_j) = \cfrac{1}{\left| r_i{\bullet}H \right| \times \left| r_j{\bullet}H \right| \displaystyle\sum_{h \in r_i{\bullet}H, \, h' \in r_j{\bullet}H} sim_N(r_i{\bullet}h, r_j{\bullet}h')} \tag{6.6}$$

where $|r{\bullet}H|$ still denotes the number of hyper-edges involving r. It is worth noting that the neighborhood of reference r contains r. Thus, if two references r_i and r_j do not share any common neighbor, their neighborhood similarity $sim_N(r_i, r_j)$ is equal to their personal identity attribute similarity $sim_A(r_i, r_j)$. In other words, two references having the same/similar neighbors can be regarded as positive evidence to support that they are more likely to be co-referent, whereas two references not having a common neighbor will not be treated as evidence of them not being co-referent.

In addition, we can define a negative constraint based on social relationships: two references that co-occur in the same hyper-edge (e.g. a criminal incident) cannot refer to the same entity.

Furthermore, the relational similarity between two references r_i and r_j can be defined as a linear combination of the three components personal identity attribute similarity, social behavioral similarity, and social neighborhood similarity:

$$sim_R(r_i, r_j) = \alpha \times sim_A(r_i, r_j) + \beta \times sim_b(r_i, r_j) + (1 - \alpha - \beta) \times sim_N(r_i, r_j) \qquad (6.7)$$

where $0 \leq \alpha$, $\beta \leq \alpha + \beta \leq 1$ and they can be adjusted to control the importance of the three similarity scores.

Matching strategies

Given a collection of references, our goal is to determine which references co-refer to the same underlying identity and which do not. We find three commonly used strategies in existing resolution techniques, namely pairwise comparison, transitive closure, and collective clustering.

Pairwise comparison

Pairwise comparison is a basic and simple strategy for entity resolution. For each pair of references r_i and r_j, we can compute the similarity score using one of the above-mentioned functions. If the similarity score $sim(r_i, r_j)$ is greater than a predefined threshold θ, we conclude that r_i and r_j are co-referent. We use A, B, and R to denote pairwise comparison approaches using personal identity attributes only, personal identity attributes and social behavior attributes, and all three types of identity attributes respectively.

Transitive closure

The outcome of pairwise comparison tells us whether two references match or not. Strictly speaking, this still has not yet uncovered the unknown entities for the reference collection. Consider a simple example where references r_i and r_j are considered as a match, and r_j and r_k are also considered a match, while r_i and r_k are determined to be a non-match. In this case, the pairwise comparison may produce conflicting resolution outcomes. A simple strategy to uncover the underlying entities is to use transitive closure. In the previous example, even though r_i and r_k are not sufficiently similar, we still consider them as a co-referent pair because r_i matches r_j and r_j matches r_k. This process should be performed iteratively until all transitive closures are reached. Finally, each transitive closure is considered as a distinct entity. Given the pairwise comparison results, computing transitive closures is straightforward and efficient. Obviously, such a merging process lowers the threshold of the matching criteria and therefore tends to reduce false negatives but introduce more false positives. We use A*, B*, and R* to denote transitive closure approaches using personal identity attributes alone, personal identity attributes and social behavior attributes, and all three types of identity attributes respectively.

Collective clustering

Unlike computing transitive closure, a different strategy of uncovering underlying identities given pairwise similarity scores of references is collective clustering [6]. In particular, a greedy agglomerative clustering algorithm can be used to find the most similar references (or clusters) and merge them. Figure 6.2 shows the pseudo-code for the algorithm.

A fundamental difference between this clustering algorithm and the other two matching strategies is a similarity function defined on clusters of references. Here, we take an average linkage approach and define the similarity between two clusters c_i and c_j as the average similarity between each reference in c_i and each reference in c_j:

$$sim(c_i, c_j) = \cfrac{1}{\left| c_i \bullet R \right| \times \left| c_j \bullet R \right|} \sum_{r \in c_i \bullet R, \ r' \in c_j \bullet R} sim(c_i \bullet r, c_j \bullet r') \qquad (6.8)$$

where $|c \bullet R|$ represents the number of references in cluster c.

At first, clusters are initialized and each reference is assigned to a different cluster. As clusters merge one cluster may contain multiple references that are determined to be co-referents. The algorithm merges the most similar cluster pair iteratively until the similarity drops below the threshold. Every time two clusters are merged, similarity scores between clusters need to be recomputed to find the new closest cluster pairs. Specifically, merging two clusters c_i and c_j into one entity should be regarded as new evidence for computing the similarity between other references that co-occur with references in c_i and c_j. Such an iterative computational procedure distinguishes the clustering algorithm with the other pairwise comparison-based approaches. We use CA, CB, and CR to denote collective clustering approaches using

1. Initialize clusters
2. Compute the similarity between each cluster pair
3. Find the cluster pair with the maximal $sim^*(c_i, c_j)$
4. If $sim^*(c_i, c_j)$ greater than threshold
    Merge c_i and c_j
    Go to Step 2

Figure 6.2:
Pseudo-code of collective clustering.

personal identity attributes alone, personal identity attributes and social behavioral attributes, and all three types of identity attributes respectively.

Complexity analysis

Given a collection of n references, a complete pairwise comparison approach considers all possible reference pairs as potential candidates for merging. The iterative clustering approaches require a lot more computation. Apart from the scaling issue, in reality most pairs will be rejected while often only less than 1% of all pairs are true matches. Hence, certain blocking steps can be performed before matching so as to screen out highly unlikely candidate pairs for matching. There are various blocking techniques but they often employ one simple and computationally cheap function to group references into a number of buckets. Buckets can overlap where one reference can belong to multiple buckets. Only reference pairs within the same bucket are considered candidate pairs for comparing and merging, whereas a pair of references from two different buckets is not considered as co-referents. For collective clustering, two clusters must have all of their references belonging to the same bucket to make them a candidate pair to merge. Furthermore, in the agglomerative clustering process, it is not necessary to recompute the similarity scores for every single cluster pair. More strategies for reducing complexity of collective clustering can be found in Ref. [6].

6.4 Experiments

In this study, for illustration purposes, we evaluate our identity resolution approach with different matching strategies using computer-generated synthetic data. We describe our experiments and discuss our findings in this section.

6.4.1 Synthetic Data Generation

We adopted a two-stage data-generation method described in Ref. [6] with some modifications, as described in Figure 6.3.

In the creation stage the algorithm first creates N entities with a personal identity attribute x and a behavior attribute y. We differentiate these two attributes because personal identity attributes can be easily modified or falsified while social behavioral attributes tend to be more consistent and less likely to change significantly over time. Next, we create M linkages among these N entities to represent their underlying social relationships. When we create these links, two entities with a similar social behavioral attribute y are more likely to be related to each other with a probability of $P_b(e_i, e_j) = P_b^{|e_i \cdot y - e_j \cdot y|}$, i.e. two individuals with similar interests are more likely to be related. In the generation stage, we created R hyper-edges that included a set of related entities' references. An entity may join a hyper-edge of its neighbor with a probability of P_c. Whenever an entity is to join a hyper-edge, we either choose an existing

Creation Stage

1. Repeat N times
2.   Create entity e
3.   Create attribute x to represent e's identity attributes
4.   Create attribute y to represent e's behavioral attributes
5. Repeat M times
6.   Choose entities e_i and e_j with $P_b(e_i, e_j)$
7.   Set $e_i = Nbr(e_j)$ and $e_j = Nbr(e_i)$

Generation Stage

8. Repeat R times
9.   Randomly choose entity e
10.   With P_a, select reference r for e or generate r using $N(e.x, 1)$
11.   Initialize hyper-edge $h = <r>$
12.   Repeat with probability P_c
13.   Randomly choose e_j from $Nbr(e)$ without replacement
14.   With P_a, select reference r_j for e_j or generate r_j using $N(e_j.x, 1)$
15.   Add r_j hyper-edge h
16.   Assign hyper-edge h's attribute y = average($h.r.e.y$)

Figure 6.3:
Pseudo-code of synthetic data generation.

reference of this entity with a probability P_a or create a new reference with its attribute x value following a Gaussian distribution of $N(e \cdot x, 1)$. Each reference r joins at least one hyper-edge. Each hyper-edge is also assigned an attribute y, which is equal to the average of all participating entities' behavior attribute y.

It is worth noting that this synthetic data generator has two major differences compared to the one described in Ref. [6]. Firstly, for each entity, we define an additional attribute y to represent one's behavioral characteristics that can be reflected and observed in its involved hyper-edges. Secondly, our synthetic data allow a reference to join more than one hyper-edge, while in Ref. [6] each reference only joins a single hyper-edge. This is more realistic in real identity management scenarios and requires more cost in computing similarities between references.

6.4.2 Experiment Design

In our experiments, we compared nine entity resolution approaches for identity resolution based on the categorization we described in the previous section (see Table 6.1). For similarity computation, we defined three different similarity functions that use personal identity attributes alone, personal identity attributes and social behavior attributes, and all three types of identity attributes respectively. For each similarity function, we employed it using one of the three different matching strategies: pairwise comparison, transitive closure, and collective clustering.

In our experiments we chose the following parameter values for generating the synthetic data: $N = 100, M = 200, R = 500, P_a = 0.8, P_b = 0.9, P_c = 0.5$, and the value ranges of x and y were

Table 6.1: Experiment Design: Identity Attributes vs. Matching Strategy

	Personal_Identity	Personal_Identity + Social_Behavior	Personal_Identity + Social_Behavior + Social_Relationship
Pairwise comparison	A	B	R
Transitive closure	A*	B*	R*
Collective cluster	CA	CB	CR

set from 0 to 500. With such parameter settings, we generated 50 sets of synthetic data and compared the nine different resolution approaches.

The personal identity similarity between two references is defined as:

$$sim_A(r_i, r_j) = \frac{|r_i \bullet x - r_j \bullet x|}{range(x)} \qquad (6.9)$$

The similarity between two hyper-edges is defined as:

$$sim_b(h_i, h_j) = \frac{|h_i \bullet y - h_j \bullet y|}{range(y)} \qquad (6.10)$$

The two parameters that control the weights of the three types of similarity functions are set as $\alpha = 0.5$ and $\beta = 0.25$. The threshold of overall similarity score is set as 0.99.

6.4.3 Evaluation Metrics

We evaluated the performance of each resolution approach by checking the correctness of the matching decisions for each reference pair. We followed most identity resolution studies and chose precision, recall and *F*-measure as our evaluation metrics [6]. As illustrated in Table 6.2, each matching decision on a pair of references is either a "match" (positive) or a "non-match" (negative). A decision can be either true or false.

Table 6.2: Possible Outcomes of Matching Decisions

Reality	Decision	
	Match	Non-match
Match	True positive (*TP*)	False negative (*FN*)
Non-match	False positive (*FP*)	True negative (*TN*)

Based on the decision outcomes, precision, recall, and *F*-measure are defined as follows:

$$\text{Precision} = \frac{TP}{TP + FP} \tag{6.11}$$

$$\text{Recall} = \frac{TP}{TP + FN} \tag{6.12}$$

$$F\text{-measure} = \frac{2 \times \text{Precision} \times \text{Recall}}{\text{Precision} + \text{Recall}} \tag{6.13}$$

6.4.4 Results and Discussion

Figure 6.4 summarizes the performance of the nine resolution approaches. Among the nine approaches, CB achieved the highest precision (92.92%) with the lowest recall (78.66%), A* achieved highest recall (99.49%) but the lowest precision (18.81%) and lowest *F*-measure (31.57%). The collective relational clustering approach (CR) achieved the highest *F*-measure of 89.39% because it considered all three types of identity attributes and matched references in a collective and iterative manner.

With the same matching strategy, the results show that approaches using personal identity attributes alone always achieved higher recall but at the cost of very low precision and *F*-measure. As social behavioral similarity is taken into account, we observed a significant boost in both precision and *F*-measure. This shows that social behavior attributes do contribute to the performance improvement of identity resolution by reducing false positives. Furthermore, when social relational attributes were also considered, there were some minor drops in precision but with generally higher *F*-measure. In particular, the approaches using all three types of identity attributes (R, R*, and CR) outperformed its baselines in terms of *F*-measure.

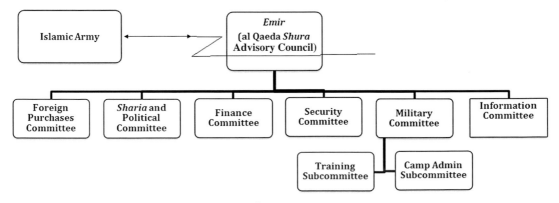

Figure 6.4:
Experiment results of nine identity resolution approaches.

6.5 Concluding Remarks

In this chapter we introduced an identity resolution technique that utilizes both personal identity attributes and social identity attributes. Guided by existing identity theories, we defined and examined three types of identity cues, namely personal identity attributes, social behavior attributes, and social relationship attributes, for identity resolution. We also evaluated three different matching strategies: pairwise comparison, transitive closure, and collective clustering. Our experimental results show that both social behavior and relationship attributes improved the performance of identity resolution as compared to using personal identity attributes alone. The collective relational clustering algorithm achieved the best overall performance in terms of F-measure among all approaches. In order to validate, improve, and operationalize these identity resolution techniques, we still need to test them on large-scale real-world identity datasets.

References

[1] J. Jonas, Identity resolution: 23 years of practical experience and observations at scale, Proceedings of the 2006 ACM SIGMOD International Conference on Management of Data, ACM Press, New York, USA, 2006, p. 718.

[2] E. Mumford, Problems, knowledge, solutions: Solving complex problems, J. Strateg. Inf. Syst. 79 (4) (1998) 255–269.

[3] US Department of State, Country reports on terrorism 2006. <http://www.state.gov/s/ct/rls/crt/2007/index.htm>, 2007.

[4] G.A. Wang, H.C. Chen, J.J. Xu, H. Atabakhsh, Automatically detecting criminal identity deception: An adaptive detection algorithm, IEEE Trans. Syst. Man. Cybern. A Syst. Hum. 36 (5) (2006) 988–999.

[5] G. Wang, H. Chen, H. Atabakhsh, Automatically detecting deceptive criminal identities, Commun. ACM 47 (3) (2004) 70–76.

[6] I. Bhattacharya, L. Getoor, Collective entity resolution in relational data, ACM Trans. Knowl. Discov. Data (TKDD) 1 (1) (2007) 5.

[7] T. Donaldson, A position paper on collaborative deceit, AAAI-94 Workshop on Planning for Interagent Communication, 1994.

[8] E. Finch, What a Tangled Web We Weave: Identity Theft and the Internet, Willan, Collompton, UK, 2003, 86–104.

[9] J.M. Cheek, S.R. Briggs, Self-consciousness and aspects of identity, Journal of Research in Personality 16 (4) (1982) 401–408.

[10] United Kingdom Home Office, Identity fraud: A study. <http://www.homeoffice.gov.uk/cpd/id_fraud-report.pdf>, 2002.

[11] H. Tajfel, J.C. Turner, The Social Identity Theory of Inter-Group Behavior, Nelson-Hall, Chicago, 1986.

[12] J.C. Turner, Some Current Issues in Research on Social Identity and Self-Categorization Theories, Blackwell, Oxford, 1999.

[13] K. Deaux, D. Martin, Interpersonal networks and social categories: Specifying levels of context in identity processes, Soc. Psychol. Q. 66 (2) (2003) 101–117.

[14] S. Stryker, R.T. Serpe, Commitment, Identity Salience, and Role Behavior: Theory and Research Example, Springer, New York, 1982.

[15] R. Conyers, F. Sensenbrenner, Real ID act of 2005, Congressional Record House 151 (14) (2005).

[16] S.T. Kent, L.I. Millett, IDs — Not That Easy: Questions about Nationwide Identity Systems, National Academy Press, Washington, DC, 2002.

[17] Privacy International, Mistaken Identity: Exploring the Relationship between National Identity Cards and the Prevention of Terrorism, Privacy International, London, UK, 2004.

[18] P.H. O'Neil, Complexity and counterterrorism: thinking about biometrics, Stud. Confl. Terror. 28 (6) (2005) 547—566.

[19] I.P. Fellegi, A.B. Sunter, A theory for record linkage, J. Am. Stat. Assoc. 64 (328) (1969) 1183—1210.

[20] M. Bilenko, R. Mooney, W. Cohen, P. Ravikumar, S. Fienberg, Adaptive name matching in information integration, IEEE Intell. Syst. 18 (5) (2003) 16—23.

[21] M.A. Hernández, S.J. Stolfo, The merge/purge problem for large databases, in: M.J. Carey, D.A. Schneider (Eds.), SIGMOD '95: Proceedings of the 1995 ACM SIGMOD International Conference on Management of Data, San Jose, CA, ACM Press, 1995, pp. 127—138.

[22] A.E. Monge, Matching algorithms within a duplicate detection system, IEEE Data Eng. Bull. 23 (4) (2000) 14—20.

[23] A.K. Elmagarmid, P.G. Ipeirotis, V.S. Verykios, Duplicate record detection: A survey, IEEE Trans. Knowl. Data Eng. 19 (1) (2007) 1—16.

[24] B. Marshall, S. Kaza, J. Xu, H. Atabakhsh, T. Petersen, C. Violette, H. Chen, Cross-jurisdictional criminal activity networks to support border and transportation security, Proceedings of the 7th International IEEE Conference on Intelligent Transportation Systems, Washington, DC, 2004.

[25] D.E. Brown, S.C. Hagen, Data association methods with applications to law enforcement, Decis. Support Syst. 34 (4) (2003) 369—378.

[26] D. Dey, S. Sarkar, P. De, A probabilistic decision model for entity matching in heterogeneous databases, Manag. Sci. 44 (10) (1998) 1379—1395.

[27] P. Ravikumar, W.W. Cohen, A hierarchical graphical model for record linkage, Proceedings of the 20th Conference on Uncertainty in Artificial Intelligence, AUAI Press, Arlington, VA, 2004.

[28] G.A. Wang, H. Chen, H. Atabakhsh, A multi-layer naïve Bayes model for approximate identity matching, Lecture Notes in Computer Science 3975, Springer. San Diego, CA 2006, pp. 479—484.

[29] W.E. Winkler, Methods for Record Linkage and Bayesian Networks, Statistical Research Division, US Census Bureau, Washington, DC, 2002. Available at <http://www.amstat.org/Sections/Srms/Proceedings/y2002/Files/JSM2002-000648.pdf>.

[30] K. Nigam, A.K. McCallum, S. Thrun, T. Mitchell, Text classification from labeled and unlabeled documents using EM, Mach. Learn. 39 (2/3) (2000) 103—134.

[31] H. Köpcke, E. Rahm, Frameworks for entity matching: A comparison, Data Knowl. Eng. 69 (2) (2010) 197—210.

[32] R. Ananthakrishna, S. Chaudhuri, V. Ganti, Eliminating fuzzy duplicates in data warehouses, Proceedings of the 28th International Conference on Very Large Data Bases, Hong Kong, China, 2002, pp. 586—597.

[33] D.V. Kalashnikov, S. Mehrotra, Z. Chen, Exploiting relationships for domain-independent data cleaning, Proceedings of SIAM International Conference on Data Mining (SDM), Newport Beach, CA, 2005.

[34] A. Culotta, A. McCallum, Joint Deduplication of Multiple Record Types in Relational Data, ACM, Bremen, Germany, 2005. http://doi.acm.org/10.1145/1099554.1099615.

[35] H. Pasula, B. Marthi, B. Milch, S. Russell, I. Shpitser, Identity uncertainty and citation matching, Adv. Neural Inf. Process. Syst. 22 (3) (2003) 1425—1432.

[36] I. Bhattacharya, L. Getoor, A latent Dirichlet model for unsupervised entity resolution, SIAM International Conference on Data Mining, Bethesda, MD, 2006, pp. 47—58.

[37] V.I. Levenshtein, Binary codes capable of correcting deletions, insertions, and reversals, Sov. Phys. Dokl. 10 (8) (1966) 707—710.

CHAPTER 7

Al Qaeda Terrorist Financing

Irina Sakharova, Bhavani Thuraisingham

University of Texas at Dallas, Richardson, Texas, USA

Chapter Outline

7.1 Importance of Cutting Terrorist Financing

"We will direct every resource at our command — every means of diplomacy, every tool of intelligence, every instrument of law enforcement, every financial influence, and every necessary weapon of war — to the destruction and to the defeat of the global terror network … We will starve terrorists of funding …" [1]

President George W. Bush, September 20, 2001

It is beyond a doubt that disrupting terrorist financing is necessary. As President George W. Bush stated in his speech on September 24, 2001, financial resources are considered to be "the lifeblood of terrorist operations" [2]. As stated by US Government authorities, "the fight against al Qaeda financing was as critical as the fight against al Qaeda itself" [3]. One of the key goals of defeating terrorism is to fight the financial structure of terrorist organizations by detecting, disrupting, and disabling their financial networks.

The General Assembly of the United Nations adopted the International Convention for the Suppression of the Financing of Terrorism in 1999; however, only a few countries had ratified the convention before September 11. The US ratified the convention only in 2002 [4] with the beginning of the campaign to "starve the terrorists of funding." Since the beginning of the War on Terror in 2001, numerous initiatives and policies at the national, regional, and international

Intelligent Systems for Security Informatics.
http://dx.doi.org/10.1016/B978-0-12-404702-0.00007-0

levels supplemented the convention. A series of new international laws that have criminalized the financing of terrorist activities were introduced by many countries.

The International Convention for the Suppression of the Financing of Terrorism gives the formal definition of the financing of terrorism [5]. The financing of terrorism essentially can be defined as any kind of financial support of terrorism or those who in any way participate in it [6].

There is a good deal of available information on various sources and methods of transferring funds used by terrorists. Funds come from a wide range of legitimate (donations to charitable organizations, front businesses) and illegitimate (petty crime, smuggling, credit card fraud, and drug trafficking) sources. Terrorists move money using the financial system and largely unregulated alternative remittance systems like *hawala* or just simply carry "bags of money" across borders. They use commodities such as diamonds, tanzanite, and sapphires to store cash value [7]. The ability to adapt which is "shown by terrorist organizations suggests that all the methods that exist to move money around the globe are to some extent at risk" [8].

Practically speaking, preventing terrorist financial flows has been extremely difficult. Nevertheless, detecting and following al Qaeda's money can be productive in tracking down and preventing terrorist activity.

Interestingly enough, al Qaeda spent only comparatively modest amounts on the planning and execution of its terrorist attacks. However, it needs significant amounts of money to satisfy the overall needs of establishing and running a terrorist network.

Costs of day-to-day operations such as organizing, recruiting, training, and equipping new recruits, paying members and their families, bribing public officials, traveling, promoting al Qaeda's ideology, and otherwise supporting their activities represent a significant drain on resources.

Disrupting terrorist financing increases the costs and risks of raising and moving funds for terrorists, and "creates a hostile environment for terrorism, constraining overall capabilities of terrorists and helping frustrate their ability to execute attacks" [8].

7.2 Description of Al Qaeda's Financial Network

There is no other terrorist organization that has built such a sophisticated, complex, robust-and-adaptive-to-changes global financial network like al Qaeda's. It is based on a system that was built by bin Laden to provide support to the mujahedin fighters in Afghanistan during the Soviet invasion in the late 1980s. It uses different sources of funding and a variety of methods of storing and transferring funds. However, as noted in the Independent Task Force Report on Terrorist Financing, "the most important source of al Qaeda's money is its continuous fund-raising efforts. Al Qaeda's global fund-raising network is built upon a foundation of charities, nongovernmental organizations, mosques, websites, intermediaries, facilitators, and banks and other financial institutions" [9].

Although al Qaeda's financial network has clearly been weakened by the War on Terror, it certainly has not been destroyed. While new financial sector regulations became a significant obstacle for terrorists to move money through the financial system, al Qaeda's financiers have quickly adapted to the new environment. Terrorists have been forced to move their organizations outside the formal financial system. Even before 9/11, al Qaeda and its cells used the global financial system to move funds very cautiously in a manner that did not arouse suspicion. As a result of the new counter-terrorism financing policies, they became increasingly careful. Most likely, instead of moving funds through the financial system, terrorist groups are using other channels of transferring funds and other means of storing wealth, such as trade in commodities like gold and diamonds, bulk cash smuggling, and underground banking systems such as hawala.

According to the former chief of the FBI's Terrorist Financing Operations section, Dennis M. Lormel, "The laws passed since 2001 have closed some gaps and addressed vulnerabilities that made it easy for al Qaeda to raise and transfer money; however, the network has responded quickly" [10]. Loretta Napoleoni, author of *Modern Jihad: Tracing the Dollars Behind the Terror Networks*, says "Terrorist financing is very different today … five years ago, we had large movement of funds which went through the international financial system" [11]. Today, cells are raising their own money as opposed to receiving funds from outside sources that could be easily detected by government authorities.

Al Qaeda's affiliated groups have become self-funded by deriving income from local legitimate businesses or from various criminal activities such as petty crime, fraud, racketeering, and kidnapping. Because of the small scale of such transactions, there is little reason to suspect terrorist involvement. As Stephen Swain, a former official at Scotland Yard, noted, "That's the cleverness of these schemes — to keep it under the radar. By doing this, they can raise significant amounts of money, fairly quickly, and there's no real way to detect it" [10].

Today's al Qaeda cannot be viewed as a single organization as it became very fragmented over the last decade. Al Qaeda has transformed from a group with hierarchical organization with a large operating budget into an ideological movement with affiliated groups around the world. Al Qaedaism inspires individuals or small groups to carry out attacks, without operational support from the central organization. Because cells become self-sufficient deriving income from local legitimate businesses or from various criminal activities, it becomes nearly impossible for authorities to detect the organization's activities and apprehend its operatives.

The weakened financial state of al Qaeda should not be underestimated as it still poses a threat. Terrorist attacks are relatively cheap. Estimates suggest that al Qaeda spent $500,000 on the 9/11 attacks, which came from an established financial network. In comparison, the group that carried out the Madrid bombings of 2004 used only $10,000–15,000, which was generated by trafficking drugs and selling counterfeit CDs. The London bombings of 2005 were even cheaper — $2000 — money that most likely was personal savings. This is a main difference between top-down al Qaeda, as it once was, when it funded operations from Afghanistan, and the new, much looser organization of localized affiliates inspired by al Qaedaism that raise their own funds and pick their own targets.

7.3 History and Development of Al Qaeda and its Financial Network

The leader of al Qaeda, Osama bin Laden, was born in Saudi Arabia in 1957. His father, Muhammad bin Laden, came from Yemen and rose from poverty to being Saudi Arabia's foremost construction developer who built his empire by winning contracts from the Saudi royal family for the construction of royal residences. Osama got his inheritance at 11 when his father died in a helicopter crash in 1968. His wealth was anywhere from $30 million to $300 million. However, it is impossible to determine what remains as he has used his wealth to finance al Qaeda and withheld details of his fortune. His wealthy and well-respected family separated itself from Osama, but US authorities believe that some family members gave him access to family funds [12].

While studying at the King Abdel Aziz University in Jidda, bin Laden was greatly influenced by Abdullah Azzam, a well-respected Palestinian Sunni Islamic theologian [13]. Azzam then became his mentor in Afghanistan and the ideological father of al Qaeda. In 1979, when the Soviet Army invaded Afghanistan, Osama left Saudi Arabia to join the Afghan rebels, the mujahedin, in their fight with the Soviets. Although bin Laden was from a wealthy family, his commitment was to Afghan and Muslim independence, and as a result his influence and popularity among the mujahedin was significant. "He not only gave us his money, but he also gave himself" [14].

In 1984, Abdullah Azzam and Osama bin Laden cofounded the Maktab al Khidmat (MAK) or Afghan Bureau of Services [15], which was later reconfigured by bin Laden into an organization called al Qaeda (The Base). Bin Laden took charge of the group's finances and was instrumental in the recruitment of Muslims to the "Afghan Arabs." MAK provided logistical help, raised funds, disseminated propaganda, recruited new members, and channeled foreign assistance to the mujahedin. "MAK distributed $200 million of Middle Eastern and Western aid, mainly American and British, destined for the Afghan jihad" [15]. MAK received the funds from various sources. Bin Laden used his family wealth to help the rebels. He also raised money among wealthy Gulf Arabs, and through charity organizations. MAK collaborated extensively with Pakistan's ISI, the Inter Services Intelligence, which allegedly was distributing arms and money from the CIA and providing training for the mujahedin [15]. "During the Afghan war, the Central Intelligence Agency provided roughly $500 million a year in material support to the mujahedin" [16]. Although Milton Bearden, a retired CIA officer, claims that the CIA had no direct relations with bin Laden, US officials admit that some of the financial aid aimed for the mujahedin may have ended up in bin Laden's hands [13].

Near the end of the Soviet—Afghan war, Azzam's and Osama's relationship deteriorated as they disagreed on a number of issues. Azzam hoped to leverage the mujahedin as a "rapid reaction force" ready to fight for the independence of all Muslims [15]. Osama and Ayman al Zawahiri, his new mentor, who at the time was the head of Egyptian Islamic Jihad, wanted to recreate the Islamic Caliphate by declaring war on corrupt governments in the Middle East and on the United States, as most of these governments were American allies. He wanted to transform MAK into "The Base" or al Qaeda, an organization that would form the basis on which a global Islamic army would be built. According to many insiders, al Zawahiri transformed Osama from a guerilla into a terrorist. The two wanted to train the mujahedin in terrorist tactics [17]. Azzam issued *fatwa* that jihadi funds used for terrorist training contravened Islamic law [15]. As this tension and Osama's desire to reconfigure MAK into al Qaeda grew, it became obvious that the power struggle between Azzam and bin Laden would end only with the removal of one of them. Azzam and his two sons were killed in 1989. Although it is uncertain who killed him, in his book *Inside al Qaeda: Global Network of Terror*, Rohan Gunaratna, an international terrorism expert, suggests that Azzam was killed by rival Egyptians who acted on bin Laden's orders. In any case, Azzam's assassination left Osama bin Laden in full control of al Qaeda's future [15].

Following the withdrawal of the Soviet Army from Afghanistan in the late 1980s, bin Laden returned to Saudi Arabia. In 1990, Iraq invaded Kuwait and Osama offered the Saudi army the help of Arab veterans of the Afghan conflict. However, the Saudis chose to accept US help instead, and invited American troops, which had never happened before. Like many other Muslims, bin Laden saw the US army's presence as an assault on Muslim lands.

Bin Laden began to give speeches accusing the Saudi regime of corruption and being un-Islamic. King Fahd placed him under house arrest in 1991, and Osama subsequently fled the country to Sudan, where he was invited by the National Islamic Front. Later in 1994, Saudi authorities revoked bin Laden's citizenship and froze his assets. "Bin Laden brought resources to Sudan, building roads and helping finance the government's war against separatists in the south" [18]. He also started a series of businesses whose proceeds he used to finance some of al Qaeda's operations. While in Sudan, bin Laden formed al Qaeda based on the MAK structure established in Afghanistan. Al Qaeda began to spread its network around the world, with its regional centers in London, New York, Turkey, and other countries. In the early 1990s, bin Laden was focused on launching attacks on the United States, "the head of the snake" as he called the country [18]. In the period between 1992 and 1996, al Qaeda carried out its first attacks in Yemen, Somalia, and Saudi Arabia aimed at Americans.

Under US and Saudi pressure, bin Laden had to leave Sudan in 1996. The Sudanese Government seized his assets after he abandoned the country. Bin Laden moved to Afghanistan, where he was offered support from the Taliban in exchange for money and a supply of numerous fighters to support the Taliban regime. In 1997 and 1998, bin Laden was working on creating alliances with other Islamist groups by sending deputies to their leaders and telling them that they had to unite in coalition to mobilize Muslims against the Americans. As a result, in 1998 al Qaeda formed an alliance with other terrorist groups: the Egyptian Islamic Jihad, Islamic Group of Egypt, Jamiat Ulema-e-Pakistan, and Jihad Movement of Bangladesh [15]. Bin Laden and Al Zawahiri, the leader of the Egyptian Islamic Jihad, issued *fatwa* in 1998, just half a year before the attacks on the US embassies in Kenya and Tanzania, in which they announced:

> *"Ruling to kill the Americans and their allies − civilians and military − is an individual duty for every Muslim who can do it in any country in which it is possible to do it, in order to liberate the al-Aqsa Mosque and the holy mosque [Mecca] from their grip, and in order for their armies to move out of all the lands of Islam"* [19]

Saudi Arabia tried to force the Taliban into extraditing bin Laden after the 1998 bombings. The Taliban's determination to protect bin Laden resulted in a breakdown in diplomatic relations between Saudi Arabia and Afghanistan.

And then there were the 9/11 attacks. The Federal Bureau of Investigation stated, "The evidence linking al Qaeda and bin Laden to the attacks of September 11 is clear and irrefutable" [20]. The attacks aimed to halt the economic and political power of the United States, and had more devastating casualties than any other terrorist attack ever known.

According to the 9/11 Commission's report:

> *"The September 11 hijackers used US and foreign financial institutions to hold, move and retrieve their money. The hijackers deposited money into US accounts primarily by wire transfers and deposits of cash or travelers' checks brought from overseas. Additionally, several of them kept funds in foreign accounts, which they accessed in the United States through ATM and credit card transactions. The hijackers received funds from facilitators in Germany and the United Arab Emirates or directly from Khalid Sheikh Mohammed[1] as they transited Pakistan on their way to the United States"* [3]

---

[1] Khalid Sheikh Mohammed (KSM) was arrested in Rawalpindi, Pakistan on March 1, 2003 and sent to the US detention center in Cuba in 2006. According to the tribunal hearing transcripts released, he "served as the head of al Qaeda military committee and was Osama bin Laden's principal al Qaeda operative who directed September 11 2001 attacks in the United States" [69]. He also admitted responsibility for the 1993 attack on the World Trade Center in New York, the bombing of nightclubs in Bali in 2002 and a Kenyan hotel in the same year, and some other terrorist attacks plots.

The hijackers responsible received funds for pilot training, living and travel expenses, and returned about $26,000 "unused" money to a facilitator in the UAE a few days before carrying out the attacks [3].

Osama bin Laden's foremost accomplishment was building al Qaeda's financial network based on MAK's system. It was built from the foundation of MAK's system used to provide financial support to the mujahedin during the Afghan war. Most of al Qaeda's infrastructure was developed in the late 1980s. At that time bin Laden started to develop a strategy to make his organization financially self-sufficient. Not only did he want to establish a fundraising system, he also was interested in finding ways of transferring funds to finance al Qaeda's operations around the world. Bin Laden used a variety of sources to raise funds for al Qaeda. Besides the network of charities developed by Azzam and bin Laden's personal contacts with Saudi charities and wealthy donors, bin Laden's brother-in-law, Mohammed Jammal Khalifa, founded a number of charitable organizations in the Philippines; several additional charities were established in Malaysia and Indonesia. One of the reasons why Southeast Asia was ideal for al Qaeda was the existence of Islamic charities and banks with lax regulations, and widespread money laundering [21]. These conditions simplified the process of collecting and transferring funds around the world. Charities were the main pillar of al Qaeda's financial structure. As well as helping to raise funds, some charities could also move these funds between their offices around the world. However, it was unknown to the majority of charities that al Qaeda members were employed by these charities or that donations were used to support terrorist activities.

For many years, it was thought that bin Laden used his personal wealth to finance the organization. It was thought that he inherited about $300 million, money that he used in Sudan and Afghanistan. However, the National Commission on Terrorist Attacks on the United States, in Monograph on Terrorist Financing, dispels this myth. Between 1970 and 1993 or 1994, bin Laden was given approximately a million dollars per year, which makes $23–24 million in total, but not the $300 million fortune [3]. As mentioned before, the Saudi Government froze his assets when he left the country. Also, his assets in Sudan cannot be viewed as the source of the money since the Sudanese Government expropriated these assets. After moving back to Afghanistan, bin Laden was in a weak financial state. After its proliferation in Afghanistan, al Qaeda supported itself through fundraising. It appears that al Qaeda directly received funding from wealthy donors through financial facilitators. Most of these wealthy donors were from the Persian Gulf region and known as the Golden Chain. As with charities, not all of the individual donors who were approached by the facilitators, charity officials, and fundraisers knew of the destinations of their donations.

It was long thought that Saudi Arabia was one of the leading sources of al Qaeda financing. However, there was no evidence found to support that allegation. Moreover, there was no conclusive proof that any government provided financial support to al Qaeda. Still, some governments may have known about al Qaeda's fundraising activities in their countries but turned a blind eye to it [18].

As noted earlier, after the 9/11 attacks and the beginning of the War on Terror, al Qaeda's funding suffered substantially. Despite the reduction in al Qaeda's funding, it is important to remember that little funding is needed to implement a terrorist attack. With al Qaeda's decentralization, individual cells became self-sufficient, with charities and individual donors still being the main source of funding for these groups.

7.4 Organizational Structure: Control Over Finances Within Al Qaeda

Before 9/11, al Qaeda was largely centralized, with headquarters located in Afghanistan. Osama bin Laden was in firm control of the organization — he had the final decision over all of al Qaeda's missions. Some terrorist experts compare the al Qaeda structure to a business enterprise. Peter Bergen thinks that al Qaeda resembled Saudi Binladin Group, the giant construction company founded by Osama's father [22], where bin Laden acted as director and established its overall direction with input from his *shura* or advisory council (which represented bin Laden's close associates). These top advisers made executive decisions for the group. There were six committees reporting to the *shura* council[2]: "Sharia" and the Political Committee responsible for issuing *fatwa*; the Military Committee responsible for proposing targets and planning of attacks; the Security Committee responsible for physical protection and intelligence collection; the Information Committee responsible for propaganda; the Finance Committee; and the Foreign Purchase Committee [18] (see Figure 7.1).

There were two committees in this structure that were related to finance: the Finance and Foreign Purchases Committees that consisted of professional bankers, accountants, and financiers [15]. The Finance Committee was responsible for fundraising and budget planning issues, such as support for training camps, living expenses, travel, housing costs, salaries, etc. The purpose of the Foreign Purchase Committee was to acquire weapons, explosives, and technical equipment from abroad. However, the National Commission on Terrorist Attacks stated that this structure "served as means for coordinating functions and providing financial support to operations. Specific operations were assigned to carefully selected cells, headed by senior al Qaeda operatives who reported personally to bin Laden" [3].

For instance, Indonesia's civilian intelligence service has linked Hambali, whose real name is Riduan Isamuddin, with the 2002 Bali attack. He is believed to have been in control of the operation, as well as the financial conduit [23]. Financial operations worldwide were managed by regional managers. For example, Mohammed Jamal Khalifa, bin Laden's brother-in-law, was responsible for worldwide investments in Mauritius, Singapore,

---

[2] Gunaratna and Bergen name only four committees: military, finance, ideological, and media.

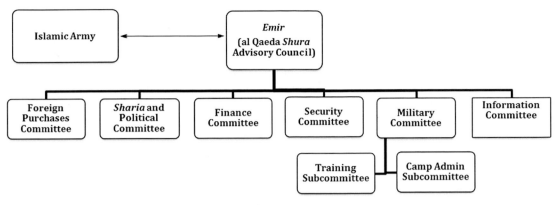

Figure 7.1:

Al Qaeda organizational structure. *Source: Overview of the enemy, National Commission on Terrorist Attacks on the United States, June 16, 2004 [18].*

Malaysia, and the Philippines [15]. He was also in charge of financial support for the Operation Bojinka plot [24], the large-scale terrorist attack by Ramzi Yousef and Khalid Shaikh Mohammed to blow up 12 airliners over the Pacific, planned to take place in January 1995.

As the US military's Operation Enduring Freedom in Afghanistan was launched on October 7, 2001 in response to the September 11, 2001 attacks on the US, al Qaeda lost its "safe haven" for planning terrorist attacks, as well as the majority of its senior leadership, and was forced to decentralize. However, experts fear that al Qaeda's structure has allowed its operation even in the absence of centralized control.

Ongoing counter-terrorism operations have isolated al Qaeda's leadership. Al Qaeda's command cadre has been on the run and they are more preoccupied to evade being captured or killed. Communication and coordination of complex operations as well as raising and transferring funds between center and cells have become extremely difficult and risky for terrorists due to isolated leadership. However, new operatives are emerging to replace old leaders. These emerging leaders can be viewed as proof that al Qaeda can adapt to new circumstances and regain its leadership [25]. They are no longer old school veterans of the 1980s Afghan war, but they are assuming greater responsibilities and autonomy. They are less able to communicate with each other. Al Qaeda has not been eradicated but instead has been spread around the world. Authorities have found it more difficult to apprehend terrorist operatives and detect their activities.

Al Qaeda went through a transformation, from a territorially based group with hierarchical organization to a more decentralized, ideological movement relying on both self-sufficient cells and affiliated groups. The 2003 suicide attacks in Casablanca and Istanbul were carried out by attackers from different groups, but all of them were linked to al Qaeda [26].

Prior to September 11, cells were encouraged to be self-sufficient for all their expenses apart from operational expenses. Al Qaeda's headquarters raised funds for training, propaganda, and operational expenses. Cells were expected to raise money to cover living expenses. As al Qaeda has become decentralized, its financial network has also become decentralized. The September 11 attacks were the last attacks that were planned, funded, and carried out under direct supervision of al Qaeda's command cadre. The consequent attacks were executed by individuals and groups that were only linked to al Qaeda ideologically [27].

A network of self-sufficient cells is more adaptable and less likely to be detected. Local cells and affiliated groups need less funds, the means used to raise money vary widely and depend on local conditions, there is less need for fund transfers, and communication between groups is minimal [28]. These groups are more autonomous in their operation and self-funded by deriving income from local legitimate businesses or from various criminal activities. The small scale of their fundraising operations generally does not raise suspicion of terrorist involvement. Also, in case of attack on one source of the funding, terrorists can easily shift to another.

Since the beginning of the War on Terror, the US Government, together with the European Union and other members of the international community, have made a major effort to disrupt terrorist financing around the world, enforcing numerous laws and regulations. Dozens of charities have been closed, more than 172 countries have frozen millions of terrorist assets, and more than 100 countries have implemented new anti-terrorism regulations and policies, including anti-money laundering legislation [26]. Al Qaeda's financial network has been disrupted significantly. With several important financial facilitators being killed or arrested, the amount of funds raised has decreased and risks of raising and transferring money have increased. In a taped message detected by CBS News in 2009 and sent by Mostafa Abul Yazid[3], the terror group's chief financial manager asks a contact in Turkey for immediate funds. "We are lacking funds here in the Afghan jihadi arena ... The slow action in the operations here nowadays is due to the lack of funds, and many mujahedin could not carry out jihad because there's not enough money" [29]. According to US Treasury official David Cohen, al Qaeda had often requested funds in 2009. He said "We assess that al-Qaeda is in its weakest financial condition in several years and that, as a result, its influence is waning" [30]. However, he asserted that if the organization had donors who were "ready, willing and able to contribute," the situation could be quickly changed [30]. Al Qaeda has regularly instructed followers that donating is a viable alternative to fighting [31]. Despite being seriously wounded and forced to decentralize, al Qaeda still poses a threat as it is a flexible, adaptive, and patient organization that can draw on global support around the world.

---

[3] Al Qaeda confirmed that its top leader in Afghanistan and chief financial official Mostafa Abul Yazid was killed in a US airstrike in Pakistan in May 2010 [70].

7.5 Al Qaeda's Portfolio and Sources of "Revenues"

The size of al Qaeda's portfolio as well as its annual budget is unknown. Various sources give estimates that differ to a large extent. For example, in 2002, the United Nations Monitoring Group referred to an estimated figure of donations from individual donors of between $16 million and $50 million. However, there was little information to back up these numbers [32]. The 9/11 Commission Report stated that the CIA estimated that, prior to September 11, al Qaeda's annual budget was about $30 million per year. For many years, it was thought that Osama bin Laden financed al Qaeda's expenses by his personal wealth. He allegedly inherited a fortune, with estimates ranging from $25–30 million to $250–300 million. However, as noted before, this is a myth. As stated in a Task Force Report on Terrorist Financing, "The most important source of al Qaeda's money is its continuous fund-raising efforts" [9]. The key sources of al Qaeda's funding can be divided into three groups:

1. Donations (through financial facilitators or charities)
2. Legitimate businesses
3. Criminal proceeds.

7.5.1 Donations

Direct contributions from wealthy individuals and funds raised through charities and financial facilitators are primary sources of funding for al Qaeda.

One of the main pillars of Islam is a religious duty for all Muslims to donate annually 2.5% of their income to the charitable causes known as *zakat*. "In many communities, the *zakat* is often provided in cash to prominent, trusted community leaders or institutions, who then commingle and disperse donated moneys to persons and charities they determine to be worthy" [9]. These practices are unaudited, generally undocumented, and therefore are easy to be abused by groups like al Qaeda. Besides mandatory *zakat*, there are voluntary donations — *infaq* and *shadaqah*. Many Muslim governments do not collect taxes, and therefore devout Muslims, through their payment of *zakat* and *sadaqah*, contribute to social welfare [17]. Some governments, for instance in Indonesia, made *zakat* tax deductible to stimulate charitable donations.

Al Qaeda continues to raise funds through direct donations from wealthy supporters and through charities. Some of the donors know the jihadi purposes that their donations will serve. Others believe that their donations are used to provide humanitarian assistance, education, and medical services to those who are in need. In the case against the Global Relief Foundation, which was established in Bridgewater, Illinois in 1992, US agents obtained donors' checks with pro-jihad notes on them [3].

Also, not all charities knowingly supported al Qaeda. Most of them were not aware that some of their officials were working for al Qaeda and diverting "thousands of dollars to fund terrorist activities and to build al Qaeda's global network, which supported jihadist fighters in Chechnya, the Balkans, Kashmir, Afghanistan, Central Asia, and Southeast Asia" [17].

Most of the charity networks were developed in the late 1980s and early 1990s by Azzam and bin Laden's personal contacts with Saudi charities and wealthy donors. These charity networks were built to support the fight against Soviet troops in Afghanistan. The United States, the United Kingdom, Saudi Arabia, Pakistan, and many Muslim countries encouraged Islamist leaders to establish these networks [17]. Donations were used to assist mujahedin fighters, to build training camps, to cover the travel expenses of young Muslims interested in joining the war against the Soviets, and to support the families of the fighters. These charities established a strong presence in the Middle East, especially in the Persian Gulf region, and in Western countries, including the United States.

It is known that al Qaeda relied on financial facilitators who played a big role in raising, transferring, and retaining the money for al Qaeda. They received money from knowing and unknowing donors mostly in the Gulf countries, but also from countries around the world. These financial facilitators also allowed al Qaeda to build an extensive financing web in Southeast Asia, Europe, and Africa.

Wealthy donors are an integral part of al Qaeda's financial network. A few wealthy donors can sponsor considerable terror. "Mustafa Ahmed al-Hasnawi, the Saudi national and bin Laden money man, sent the September 11 hijackers operational funds and received at least $15,000 in unspent funds before leaving the UAE for Pakistan on September 11" [33]. Evidence found in March 2002 in the offices of the Benevolence International Foundation in Bosnia included handwritten documents scanned into computer formats with a file titled "Osama's history" that contained a list of 20 wealthy donors referred to as the "Golden Chain," with indication of the amount donated and name of the facilitator. According to the list, at least seven of the donors knew bin Laden personally and gave money directly to him, and six of the others donated money to the Muslim charity founder [34]. Surely they knew the destination of the donations. "These financial facilitators also appeared to rely heavily on certain imams at mosques who diverted *zakat* donations to the facilitators and encouraged support of radical causes" [3].

A primary aim of international governments has been to capture financial facilitators. Although many of these facilitators have been apprehended or placed on designated lists, some of them remain undetected. "When experienced financial facilitators such as Mostafa Abul Yazid are arrested or killed, al Qaeda is forced to turn over their duties to increasingly junior and untested members. These new leaders often do not know and are not trusted by potential donors. They also lack a deep understanding of the most effective ways to move money" [35]. Based on the above, we can conclude that al Qaeda faces financial troubles. But this can change given there are donors willing to fund groups such as al Qaeda.

Charities are a fundamental part of al Qaeda's financial structure. Charities are based on public trust, they have access to a continuous source of money, and most of them have branches around the world (which is useful for transferring funds). Also, most charities collect funds informally, and therefore it is difficult to monitor their activities. These characteristics make charities attractive and vulnerable to misuse by terrorist groups.

A number of Islamic charities and related nonprofit organizations are used by terrorist groups. A National Commission report suggested two forms of involvement. In some cases, al Qaeda infiltrated foreign branch offices of large charities. And because of the lack of oversight and controls within charities, al Qaeda operatives were able to siphon money away from charities. Additionally, whole charitable organizations were established for the purposes of terrorist funding. In those cases, the entire organization was under al Qaeda control, with operatives having access to bank accounts. Such corrupt charities, including the WAFA Charitable Foundation, have now been shut down [3].

Saudi charities play a central role in terrorist financing. Saudi Arabia has been criticized for turning a blind eye to terrorist financing. Since the September 11 attacks, Saudi Arabia implemented various policies to strengthen financial system control, collaborated extensively with the United States on detection of terrorist financing, shut down suspected charities, and prohibited cash collections at mosques and unlicensed money exchanges [36]. As a result of the joint collaboration between the US and Saudi governments, eleven branches of the **Al Haramain Islamic Foundation (IBID)**, a charity linked to Saudi royalty, have been designated. It was proven that al Qaeda received financial, material, and logistical support from these branches. Moreover, an ex-employee at Al Haramain was linked to the 1998 bombing of the US embassy in Tanzania [36]. Another Saudi charity financing al Qaeda was the **al WAFA Humanitarian Organization**, which was a "militant supporter of the Taliban." Evidence discovered in Afghan offices of WAFA demonstrated the involvement in terrorist plots against US citizens. US authorities have identified WAFA "as a key component of bin Laden's organization" [37]. One authority said that al WAFA and other groups listed "do a small amount of legitimate humanitarian work and raise a lot of money for equipment and weapons" [33].

The International Islamic Relief Organization (IIRO), which is part of the Muslim World League, was established in 1978 and has branches in more than 20 countries around the world. Abd Al Hamid Sulaiman Al-Mujil, a senior official at the IIRO branch office in Saudi Arabia, has been referred to as the "million dollar man" for providing funds directly to al Qaeda and other Islamic militant groups such as Abu Sayyaf Group and Jemaah Islamiyah [37]. Accusations have been made that a branch in the Philippines has been involved in funding al Qaeda since the mid-1990s, when it was headed by Mohammed Jamal Khalifa, bin Laden's brother-in-law, who funded the Bojinka plot in the early 1990s. The Philippines and Indonesian branches of the IIRO were designated as a financier of terrorism by the US and

UN in 2006. Al-Mujil was designated as well. According to CIA reports, the IIRO funded several al Qaeda training camps in Afghanistan before 9/11. Also, the IIRO had direct links to groups responsible for the 1998 bombings of the American embassies in Dar es Salaam and Nairobi [38].

The **Saudi High Commission for Aid to Bosnia** was established in 1993 by Prince Salman bin Abdul Aziz. During NATO raids, before-and-after photographs of the World Trade Center, US embassies in Kenya and Tanzania, and the USS Cole; maps of government buildings in Washington; materials for forging US State Department badges; and files on the use of crop duster aircraft were all discovered [33].

During the 2001 trial regarding the 1998 embassy attacks, a number of organizations were involved in assisting the attackers, including **Mercy International Relief Agency**. L'Houssaine Kherchtou, a man found guilty of the 1998 bombings of the US embassies in Nairobi and Tanzania, testified, "People of al Qaeda were dealing with the Mercy International" and a number of employees there were actually al Qaeda operatives [39]. Telephone records were uncovered demonstrating that bin Laden's satellite phone was used to contact Mercy director Ahmad Sheik Adam. Moreover, Wadih el Hage, an influential al Qaeda operative, testified that he kept terrorist utensils, such as sensitive documents, at the Mercy International office in Kenya. Among these were found the business cards of Mercy employees. Also, Mercy International receipts from 1998 disclosed "getting the weapons from Somalia" [40].

One of the first organizations to be named as a financial facilitator of terrorists and to have its assets frozen was the **Al Rashid Trust**, which had been financing al Qaeda and the Taliban and is related to the al Qaeda-linked terrorist group Jaish Mohammed. The body of Daniel Pearl, a Wall Street Journal reporter kidnapped and beheaded in 2002, was found in property owned by local businessman Saud Memon, a jihadi with ties to the al-Rashid Trust. The Global Jihad Fund, a British website linked with bin Laden, was used by Al Rashid and other terrorist groups to raise funds and promote jihad movements worldwide [37].

Two charities, the **Global Relief Foundation (GRF)** and the **Benevolence International Foundation (BIF)** from the United States, provided funds to al Qaeda and other terrorist groups. GRF was founded in 1992 by people who had been associated with the MAK during the Afghan war in the 1980s [3]. GRF was a private charity that provided aid to Muslims worldwide, particularly in Bosnia, Kashmir, Afghanistan, Lebanon, and Chechnya. Global Relief raised more than $5 million annually [3]. As noted by US authorities in 2001, "GRF is a highly organized fundraising machine, which raises millions of dollars annually" [3]. A prominent figure in the organization "has been and continues to be a supporter of worldwide Islamic extremist activity" and "has past and present links and associations with a wide variety of international Muslim extremists," including al Qaeda and bin Laden [3]. BIF was a nonprofit organization founded in 1992 which also provided aid to Muslims worldwide.

BIF's accounts were initially frozen as an investigation was opened in December 2001, and BIF was later designated by the US and UN in 2002. BIF had offices in Bosnia, Chechnya, Pakistan, China, Ingushetia, and Russia [37]. Evidence seized by Bosnian criminal investigators during a raid of BIF's office in Bosnia directly documented BIF's association with al Qaeda going back to the early years. Among this evidence was the "Golden Chain" list of donors, in addition to correspondence between bin Ladin and the CEO of BIF, Enaam Arnaout. Arnaout declared that the donations were intended for humanitarian aid, but instead withheld "from donors, potential donors, and federal and state governments in the United States that a material portion of the donations received by BIF based on BIF's misleading representations was being used to support fighters overseas" [37]. BIF siphoned $315,624 away from humanitarian aid to fund terrorism in Chechnya and Bosnia-Herzegovina [37].

These are a handful of the many examples of charities associated with al Qaeda. Many charities linked to terrorist financing have been designated and shut down. Several have been hit by decreased funding as their operations have been investigated. However, in their place have arisen many small entities around the world whose activity goes largely unnoticed given their small scale. Also, charities shut down in one country are often reopened under a different name elsewhere. For instance, al Haramain, after being designated in 2002 as al Qaeda's front in Bosnia and Sudan, opened an Islamist school in Jakarta in 2003. It also reopened in Bosnia twice under a different name [27]. The Financial Action Task Force (FATF) admitted that charities can be relocated as quickly as money can be wired from one place to another [27].

7.5.2 Legitimate Business

Terrorist groups use proceeds from legitimate businesses as a source of funds for their activities. This method of fundraising is particularly difficult to detect and prevent as their operations are legitimate and do not need to resort to money laundering. A wide array of businesses worldwide, such as fishing, farming, banking, and honey production, has been connected to terrorism.

Legitimate businesses supporting terrorist groups often exist in the sectors that do not require formal qualifications and where start-up capital is not substantial, for example, cells in Europe running small businesses, such as car repair and providing home repair services, hired operatives coming from areas in conflict, such as Bosnia [41].

In 2001, several honey production companies in Yemen were suspected and listed as having links to terrorism. Yemen honey is considered among the best and most expensive in the world. The honey shops often sell other Yemeni specialties such as perfume, incense, and spices. The owner of two of these enterprises (Al Nur Honey Press Shops and Al Hamati Sweets Bakeries), Mr Al Ahdal, also known as Al Hamati, was one of the first Arab fighters in Afghanistan and Bosnia. He was arrested in Saudi Arabia in 1998 for "planning terrorist activities," and then deported from the country in 1999 [42]. The third honey business on the US government's list was al Shifa Honey Press for Industry and Commerce. Allegedly, besides generating income for al Qaeda through the legitimate economy, honey production also provided a useful method for the transportation of weapons and funds concealed within honey shipments. "The smell and consistency of the honey makes it easy to hide weapons and drugs in the shipments. Inspectors don't want to inspect that product. It's too messy," [42] said one of the officials. However, two of these enterprises, Al Nur Honey Press Shops and Al Shifa Honey Press for Industry and Commerce, were de-listed by the UN on July 10, 2010 [43].

Another example of an al Qaeda front company is Maram, a Turkish company founded at a time when al Qaeda was spreading into Europe. The company provided both travel agency as well as import—export services. It was suspected of assisting al Qaeda operatives passing between Europe and Afghanistan. The company literally vanished when one of its directors, Mamdouh Mahmud Salim, an alleged cofounder of al Qaeda, was apprehended while traveling to Germany and deported to the US on suspicion of terrorism in 1998 [44]. In the 1990s, al Qaeda operatives would often go through Turkey while passing between Afghanistan, Sudan, and Europe. According to German authorities, Muhammad Heidar Zammar, a suspected al Qaeda operative, traveled through Turkey 40 times while passing between Europe and Afghanistan [44].

A US authority suspected Maram of providing al Qaeda with transportation assistance and acquiring parts for the construction of nuclear arms. According to the accountant who handled Maram's books, the company was not engaged in legitimate business activity, but Salim regularly visited countries known to have black markets for components of nuclear weapons, such as Russia, Romania, and Bulgaria [44].

Terrorists leverage shell companies and offshore accounts to conceal assets and those individuals or businesses that have financed al Qaeda. Wadi al Aqiq, a holding company started by Osama bin Laden while in Sudan, was one of the shell corporations. Other companies in Sudan were import—export business Ladin International Company, foreign exchange trader Taba Investment, and construction company Hijra Construction [38]. The Sudanese Government shut down these companies when bin Laden left Sudan in 1998 [3].

A number of front companies were established in Southeast Asia by al Qaeda operatives. Green Laboratory Medicine was founded in Malaysia in 1993. Its director, Yazid Sufat, who received his biochemistry education in the US, was recruited by al Qaeda while in Pakistan. Sufat was apprehended on his arrival to Malaysia from his al Qaeda training in Afghanistan in 2001. His firm was ordered by al Qaeda to acquire 21 tons of ammonium nitrate for use in attacks in Singapore [21]. Konsojaya, which was founded in 1994, was an import—export company trading in honey and palm oil. The company had strong links to Ramzi Yozef and Khalid Sheikh Mohammed's Bojinka plot as a cover-up of the transfer of funds and acquisition of ingredients for explosives [21]. Bermuda Trading Company was another company used as a front for importing bomb-making ingredients. The alleged 20th hijacker, Zacarias Moussaoui, was employed by Infocus Technology and was to be paid $35,000 initially and then $2000 every month to pay for his flight training in the USA [21]. In the Philippines a number of businesses, corporations, and charitable institutions were founded by Jamal Khalifa, bin Laden's brother-in law. Among these are Khalifa Trading Industries, ET Dizon Travel Pyramid Trading, Manpower Services. and Daw al-Iman al-Shafee Inc [38].

Al Qaeda operatives use legitimate businesses and employment to support themselves and their activities. It offers them cover and livelihood.

7.5.3 Criminal Proceeds

Post 9/11, financial troubles have pressed al Qaeda to find financial and logistical support from non-traditional resources. Terrorist groups have become involved in criminal activity. The nexus between criminals and international terrorists is growing. This is the by-product of shared financial benefit. Terrorist and criminal groups have much in common.

As Rollins, Wyler, and Rossen note, these groups overlap in several ways: through using the same tactics and methods; through switching from one type of group to the other; and "through short-term or long-term transaction-based service-for-hire activities between groups" [45].

The growing terrorist—criminal nexus leaves the US open to terrorist attack due to further opportunities for financing and stronger criminal support.

Terrorist use of criminal activities for financing their activities ranges from petty crime and low-level fraud to involvement in organized crime. For instance, the cell that carried out the Bali attack received funding partially through theft from jewelry shops. Imam Samudra, one of the leaders of the Bali plot, was also involved in credit card fraud [21].

There is a lot of evidence that many al Qaeda cells arc actively using credit card fraud. Terrorists use credit card cloning and skimming. "Terror groups and criminal organizations use credit card cloning and skimming to fund themselves," says Loretta Napoleoni, author of *Modern Jihad: Tracing the Dollars Behind the Terror Networks.* "Cloning is done primarily via the Internet. Skimming requires use of the actual card, so it is done in restaurants and stores," she says. "It is a very popular and easy technique" [46]. Credit card details are obtained from shops and restaurants or bought on the black market and then bogus cards are produced that are used to steal funds from accounts. In Europe, al Qaeda's financial network relies heavily on credit card fraud. An Algerian cell discovered in Britain in 1997 raised nearly $200,000 in 6 months [15]. There were even special camps established in Afghanistan to provide training in financial fraud, including credit card counterfeiting [15]. In 2008 in the UK, detectives were investigating a sophisticated credit card fraud that could have been linked to extremists in Pakistan. Small devices inserted into the stores' "Chip and Pin" credit card readers were reading and storing credit card information. Then the information was transmitted by wireless technology to Lahore, Pakistan. The stolen information was used to clone the cards and use them to steal money from credit and current accounts and to pay for items such as airline tickets on the Internet [47].

Interpol officials note that terrorist groups such as al Qaeda are profiting from the trafficking of counterfeit goods such as fake Nike sneakers, stereo equipment, designer bags and clothes — products that are commonly sold on streets throughout America or via the Internet [48]. In 2001, counterfeit or pirated goods worth almost $2 billion were confiscated in Europe. It has been estimated that counterfeiting has resulted in the loss of $200–250 billion commercially per year in the USA [48]. Returns generated by the sale of counterfeit goods and losses for legitimate businesses are significant.

Due to the squeeze in their funding, terrorist groups are seeking broader means for their financing, both in legitimate business practices and in counterfeiting. John Newton, an Interpol officer, said: "North African radical fundamentalist groups in Europe, al Qaeda and Hezbollah all derive income from counterfeiting. This crime has the potential to become the preferred source of funding for terrorists" [49]. In 2002, fake goods from Dubai that allegedly were sent by al Qaeda members were intercepted in Britain. In France, members of the Salafist Group for Preaching and Combat, a group associated with al Qaeda, were apprehended on suspicion of counterfeiting clothing goods [49].

Cells in Europe are becoming very creative in their attempts to raise money. For example, three men in Germany were involved in insurance fraud where they attempted to collect $6.3 million from nine life insurance policies due to a fake death [10]. In Spain and Switzerland, operatives were reselling stolen goods on the black market. Two of the 2005 London suicide bombers secured loans totaling $34,000, one of which was in default [10].

Cigarette smuggling is a highly profitable way to earn money for terrorists. The scheme is very simple but difficult to stop. The smugglers buy cheap cigarettes in regions where state tax is relatively low, such as North Carolina, and then travel to sell cigarettes at a higher price even though they did not pay the higher taxes in states such as New York. The profits are enormous and the penalties are low.

Traditionally, al Qaeda's core leadership has mostly avoided organized crime involvement due to their strong beliefs against particular crimes that violate Islam. The 9/11 Commission asserted that it cannot be proved that Osama bin Laden profited in any way from drug trafficking. The organization is currently in its weakest state, which would have been avoidable if al Qaeda had been involved in the highly profitable heroin trade in Afghanistan [45]. However, while al Qaeda leaders are not openly associated with criminal actions, its affiliates may be involved in such activities. For instance, for al Qaeda in the Islamic Maghreb (AQIM), abducting civilians and demanding ransoms is a new way to generate money. In 2009, several European tourists in Mali were released after being abducted for several months for ransoms allegedly up to $5 million each. However, a British citizen was murdered after the refusal of Great Britain to release the radical Islamist Sheikk Abu Qatada from imprisonment [50].

Another area of big concern is narcoterrorism. More often local terrorist cells are becoming increasingly involved in the drug trade. The cell that was responsible for the 2004 Madrid bombings used solely criminal connections to fund a terrorist operation. Few members were involved in drug trafficking before they joined al Qaeda. Jamal Ahmidan, a major 1990s hashish and Ecstasy dealer in Western Europe, was one of the masterminds behind the Madrid bombings plot. Ahmidan exchanged hashish for dynamite with Jose Emilio Suarez Trashorras, a former miner [45].

From 2003 to 2008, the number of designated foreign terrorist groups involved in the narco-trade increased from 14 to 18 according to the US Drug Enforcement Administration [45].

In December 2009, three members of AQIM were arrested in Ghana after a sting operation. The three men believed they were arranging a deal with members of Colombia's Marxist FARC guerrillas to smuggle up to 1000 kilograms of cocaine. They guaranteed transit of the drugs through territory under their control for the payment of $2000 per kilogram [50]. These "arrests are further proof of the direct link between dangerous terrorist organizations, including al Qaeda, and international drug trafficking that fuels their violent activities," said DEA Acting Administrator Michele Leonhart [51].

Although the 9/11 Commission reported that "no persuasive evidence exists … that al Qaeda had any substantial involvement with conflict diamonds" [3], other experts like Douglas Farah, author of *Blood From Stones: The Secret Financial Network of Terror*, are convinced that al Qaeda used African diamonds to convert cash into diamonds "in response to a move by the United States in 1998 to freeze al Qaeda assets after attacks on US embassies in Africa" [52]. The Global Witness Report "For a Few Dollars More: How al Qaeda Moved into a Diamond Trade" argues that al Qaeda used diamonds for several reasons: to raise funds, to hide money targeted by financial sanctions, and to use diamonds as a means of transferring wealth.

7.6 Methods of Transferring and Storing Funds

Al Qaeda uses various mechanisms to move and store its funds. According to the Financial Action Task Force (FATF) report on Terrorist Financing [8], there are three main methods terrorists use to move their funds or transfer value. They are:

1. Use of the financial system
2. Physical movement of money
3. International trade system.

Besides these methods, terrorists abuse alternative remittance systems (ARS), charities, and businesses, and smuggle precious stones and metals as a cover of moving funds.

Prior to 9/11, al Qaeda relied on the financial system to transfer funds. It extensively used commercial banks, shell banks, front companies, charities, and financial service businesses to move money around the world. Al Qaeda used the international banking system from the beginning. Bin Laden, as well as other top cadre members and financial facilitators, had bank accounts around the world. For a period of time, al Qaeda has targeted areas with lax financial regulations and anti-money laundering laws and inefficient banking oversight. Over the years, regional banking centers in the Middle East have avoided building anti-money laundering regimes and oversight of the banking system consistent with international standards. For instance, funds for the attempted assassination of President Mubarak went through the National Commercial Bank (NCB), the largest bank in Saudi Arabia. It transferred millions of dollars to al Qaeda's accounts via corresponding banks in London and New York [15]. The NCB chairman, Khalid bin Mahfouz, denied that his bank was involved in funding an al Qaeda group. He stated that he could not have been aware of every wire transfer moving through the bank, and that if he knew that such transactions were taking place, he would not have allowed it. There was no evidence found that Mahfouz was personally involved in any of these transactions. He was also involved with the Bank of Credit and Commerce International (BCCI), another bank from al Qaeda's infrastructure. BCCI was a major international bank founded in 1972 by Pakistani financier Agha Hasan Abedi, with operations in 69 countries. However, the bank suffered significant losses from its businesses in lending, currency trade, and deposits. Khalid bin Mahfouz was a principal shareholder and director of the BCCI Group. He was convicted in the USA for large-scale redemptions on investments prior to the bank's failure in 1991, "which resulted in a gross misstatement of the true financial picture of the bank" [53]. The BCCI's worldwide Ponzi scheme collapse resulted in large losses for investors. Although Mahfouz denied all allegations, he paid a fine of $225 million [53].

BCCI was involved in fraudulent operations and was a popular bank among money launderers, drug cartels, weapons smugglers, and terrorist organizations. When BCCI was shut down, it was discovered that bin Laden as well as other terrorists held accounts there [54]. Apparently, the bank was also used to channel money from various donors to the mujahedin in Afghanistan.

Gunaratna writes that al Qaeda's financial network was derived from BCCI [15]. Al Qaeda maintains a network with "feeder" and operational accounts to channel funds to the user of this money. Feeder accounts are set up for legitimate charities or businesses. The operational accounts belong to al Qaeda's operatives whose identity is concealed from the public. Cells have access to these accounts to fund their operations. Transfers from the feeder to operational accounts are done through several other bank accounts to conceal the real motive of the transfer [15].

The Islamic banking system provides legitimate banking services to Muslims and adheres to sharia, or Islamic law, which prohibits making money on loans and charging of interest. There are five ways in which Islamic banks provide money to their customers: (1) *mudahara*, money provided to an investor and losses and gains are co-shared; (2) *quard al-hasanah*, an interest-free loan; (3) *musharaka*, where the lending institution becomes a shareholder; (4) *murabaha*, when a bank buys and sells assets with a mark-up; (5) *ijara*, a leasing agreement, when the bank buys an object and rents it to the customer. There are three types of accounts used by Islamic lending institutions: (1) current deposit accounts with no interest earned; (2) limited *murabaha* deposits where funds can be used by the bank for the investment projects; (3) limited *mudaraba* deposits where the bank together with the customer determine the investment project and share the returns [55]. Although the Islamic banking has been growing rapidly, the regulation and oversight of the banking system is not up to international standards. Many Islamic banks possess a greater degree of autonomy and operate under lax regulatory oversight and controls. Moreover, al Qaeda and other Islamic terrorist groups can often find sympathizers from within Islamic banking.

After 9/11, al Qaeda's financial network has been largely disrupted due to increased regulations in the banking system. As a result, terrorists adapted by using tactics that have allowed them to better hide their assets and move them in informal or alternative ways of transferring funds.

Terrorists are attracted by alternative remittance systems (ARS) because they are convenient, reliable, and available 24 hours, and they are generally not subject to strict regulatory oversight. Due to rapidity and anonymity of these systems, they are one of the favorable methods of transferring funds used by terrorists. The main feature of ARS is the ability to move funds without physical movement of currency. The most widespread network for informal transfers is *hawala*.

Hawala appeared many centuries before the current financial system was formed. The word comes originally from the Arabic language and means transfer or remittance. There are other similar systems known in Pakistan (*hundi*), Philippines (*padala*), and Somalia (*xawilaad*).

Hawala is a fast and cost-effective way to transfer funds, especially for those who are beyond traditional financial services. It is challenging to accurately measure the value of funds passing through these systems; however, estimates are at tens of billions of dollars. For instance, it is estimated that in Pakistan more than $7 billion passes through *hawala* channels each year [56].

Hawala works in a similar way to Western Union or MoneyGram. Figure 7.2 shows how it works. First, a person in one country who wishes to send money to a recipient in another country contacts *hawaladar* and gives him instructions. *Hawaladar*, a *hawala* operator, contacts a counterpart *hawaladar* in the recipient country via phone, email, etc., who in turn

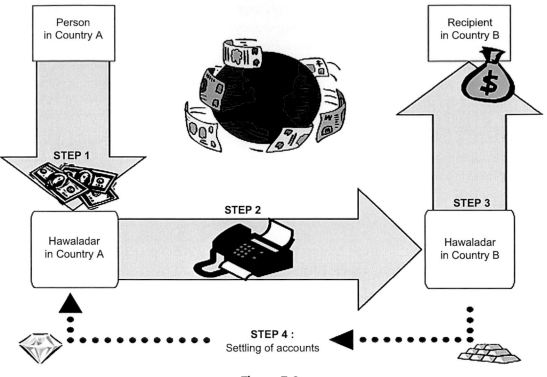

Figure 7.2:

Example of *hawala* transaction. *Source: GAO Report to Congressional Requesters Terrorist Financing: US agencies should systematically assess terrorists' use of alternative financing mechanisms, November 2003 [68].*

distributes funds to the intended recipient. The recipient has to be verified by some kind of code passed to him from the sender. Over time, the accounts between the two *hawaladars* may become unbalanced and must be settled. The settlement can take various forms, such as "reciprocal payments to customers, physical movement of the money, wire transfer or check, invoice manipulation, trade or smuggling precious stones or metals such as gold and diamonds" [57].

There are numerous reports that terrorists have used *hawala* prolifically. The 1998 US embassy attacks in Africa were financed partially by a Pakistani *hawaladar* [57]. When, following the 9/11 attacks, the United States began Operation Enduring Freedom in Afghanistan, the ruling Taliban and al Qaeda's operatives used hawala to transfer millions of dollars to Pakistan [58]. *Hawala* can be abused by narco-traffickers and other criminals. According to an anonymous source associated with a *hawala* business, "*Hawala* dealers do not care about where the money comes from or what it is being used for … They only concern themselves with the deal" [59].

Terrorists have been using charities not only as a source of financing but also as a method to move funds. Terrorists abuse the fact that foundations and charities often use financial transactions that appear legitimate. For example, the Global Relief Foundation reported that 90% of donations were transferred abroad between 1994 and 2000 [3]. As previously discussed, GRF has been linked to and has provided support and assistance to the al Qaeda network, and other known terrorist groups. Another US charity, Benevolence International Foundation, also transferred donations abroad for use in terrorism [3].

Criminal organizations and terrorist groups have long been misusing the international trade system to move funds. The FATF stated that "the international trade system is clearly subject to a wide range of risks and vulnerabilities that can be exploited by criminal organizations and terrorist financiers" [60]. Officials estimate that hundreds of billions of dollars are laundered through international trade [61].

The means for money laundering through trade channels vary greatly in complexity. The basic methods of abusing the system of international trade include the "over- and under-invoicing of goods and services, multiple invoicing of goods and services, over- and under-shipments of goods and services, and falsely describing goods and services" [61].

More complicated schemes besides involvement of various fraudulent trade practices can also involve other illegal techniques such as smuggling, corruption, narcotics trafficking, and tax avoidance. These illegal practices can be so complicated and intertwined that it is extremely difficult for effective law enforcement.

One of the most basic and oldest methods of misuse of the international trade system is over- and under-invoicing of goods and services by importers and exporters. The exporter transfers value to the importer by under-invoicing goods, because the goods are undervalued and thus the exporter receives less and the importer is able to make a profit by selling the goods on the market for their true higher value. *Vice versa*, by overvaluing the goods, the exporter will receive a greater amount than the true value from the importer, and thus profit from the difference. Figure 7.3 shows a case study illustrating over- and under-invoicing schemes.

In this example, a terrorist or criminal wants to launder money to a foreign country. A foreign exporter ships 1 million widgets worth $2 each, but invoices a domestic importer for 1 million widgets at a price of $1. Therefore, the exporter launders $1,000,000 abroad, as the importer pays $1,000,000 and receives the shipment worth $2,000,000, which is then sold in the domestic market [61].

In the opposite example, when a terrorist or criminal needs to launder money into the country, the domestic exporter ships 1 million widgets worth $2 each, but on the invoice states a price of $3 per widget. In this case, the exporting company receives a $1,000,000 extra payment, as it receives a payment of $3,000,000 and ships goods worth only $2,000,000 [61].

The use of over- and under-invoicing techniques is only possible when there is an agreement between exporter and importer, which often are controlled by the same company.

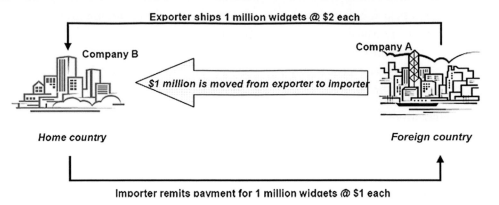

Figure 7.3:

Case study illustrating over- and under-invoicing schemes. *Source: FATF, Trade based money laundering, June 2006 [61].*

John Zdanowicz, a professor of finance at Florida International University, developed a statistical program called the International Price Profiling System (IPPS) to track money laundering through international trade. He analyzed US Government trade figures, calculated average prices for merchandise, and identified abnormally priced products.

> *"The IPPS analysis evaluates an international trade price and produces a 'Risk Index' that ranges between '−4' and '+4.' A negative [figure] indicates the potential of money being moved out of the United States to a foreign country. A positive [number] reflects the potential of money being moved into the United States from a foreign country. The magnitude of the index reflects the probability or likelihood that a price is overvalued or undervalued" [62].*

In his article "Trade Based Money Laundering and Terrorist Financing," Zdanowicz details how fraudulent invoicing is used to transfer money across borders. By comparing invoice prices with average world prices, Zdanowicz estimated that $192 billion was moved out of the USA in 2005 via undervalued and overvalued imports, and $189 billion in 2006 [63].

As government control and oversight over banks, charities, and other financial service sector businesses has become stricter, terrorist groups find it more challenging to raise and move funds. As a result, terrorists are turning from formal financial systems to the most basic and oldest method of moving funds — the physical movement of bulk cash using cash couriers. According to Stuart Levey, undersecretary of Treasury for terrorism and financial intelligence, there is "a trend toward bulk-cash smuggling and use of cash couriers" [64].

Cash smuggling is widespread in the Middle East, Southeast Asia, and Africa, assisted by ineffective border security and lax anti-money laundering enforcement practices. Unlike in the West, many people carry cash and most transactions are conducted in cash. Therefore, in such cash-based economies with the electronic banking system in an embryonic state, large cash movements can be viewed as normal and not always raise suspicion of authorities.

To terrorists, the main advantages of this method of moving funds are that there are no traceable paper trails left and no third party such as bank officials that can suspect the illicit purpose of the transfer involved. As the cost of attacks can be relatively cheap, cash moved across borders for terrorist purposes is at very low levels, making it difficult to detect and stop. But it also can be a less efficient method as there is a possibility of getting caught, and some couriers can be tempted to steal the money. Also, it is more expensive than moving money using wire transfers as it involves arrangement of the travel documents. Al Qaeda assists in travel arrangements for the courier, who passes over the package to a contact at the airport. It is often the case that the courier has no information on the purpose of the mission beyond delivering the package [58].

The attempts by international authorities to prevent cash smuggling have not been successful, especially in regions where carrying large sums of cash is normal. It is almost impossible to stop cash smuggling as it is impossible to search everyone coming to the country. According to an Indonesian authority, "you could bring a container of cash into the country without being noticed" [21]. According to Malaysian and Singaporean intelligence reports, the Jemaah Islamiya received about $40,000 in 1997 and $70,000 in 2000. Omar al-Faruq[4] testified of transferring $200,000 to the Jemaah Islamiya Indonesian cell after 2000 [21].

A leader of the Jemaah Islamiya network in Malaysia used a cash courier to transfer approximately $15,000 used in the Bali bombings. Khalid Sheikh Mohammed used a Pakistani courier, Majid Khan, to deliver $50,000 to Hambali in Thailand in early 2003 [21]. The case of Jamal al Fadl provides another example.

In 1993 Jamal al Fadl, a key witness in the 1998 US embassy bombings trials and bin Laden's finance officer from 1991to 1996, revealed his mission from Sudan to Amman in Jordan with funds for a group associated with al Qaeda in Jordan and the Palestinian territories. He smuggled $100,000 in cash, which was concealed among clothes in his suitcase. His contact in Jordan met him and enabled him to pass through customs. "He talked with one of the customs people and they didn't check my bag," al Fadl revealed [65].

Terrorist organizations also move their assets in the form of precious stones and metals such as diamonds and gold because they are highly valuable, convertible, easy to conceal, and as with cash smuggling of this method also does not leave a paper trail.

Although a link between al Qaeda and the diamond trade is a contentious issue, officials from the UN Special Court for Sierra Leone, representatives of Global Witness, media and other

---

[4] Omar al-Faruq was an Iraqi citizen brought up in Kuwait, and a senior al Qaeda member. He was a liaison between al Qaeda and Islamic terrorism in the Far East, particularly Jemaah Islamiya [71].

experts have pointed to evidence that al Qaeda was involved in the West African diamond trade. According to Douglas Farah, a Washington Post reporter and the author of *Blood From Stones*, al Qaeda was interested in profiting from gemstones in West Africa, East Africa, and Europe almost since its beginnings. West Africa is attractive to terrorist groups like al Qaeda because in countries like "Liberia, Sierra Leone and others in the region, governments are weak, corrupt and exercise little control over much of the national territory. Some states, like Liberia under Charles Taylor, were in fact functioning criminal enterprises" [66].

Al Qaeda's diamond purchases in West Africa picked up at the end of 2000 and lasted until just before 9/11. Al Qaeda operatives were paying above market value because their goal was to transfer funds into the stones and not to make money. Farah states that al Qaeda allegedly accumulated $20 million worth of diamonds prior to 9/11 to move the funds out of the banking system and into more undetectable commodities [67].

Gold presents another opportunity for moving and storing funds. A former senior Treasury official, Patrick Jost, noted, "There can be no doubt that al Qaeda has placed a large share of its assets in gold. This metal is indeed the best means of transferring secret funds. Jewelers in the Middle East and Indian subcontinent act as virtual bankers and due to its secret and archaic nature, this trade is particularly difficult to track down and infiltrate" [67].

Gold is a favorite commodity of groups like al Qaeda used to store and move funds. A large amount of cash deposited into the bank account can raise red flags and be tracked by automated systems and monitored by the authorities. Gold can be melted, smelted, and broken down into smaller pieces, making it harder to track down the original value. Gold stored in a deposit box does not have an audit trail in the banking system and can go unnoticed. Gold is a "near cash" commodity and is used by terrorists not only to store and move funds but also as a means of payment. Gold is an international market commodity and it can be converted into any currency. While gold's value can fluctuate over time, gold is considered a traditional hedge against inflation. Moreover, any loss will be a small price to pay for the security and secrecy afforded by converting the hard currency to an untraceable asset.

References

[1] Transcript of President George W. Bush, Address before a joint session of Congress on the United States response to the terrorist attacks of September 11. Available at: <http://www.presidency.ucsb.edu/ws/index.php?pid=64731#axzz1WRxfaFna>, September 20, 2001.

[2] Transcript of President George W. Bush, Remarks on United States financial sanctions against terrorists and their supporters and an exchange with reporters. Available at: <http://www.presidency.ucsb.edu/ws/index.php?pid=64040#axzz1WRxfaFna>, September 24, 2001.

[3] National Commission on Terrorist Attacks on the United States, Monograph on Terrorism Financing, Government Printing Office, Washington, DC, 2004. Available at: <http://www.9-11commission.gov/staff_statements/911_TerrFin_Monograph.pdf>.

[4] United Nations Treaty Collection. <http://treaties.un.org/Pages/ViewDetails.aspx?src=IND&mtdsg_no=XVIII-11&chapter=18&lang=en>.

[5] Text of the International Convention for the Suppression of the Financing of Terrorism is available at: <http://treaties.un.org/Pages/DB.aspx?path=DB/studies/page2_en.xml&menu=MTDSG>.

[6] United States Government Accountability Office. "Terrorist financing" testimony before the Committee on Financial Services, Subcommittee on Oversight and Investigations, House of Representatives. Available at: <http://www.gao.gov/new.items/d0619.pdf>, April 6, 2006.

[7] L.K. Donohue, Anti-terrorist finance in the United Kingdom and United States. Available at: <http://students.law.umich.edu/mjil/article-pdfs/v27n2-donohue.pdf>.

[8] Terrorist Financing: Report of an Independent Task Force. Available at: <http://www.fatf-gafi.org/dataoecd/28/43/40285899.pdf>, February 2009.

[9] Terrorist Financing, Report of an Independent Task Force sponsored by the Council on Foreign Relations, Council on Foreign Relations, New York, October 2002. Available at: <http://www.cfr.org/publication/5080/terrorist_financing.html?breadcrumb=%2Fpublication%2Fpublication_list%3Fgroupby%3D3%26type%3Dtask_force_report%26filter%3D2002>.

[10] C. Whitlock, Al-Qaeda masters terrorism on the cheap, Washington Post Foreign Service. Available at: <http://www.washingtonpost.com/wp-dyn/content/article/2008/08/23/AR2008082301962.html>, August 24, 2008.

[11] M. Rice-Oxley, Why terror financing is so tough to track down. Available at: <http://www.csmonitor.com/2006/0308/p04s01-woeu.html>.

[12] Council on Foreign Relations, Profile: Osama bin Laden. Available at: <http://www.cfr.org/publication/9951/profile.html>.

[13] L. Beyer, The most wanted man in the world. Available at: <http://www.time.com/time/magazine/article/0,9171,1000871,00.html>.

[14] The Jihad Fixation, cited in R. Gunaratna, Inside al Qaeda: Global Network of Terror.

[15] R. Gunaratna, Inside al Qaeda: Global Network of Terror, Columbia University Press, 2002.

[16] A. K. Cronin, Foreign terrorist organizations, CRS Report for Congress. Available at: <www.fas.org/irp/crs/RL32223.pdf>, February 6, 2004.

[17] T. Koker, C.L. Yordan, Microfinancing terrorism: a study in al Qaeda financing strategy. Available at: <http://papers.ssrn.com/sol3/papers.cfm?abstract_id=1287241>.

[18] National Commission on Terrorist Attacks Upon the United States, Overview of the enemy, Staff Statement No. 15. Available at: <http://www.9-11commission.gov/staff_statements/staff_statement_15.pdf>.

[19] World Islamic Front Statement, Jihad against Jews and Crusaders. Available at: <http://www.fas.org/irp/world/para/docs/980223-fatwa.htm>, February 23, 1998.

[20] D.L. Watson, The terrorist threat confronting the United States, Congressional Testimony before the Senate Select Committee on Intelligence, Federal Bureau of Investigation. Available at: <http://www.fbi.gov/news/testimony/the-terrorist-threat-confronting-the-united-states>, Frebruary 6, 2002.

[21] Z. Abuza, Funding terrorism in Southeast Asia: The financial network of Al-Qaeda and Jemaah Islamiyah, Contemp. Southeast Asia 23 (2) (2003) 169−199.

[22] P. Bergen, Holy War, Inc.: Inside the Secret World of Osama bin Laden, Simon & Schuster, New York, 2002.

[23] BBC News Hambali, Asia's Bin Laden. Available at: <http://news.bbc.co.uk/2/hi/asia-pacific/2346225.stm>, Wednesday, September 6, 2006.

[24] The House Permanent Select Committee on Intelligence and the Senate Select Committee on Intelligence, Report of the Joint Inquiry into the Terrorist Attacks of September 11, 2001. Available at: <http://news.findlaw.com/usatoday/docs/911rpt/part2.pdf>, July 24, 2003. Cited in Dissertation: "Financing Terror: An Analysis and Simulation for Affecting Al Qaeda's Financial Infrastructure" by Steve Kiser Pardee, RAND Graduate School.

[25] S. Schmidt, D. Farrah, Al Qaeda's new leaders: Six militants from ranks to fill void, Washington Post. Available at: <http://www.washingtonpost.com/ac2/wp-dyn/A32695-2002Oct28?language=printer>, October 29, 2002.

[26] J. Coffer Black, Al-Qaida: The threat to the United States and its allies, Testimony to the House Committee on International Relations. Available at: <http://commdocs.house.gov/committees/intlrel/hfa92869.000/hfa 92869_0.htm>, April 1, 2004.

[27] L. Napoleoni, Terrorism financing in Europe, in: Giraldo, Trinkunas (Eds.), Terrorist Financing and State Response, Stanford University Press, Stanford, CA.

[28] N. Passas, Terrorism financing: Mechanisms and policy dilemmas, in: Giraldo, Trinkunas (Eds.), Terrorist Financing and State Response, Stanford University Press, Stanford, CA.

[29] K. Wassef, Recession tough for Al Qaeda, too? Available at: <http://www.cbsnews.com/8301-503543_162-5076823-503543.html>, June 10, 2009.

[30] G. Corera, Al-Qaeda 'faces funding crisis', BBC News. Available at: <http://news.bbc.co.uk/2/hi/8303978.stm>, October 13, 2009.

[31] W. Maclean, Al-Qaeda's money trouble, Reuters, June 15, 2009.

[32] R. Lee, Terrorist financing: The US and international response, Congressional Research Service. Available at: <www.law.umaryland.edu/marshall/./RL31658_12062002.pdf>, December 6, 2002.

[33] M.A. Levitt, Hearing on "The role of charities and NGOs in the financing of terrorist activities," Subcommittee on International Trade and Finance. Available at: <http://banking.senate.gov/02_08hrg/080102/levitt.htm>.

[34] Fox News, Al Qaeda financing documents turn up in Bosnia raid. Available at: <http://www.foxnews.com/story/0,2933,78937,00.html>, February 19, 2003.

[35] S.A. Levey, Loss of moneyman a big blow for al-Qaeda. Available at: <http://www.washingtonpost.com/wp-dyn/content/article/2010/06/04/AR2010060404271.html>, June 6, 2010.

[36] C.M. Blanchard, A.B. Prados, Saudi Arabia: Terrorist financing issues, CRS Report for Congress. Available at: <www.fas.org/sgp/crs/terror/RL32499.pdf>, December 8, 2004.

[37] Department of the Treasury, Additional background information on charities designated under executive order 13224. Available at: <http://www.treasury.gov/resource-center/terrorist-illicit-finance/Pages/protecting-charities_execorder_13224-p.aspx#w>.

[38] V. Comras, Al Qaeda finances and funding to affiliated groups, Strategic Insights IV (1) (2005). Available at: <http://www.apgml.org/frameworks/docs/7/Al%20Qaeda%20Financing_%20V%20Comras_Jan05.pdf>.

[39] Trial Transcripts of the United States of America v. Usama bin Laden et al., Day 8. Available at: <http://cryptome.org/usa-v-ubl-08.htm>, February 21, 2001.

[40] M. Epstein, B. Schmidt, Operation support-system shutdown, National Review, Online. Available at: <http://www.investigativeproject.org/170/operation-support-system-shutdown>, September 4, 2003.

[41] D. M. Lormel, Financing patterns associated with Al Qaeda and global terrorist networks, Federal Bureau of Investigation. Available at: <http://www.fbi.gov/news/testimony/financing-patterns-associated-with-al-qaeda-and-global-terrorist-networks>, February 12, 2002.

[42] J. Miller, J. Gerth, A nation challenged: Al Qaeda; Honey trade said to provide funds and cover to bin Laden, New York Times. Available at: <http://www.nytimes.com/2001/10/11/world/nation-challenged-al-qaeda-honey-trade-said-provide-funds-cover-bin-laden.html?sec=&spon=&pagewanted=print>, October 11, 2001.

[43] Security Council, Al-Qaida and Taliban Sanctions Committee approves deletion of two entries from consolidated list. Available at: <http://www.un.org/News/Press/docs//2010/sc9977.doc.htm>.

[44] D. Frantz, Threats and responses: Qaeda's bankrolls; Front companies said to keep financing terrorists, New York Times. Available at: <http://www.nytimes.com/2002/09/19/world/threats-responses-qaeda-s-bankrolls-front-companies-said-keep-financing.html?sec=&spon=&pagewanted=print>, September 19, 2002.

[45] J. Rollins, L. Sun Wyler, International terrorism and transnational crime: Security threats, US policy, and considerations for Congress, Congressional Research Service. Available at: <www.fas.org/sgp/crs/terror/R41004.pdf>, March 18, 2010.

[46] J.M. Simon, The credit card-terrorism connection: How terrorists use cards for everyday needs and to fund operations (2008). Available at: <http://www.creditcards.com/credit-card-news/credit-cards-terrorism-1282.php>.

[47] D. Leppard, Fraudsters' bugs transmit credit card details to Pakistan, Sunday Times. Available at: <http://www.timesonline.co.uk/tol/news/uk/crime/article4926400.ece>, October 12, 2008.

[48] Fox News, Officials: Counterfeit goods fund terrorism. Available at: <http://www.foxnews.com/story/0,2933,92094,00.html>, July 16, 2003.

[49] J. Ungoed-Thomas, Designer fakes 'are funding Al-Qaeda'. Available at: <http://www.timesonline.co.uk/tol/news/uk/article432410.ece>, March 20, 2005.

[50] P. Sherwell, Cocaine, kidnapping and the Al-Qaeda cash squeeze. Available at: <http://www.telegraph.co.uk/news/worldnews/africaandindianocean/mali/7386278/Cocaine-kidnapping-and-the-Al-Qaeda-cash-squeeze.html>, March 6, 2010.

[51] News Release, Three Al Qaeda associates arrested on drug and terrorism charges, US Drug Enforcement Administration Press. Available at: <http://www.justice.gov/dea/pubs/pressrel/pr121809.html>, December 18, 2009.

[52] D. Farah, Terror assets hidden in gem-buying spree, Washington Post. Available at: <http://www9.georgetown.edu/faculty/irvinem/CCT510/Sources/washingtonpost-Africans_Al-Qaeda_Diamonds-12-29-02.html>.

[53] R. Ehrenfeld, The Saudi buck stops here. Available at: <http://www.acdemocracy.org/viewarticle.cfm?id=202>.

[54] A. Dodds Frank, M. Perez-Rivas, Bin Laden's global financial reach detailed, CNN. Available at: <http://archives.cnn.com/2001/US/09/26/inv.drug.money/index.html>, September 26, 2001.

[55] S.M. Aubrey, The New Dimension of International Terrorism, vdf Hochschulverlag AG, 2004.

[56] US Department of the Treasury, Hawala and alternative remittance systems. Available at: <http://www.treasury.gov/resource-center/terrorist-illicit-finance/Pages/Hawala-and-Alternatives.aspx>.

[57] S. Kiser, Financing terror: An analysis and simulation for affecting Al Qaeda's financial infrastructure, Dissertation, Pardee RAND Graduate School. Available at: <http://www.rand.org/pubs/rgs_dissertations/RGSD185.html>.

[58] D. Farah, Al Qaeda's road paved with gold, Washington Post Foreign Service. Available at: <http://www.library.cornell.edu/colldev/mideast/qdagold.htm>, February 17, 2002.

[59] M. Ganguly, A banking system built for terrorism. Available at: <http://www.time.com/time/world/article/0,8599,178227,00.html>, Friday, October 5, 2001.

[60] FATF, Trade based money laundering. Available at: <http://www.fincen.gov/news_room/rp/files/fatf_typologies.pdf>, June 2006.

[61] United States Department of State Bureau for International Narcotics and Law Enforcement Affairs, Money laundering and financial crimes, International Narcotics Control Strategy Report (Volume II). Available at: <http://www.state.gov/p/inl/rls/nrcrpt/2009/vol2/116537.htm>, February 27, 2009.

[62] International Trade Alert, Inc. Available at: <http://www.internationaltradealert.com/products.asp>.

[63] J.S. Zdanowicz, Trade based money laundering and terrorist financing, Ph.D. Dissertation. Available at: <http://ciber.fiu.edu/workingpaperseries.php>, October 2009.

[64] J. Diamond, Terror funding shifts to cash, USA Today. Available at: <http://www.usatoday.com/news/washington/2006-06-18-terror-cash_x.htm>, June 18, 2006.

[65] J. Willman, Trail of terrorist dollars that spans the world. Available at: <http://specials.ft.com/attackonterrorism/FT3RNR3XMUC.html>, November 29, 2001.

[66] Testimony of Douglas Farah, Terrorist responses to improved US financial defenses, before the House Subcommittee on Oversight and Investigations, Committee on Financial Services. Available at: <http://financialservices.house.gov/media/pdf/021605df.pdf>, February 16, 2005.

[67] Global Witness, For a few dollars more: How Al Qaeda moved into the diamond trade. Available at: <http://www.globalpolicy.org/security/issues/diamond/2003/Liberia-GW.pdf>, April 2003.

[68] Verbatim Transcript of Combatant Status Review, Tribunal Hearing for ISN 10024. Available at: <www.defense.gov/news/transcript_isn10024.pdf>.

[69] T. Joscelyn, On the death of Mustafa Abu Yazid: The top terrorist's career dispels some myths about our enemies, Weekly Standard. Available at: <http://www.weeklystandard.com/blogs/death-mustafa-abu-yazid>, Jun 1, 2010.

[70]   BBC News, Profile: Omar al-Faruq (2006). Available at: <http://news.bbc.co.uk/2/hi/middle_east/5379604.
        stm>.

[71]   GAO Report to Congressional Requesters, Terrorist financing: US agencies should systematically assess
        terrorists' use of alternative financing mechanisms. Available at: <http://www.gao.gov/new.items/d04163.
        pdf>, November 2003.

CHAPTER 8

Study on Covert Networks of Terrorists Based on Interactive Relationship Hypothesis

Duoyong Sun, Wenju Li, Xiaopeng Liu

College of Information System & Management, National University of Defense Technology, P.R. China

Chapter Outline

Intelligent Systems for Security Informatics.
http://dx.doi.org/10.1016/B978-0-12-404702-0.00008-2

155

8.1 Introduction

The events of 9/11 have made terrorism become the common enemy of people internationally. Striking against and facing up to terrorism are now global issues. Important measures have been taken by many countries as regards counter-terrorism, including understanding the terrorist organizations, breaking up terrorist organizations, and making emergency preparations. Currently, with the development of information technology and the international community's fight against terrorism, great changes have taken place in the structure of terrorist organizations and the traditional pyramidal structure has been replaced by a network structure, which has become the most important feature of contemporary terrorist organizations [1]. Terrorist organizations can be regarded as relationship networks formed on the basis of specific beliefs. According to social network theory, any action of actors is not isolated but correlated. The relationship ties among them are transmission channels of information and resources, and the network relation structure decides their opportunities for action and results. It has become an important way to understand and break up networks of terrorist organizations by analyzing network characteristics of terrorist organizations by constructing a social network model of the terrorist organization's members. Because of the concealment and dispersiveness of terrorist organization activities, the traditional social network modeling method is difficult to put into effect. Therefore, it is a very important task to develop new research means, construct social network models according to public information and clues of the activities of terrorist organization members, and explore the characteristics of the activities of terrorist organizations.

Public information contains telephone records, court trail records, bank transaction records, traffic violation records, boarding records, trade records, text records, mail records, Internet forum records, video records, involved event records, interactive relationship records, interrelationship records, and so on. In principle, any trace that reflects the activities of terrorist organization members can be taken as the basis for the construction of a social network model. However, we should also see that terrorist organization members usually live in a covert way and they seldom contact each other in normal time for reasons of personal safety and evading attack. Therefore, it is seen that the network of terrorist organization members has entirely different relationship characteristics from those of general interpersonal relationship networks. Due to the covert nature of the terrorist network, the terrorist organization may conceal the information positively, so a social network model established on the basis of public data information may omit some important relationships, and the result may therefore deviate from the actual situation. Hence, solving the problems of missing data is the unavoidable issue in constructing social networks of terrorist organizations.

This chapter takes text information from two groups of terrorist organization members published by the Ministry of Public Security of the People's Republic of China in December 2003[1] and October 2008[2] as data sources[3]. The social network model of terrorist organization members is established by extracting the involved event records, interactive relationship records, and affiliations of personnel organizations in the public domain. The model aims to acquire missing information regarding individuals and relationships, and detect spurious relationship screening issues possibly encountered in the network model construction, and to conduct relationship deduction by introducing an interactive relationship hypothesis, perfect the network, and verify the rationality by empirical research.

The chapter is arranged as follows. Section 8.2 mainly introduces the relevant research and literature. Section 8.3 puts forward the initial network construction methods of terrorist organizations on the basis of affiliations. Section 8.4 aims to find the deficiencies in the data, discovers the basis, proposes a forward interactive relationship hypothesis, and improves the initial network. Section 8.5 refines the terrorist organization and incident relationship networks, and establishes the final relationship networks. Section 8.6 carries out the relevant network calculations, experimental analysis, and result verifications. Section 8.7 considers the conclusions and future prospects.

8.2 Relevant Works

Before the events of 9/11, many scholars attempted to use social network analysis methods to research the covert networks of terrorist organizations. In 1981, Bonnie Erickson proposed that the effective associations in a secret society depended on the trust between them [2]. For instance, whether receiving training together, living together, being close friends in a dormitory, or blood relationships might directly influence the reliability of the network relationships. In 1991, Malcolm Sparrow studied the existing problems in crime networks [3], i.e. a covert network would inevitably introduce imperfections of the node and relationship data, vagueness of network boundaries, and dynamic variability. In 1993, Baker and Faulkner found that terrorist organization networks and other covert networks were different from the

---

[1] http://news.sina.com.cn/c/2003-12-29/12582490000.shtm
[2] http://news.ifeng.com/photo/news/200810/1021_1397_839722.shtml. 2008-10
[3] http://www.chinanews.com.cn/gn/news/2008/10-21/1419010.shtml. 2008-10

normal interpersonal networks, and that their members rarely contacted each other, which constituted weak connections in models [4]. Strong connections might be the experience of receiving training or learning together several years ago. They suggested exploring the terrorist network relationship data using archive files, such as evidence of court proceedings and information provided by various witnesses. After 9/11, this field attracted much attention and gradually became a focus of research. Valdis E. Krebs constructed a terrorist organization member relationship network for 9/11 by using telephone records [5]. Aparna Basu constructed a social network structure of terrorist organizations according to records of terrorist incidents launched by 61 terrorist organizations in India between 2001 and 2003 [6]. Richard Rothenberg established an "Al-Qaeda" network structure according to newspapers and radio station information records [7]. Kathleen Carley clarified the application potential of the social network analysis and modeling method on the basis of the use of intelligent agents in breaking up the terrorist organizations [8].

Data missing from public information is a common problem in the construction of covert network models. Dombroski and colleagues paid close attention to the missing data phenomenon in the construction of social network models, and studied the construction of a covert network model under the condition of missing information [9]. José A. Rodriguez pointed out that "Incomplete connections make the terrorist organization members able to maintain the foremost relationship in the large network, providing substantial support and spiritual arousal for them" [10]. Sageman stated the importance of weak relationship contact in terrorist organization networks [1]. Jonathan Kennedy researched the weak relationship problems of the terrorists, and deemed that its importance was greater than knowing strong relationships [11]. This research laid the foundations for the hypothesis and network refinement considered in this chapter.

8.3 Initial Network Construction

The initial network mainly involves the construction of figures and incident relationship network, the construction of figures and organization relationship network, and the relationship network among figures and among organizations relevant to the terrorist organization members, with the purpose of providing the basis for finding the missing data.

8.3.1 Relationship Network Construction of Terrorist Organization Members and Terrorist Incident Participation

Analyzing the data sources, we found that 42 terrorist organization members and 28 terrorist incidents were involved by classifying the data obtained. We numbered the terrorist organization members as A01−A42, numbered terrorist incidents as E01−E28, and defined the matrix elements Z_{ij} according to whether members participated in the incidents or not.

Table 8.1: Relationship Matrix of Terrorist Organization Members and Terrorist Incidents

	E01	E02	E03	E04	E05	E06	E07	E08	E09	...	E28
A01	1	0	0	0	0	0	0	0	0	...	0
A02	0	1	0	0	0	0	0	0	0	...	0
A03	0	0	1	0	0	0	0	0	0	...	0
A04	0	0	1	0	0	0	0	0	0	...	0
A05	0	0	1	0	0	0	0	0	0	...	0
A06	0	0	1	1	0	1	0	0	0	...	0
A07	0	0	0	1	0	0	0	0	0	...	0
A08	0	0	0	0	1	0	0	0	0	...	0
A09	0	0	0	0	1	0	0	0	0	...	0
...	...	...	...	...	...	...	...	...	...	...	...
A42	0	0	0	0	0	0	0	0	0	...	0

$Z_{ij} = 1$ indicated that member i participated in incident j, and $Z_{ij} = 0$ indicated that member i did not participate in incident j. Based on this definition, the relationship matrix of incident participation of terrorist organization members was established as shown in Table 8.1. See Figure 8.1 for the corresponding network topology.

8.3.2 Network Construction of Terrorist Organization Members and Terrorist Organization Affiliation

In the obtained text data, eight terrorist organizations are involved, numbered as G01−G08. We defined the matrix element Z_{ij} according to whether the members were affiliated to an organization or not. $Z_{ij} = 1$ indicated that member i was affiliated to organization j, and $Z_{ij} = 0$ indicated that member i was not affiliated to organization j. Based on this definition, the relationship matrix of terrorist organization members and organization affiliations was established as shown in Table 8.2. See Figure 8.2 for the corresponding network topology.

8.3.3 Assignment and Interactive Relationship Network Construction among Terrorist Organization Members

The assignment relationship among the terrorist organization members was largely determined by specific terms in public text information, such as dispatch, recruitment, command, and instigation. The matrix element Z_{ij} was defined according to whether the members were involved in the assignment relationship or not. $Z_{ij} = 1$ indicated that member i received an assignment from member j, and $Z_{ij} = 0$ indicated that member i did not receive an assignment from member j. The assignment relationship was unidirectional. Besides the unidirectional assignment relationship, a bidirectional interactive relationship also existed among terrorist organization members. The interactive relationship among

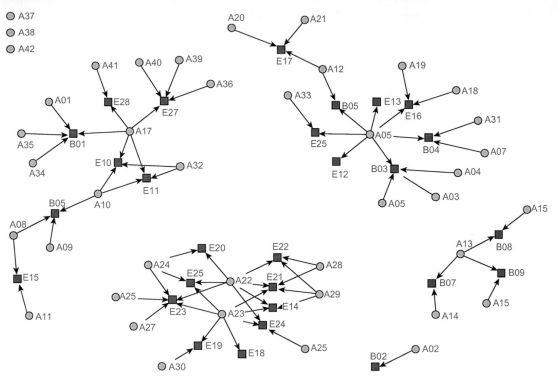

Figure 8.1:

Relationship network of terrorist organization members and terrorist incidents.

terrorist organization members was mainly determined by terms such as deciding through consultation, discussion and reaching consensus, and was indicated as $Z_{ij} = Z_{ji} = 1$ in the matrix, as shown in Table 8.3. See Figure 8.3 for the corresponding network topology.

Table 8.2: Relationship Matrix of Terrorist Organization Members and Terrorist Organizations

	G01	G02	G03	G04	G05	G06	G07	G08
A01	0	1	0	0	0	0	0	0
A02	1	0	0	0	0	0	0	0
A03	0	1	0	0	0	0	0	0
A04	0	0	0	0	0	0	0	0
A05	0	0	0	0	0	0	0	0
A06	0	1	0	0	0	0	0	0
A07	0	1	0	0	0	0	0	0
A08	1	0	0	0	0	0	0	0
A09	1	0	0	0	0	0	0	0
...	...	...	...	...	...	...	...	...
A42	0	0	0	0	0	0	0	0

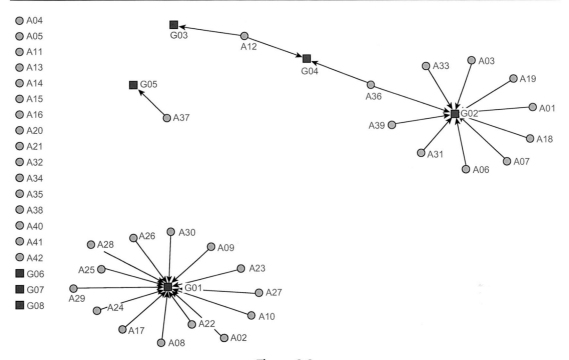

Figure 8.2:
Relationship network of terrorist organization members and terrorist organizations.

The assignment and interactive relationship records in public information is actually the information about interactive relationships among terrorists in incidents released by relevant departments of the state based on facts. The relationship network of terrorist organization members established by the above is explicit and reliable, and its defects may be problems of individual deficiency and missing relationships.

Table 8.3: Relationship Chart of Terrorist Organization Members

	A01	A02	A03	A04	A05	A06	A07	A08	A09	...	A42
A01	0	0	0	0	0	0	0	0	0	...	0
A02	0	0	0	0	0	0	0	0	0	...	0
A03	0	0	0	1	1	0	0	0	0	...	0
A04	0	0	0	0	0	0	0	0	0	...	0
A05	0	0	0	0	0	0	0	0	0	...	0
A06	0	0	0	0	0	0	0	0	0	...	0
A07	0	0	0	0	0	1	0	0	0	...	0
A08	0	0	0	0	0	0	0	0	0	...	0
A09	0	0	0	0	0	0	0	1	0	...	0
...	...	...	...	...	...	...	...	...	...	...	...
A42	0	0	0	0	0	0	0	0	0	...	0

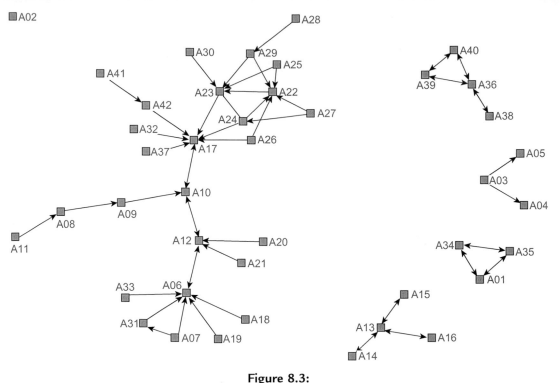

Figure 8.3:
Relationship network of terrorist organization members.

8.3.4 Supporting Relationship Network Construction among Terrorist Organizations

The text data described the relationships among terrorist organizations in detail, and the supporting relationship matrix among terrorist organizations was constructed in the light of the connection and support among terrorist organizations, and the interactions among terrorist organization leaders. The element $Z_{ij} = 1$ in the matrix indicated that the organizations i and j had this supporting relationship, and $Z_{ij} = 0$ indicated that the organizations i and j did not have this supporting relationship, as shown in Table 8.4. See Figure 8.4 for the corresponding network topology.

8.3.5 Construction of Initial Multi-Element Network

According to the above relationship matrices, the multi-element social relationship network model of terrorist organization members was established using ORA tools developed by Dr. Kathleen M. Carley of CASOS at the School of Computer Science at Carnegie Mellon University, as shown in Figure 8.5. In the figure, the round dots represent 42 terrorist organization members, the rhombus dots represent 28 terrorist incidents, and the square dots represent eight terrorist organizations. The relationships between dots are

Table 8.4: Relationship Matrix of Terrorist Organizations

	G01	G02	G03	G04	G05	G06	G07	G08
G01	0	1	1	1	1	0	0	0
G02	1	0	1	1	1	1	1	0
G03	1	1	0	1	0	0	0	1
G04	1	1	1	0	0	0	0	0
G05	1	1	0	0	0	0	0	0
G06	0	1	0	0	0	0	0	0
G07	0	1	0	0	0	0	0	0
G08	0	0	1	0	0	0	0	0

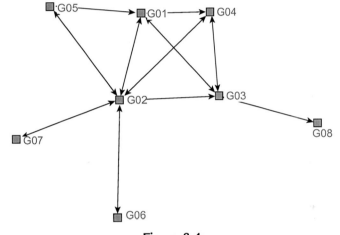

Figure 8.4:
Relationship network of terrorist organizations.

represented by the solid lines. The arrows point at the leaders, incidents and organizations, and reflect the affiliations among terrorist organization members, terrorist incidents and terrorist organizations. The bidirectional arrows indicate the interactive relationships among terrorist organization members, and supporting relationships among terrorist organizations.

Compared with Figures 8.1 and 8.3, it can be seen that some terrorist organization members are connected by some terrorist incidents or terrorist organizations, such as A03 and A06 connected by E03. If all terrorist incidents and organizations are removed from the multi-element network of terrorist organization members, the network of terrorist organization members is as shown in Figure 8.3. The structure of the network has changed significantly and more isolated groups occur. This phenomenon is likely due to the relationships of partial terrorist organization members being concealed in various affiliations.

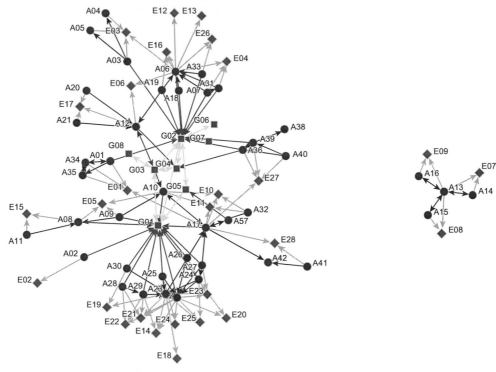

Figure 8.5:
Multi-element network of terrorist organization members.

8.4 Network Refinement Based on Interaction Relation Hypothesis

In order to compensate for potentially missing data and to improve the network, this section first constructs a possible relationship network of the members of a terrorist organization on the basis of the matrix of mutually participated events; secondly, it finds the potentially missing data by comparing the assignments obtained from the possible relationship network and public information with the interaction relation network; thirdly, the interaction relation hypothesis is proposed in accordance with the characteristics of member relationship in terrorist activities; finally, the initial network of the members of the terrorist organization is improved in accordance with the hypothesis.

8.4.1 Construction of Possible Relationship Network of Members of a Terrorist Organization Based on Mutual Participation Relationship

It is supposed that there are *m* terrorists, who separately participate in *n* terrorist incidents. The participation matrix of the event is defined as **PT**; thus **PT** is the subordinate relationship matrix of m × n rank, among which:

$$\mathbf{PT}_{ik} = \{ \begin{array}{l} 1 \\ 0 \end{array} \quad \begin{array}{l} \text{If the } i\text{th terrorist has participated in Event } k \\ \text{If the } i\text{th terrorist has not participated in Event } k \end{array}$$

In this formula, $i = 1, 2, \ldots, m$; $k = 1, 2, \ldots, n$.

In the social network theory, the interpersonal relationship network between members can be established in accordance with the fact that many people participate in some activities many times. For example, for the many people participating in club activities many times, it can be considered that a certain relationship exists between them. However, generally terrorist incidents are planned meticulously. The members involved are selected on a strict basis. Generally, the members may communicate secretly before the action in order to coordinate the action; although a single connection between members exists, the key information here is knowing this relationship in advance. Thus, we can establish the possible interpersonal relationship network (PRO) in accordance with the subordinate relationship matrix of the event. The advantage is that the relationships can be considered comprehensively while the disadvantage is that details of the relationship may be missing or a spurious relationship may exist.

Thus, in accordance with the participation matrix **PT**, we can get the adjacency matrix model **PRO**, including the possible relationships; **PRO** is an $m \times m$ rank matrix. In this situation, $\mathbf{PRO} = \mathbf{PT} \times \mathbf{PT}'$, and in this formula matrix **PT**' is the transpose of the participation matrix **PT**. Obviously, if actors i and j have jointly participated in Event k, $pt_{ip} = pt_{jp} = 1$, where $p = 1, 2, \ldots, k$; $PRO_{ij} = k$, with $k = 1, 2, \ldots, n$.

Certainly, in accordance with situations of individuals participating in the events, we can get the relation matrix **ATCK** of the event in the same way, i.e. $\mathbf{ATCK} = \mathbf{PT}' \times \mathbf{PT}$.

In accordance with the subordinate relationship matrix between the members of the terrorist organization and the terrorist incidents in Table 8.1 and the above calculation method, the relationship matrix of the members of the terrorist organization based on joint participation in the terrorist incident is shown in Table 8.5.

The relationship matrix above is a symmetrical matrix. The elements in the matrix represent the number of terrorist incidents in which the members of the terrorist organization jointly participate. For example, the value in the third line and the fifth column is 1, which means that A03 and A05 jointly participate in one terrorist incident. Inputting the content of Table 8.5 into UCINET software allows us to get a possible relationship network diagram of the members of terrorist organization based on the mutual participation relationship, as shown in Figure 8.6. In the figure, the dots represent 42 members of the terrorist organization; the lines between the dots represent the possible interrelationships between the members of the terrorist organization. Four isolated points in the figure indicate that they do not jointly participate in any terrorist incidents with other members of the terrorist organization.

Table 8.5: Relationship Matrix of the Members of a Terrorist Organization Based on Participation

	A01	A02	A03	A04	A05	A06	A07	A08	A09	...	A42
A01	1	0	0	0	0	0	0	0	0	...	0
A02	0	1	0	0	0	0	0	0	0	...	0
A03	0	0	1	1	1	1	0	0	0	...	0
A04	0	0	1	1	1	1	0	0	0	...	0
A05	0	0	1	1	1	1	0	0	0	...	0
A06	0	0	1	1	1	7	1	0	0	...	0
A07	0	0	0	0	0	1	1	0	0	...	0
A08	0	0	0	0	0	0	0	2	1	...	0
A09	0	0	0	0	0	0	0	1	1	...	0
...	...	...	...	...	...	...	...	...	...	...	...
A42	0	0	0	0	0	0	0	0	0	...	0

8.4.2 Potential Missing Data

Compared with the relationship in Figure 8.3, the relationship between the members of the terrorist organization in Figure 8.6 is changed significantly, and some new relationships appear; meanwhile, some old relationships no longer exist. The reasons for these situations are as follows. Firstly, partial members of the terrorist organization jointly participate in a terrorist incident, but public information does not include information on the relationships between these members of the terrorist organization, which results in the relationships increasing. Secondly, some members of the terrorist organization do not jointly participate in a terrorist event, but they are interrelated, which constitutes missing relationships. For the newly increased relationships, some arise from the possible data missing in the public information while others may be spurious relationships.

Entity and relationship missing cases

Common data missing includes two types: entity missing and relationship missing. Entity missing mainly means there is a figure, event, or organization missing. Relationship missing mainly refers to the relationship between the entities being missing; that is, a relationship between people or between the people and the event is missing.

Comparing Figures 8.3 and 8.6, the entity missing and relationship missing cases obviously exist in Figure 8.3. The entity missing case refers to those members of terrorist organization who participate in the terrorist incident with a clear relationship, but where no relationship data are included in the public information. For example, in terrorist event E03, the members A03, A04, A05, and A06 jointly participate in this event; however, in accordance with public information, the members of these two terrorist organizations have no contact. The relationship missing case is where members are not directly related to each other, but they are

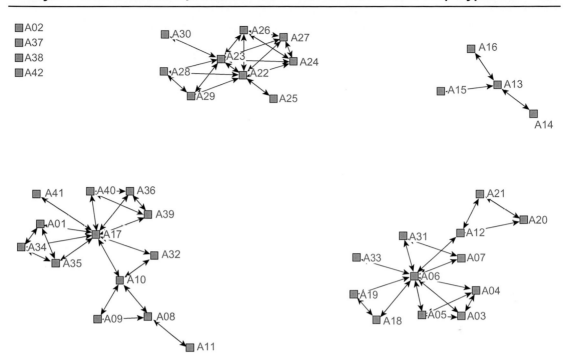

Figure 8.6:
Possible relationship network diagram of the members of a terrorist organization based on mutual participation relationships.

linked through the co-leader or the people being led. For example, if A06, A18, and A19 jointly participate in event E16, A18 and A19 are led by A06, so A18 and A19 are linked through A06; however, A18 and A19 do not contact each other directly via public information, so their relationship is missed. Possible entity missing and relationship missing cases are shown in Table 8.6.

Spurious relationships

A spurious relationship is one where a possible relationship network between members exists based on event correlation. Because these two members jointly participate in the same event, an association relationship is formed. However, due to regional and time differences, actually this relationship does not exist. The potential spurious relationships in Figure 8.6 are listed in Table 8.6. There are six spurious relationships in all, among which four are potentially spurious relationships appearing in the same chain of command. For example, A23 and A28 established a direct relationship in Figure 8.3, because both jointly participated in event E21. However, analysis of public information reveals that, in event E21, A29 went to a Middle Eastern country to develop the new member A28, which was arranged by A23. At this time, A23 was in a South Asian country. The regional difference makes the possibility of a direct

Table 8.6: Relationship Changes Between Members of a Terrorist Organization

		Team 1	Team 2
New links	Person missing	A17	A01, A34, A35
		A06	A03, A04, A05
		A17	A36, A39, A40
	Link missing	A08	A10
		A10	A33
		A18	A19
		A20	A21
	False links	A22	A28
		A23	A28
		A23	A27
		A23	A26
		A24	A26
		A27	A26
Disappeared links		A17	A23, A24, A26
		A10	A12

relationship between A23 and A28 very unlikely. The possible spurious relationships are shown in Table 8.6.

8.4.3 Interaction Relationship Hypothesis

In this section, we propose three types of inference hypotheses. They are the entity missing hypothesis based on action association, the tripartite relationship hypothesis based on the event, and the spurious relationship hypothesis based on association differences. These hypotheses can help us to find missing entities, missing relations and false relations, and lay the foundations for improvement of the initial social networks.

Entity missing hypothesis based on action association

Most terrorist incidents are carefully planned. The implementation of terrorist actions requires close communication and cooperation between members. Thus, on the basis of the action association relationship in the terrorist incident, we can propose the entity missing hypothesis. That is, the appointed and interactive relationship network between the members is based on public information. For two individuals or action groups that participate in the same terrorist incident and have clear tasks, if they do not contact each other directly and do not have an indirect relationship, we can suppose that at least one middleman AE exists between these two individuals or action groups and acts as an intermediary, who takes charge of communication and coordination, as shown in Table 8.7.

Taking event E01 as an example, A17, A01, A34, and A35 participate in this event. However, public information does not include any descriptions of a relationship between A17, A01,

Table 8.7: Entity Missing Hypothesis

Event	Team 1	Team 2	Middleman
E01	A17	A01, A34, A35	AE01
E03	A06	A03, A04, A05	AE03
E28	A17	A36, A39, A40	AE28

A34, and A35. Therefore, we can suppose that the middleman AE01 exists and is responsible for the contacts among them.

Tripartite relationship hypothesis based on the event

The tripartite relationship arises from analysis and research into the relationship between three points in the network. It is composed of a two-party relationship that researches the relationship of a pair of points in the network.

The two-party relationship includes two types in the undirected network, which are related and not related, and three types in the directed network, which are the two-way relationship, a single-way relationship, and no relationship. Similarly, the tripartite relationship includes many types of relationships in the undirected and directed networks. Cartwright and Harary [12] believe that the complex social structure is made up of simple structures. In particular, they are composed of multiple overlapping tripartite relationship groups. The simple three-party structure is the basis for a bigger social structure. Therefore, it is significant to research the tripartite relationship to analyze the network structure and the relationship between the points.

The tripartite relationship hypothesis means the assumption and reasoning of a missing relationship between three points in a network based on mathematics and probability. In 1954, Anatol Rapoport, a Russian mathematical psychologist, proposed the weak ties hypothesis [10]. The weak ties hypothesis means that if A has a certain relationship with B and C separately, there is a relationship between B and C. In 1973, Granovetter [13], an American sociologist, divided the relationships between people into strong ties, weak ties, and unrelated in accordance with the contact time, emotional intensity, familiarity, and situation of helping each other. He also proposed a tripartite relationship hypothesis based on speculation about interpersonal relationships: that is, if A and B have a strong tie, and B and C also have a strong tie, then a relationship may exist between A and C.

On the basis of the characteristics of the member relationship networks of a terrorist organization, we propose the tripartite relationship based on terrorist incidents. For three people A, B, and C jointly participating in the same terrorist incident at the same time in the same place, if B and C are related because A was the co-leader or the people being led,

Table 8.8: Interaction Relationship Hypothesis

Event	Participant	Non-Link Persons	Link Hypothesis
E05	A08, A09, A10	A08, A10	A08, A10
E10, E11	A10, A17, A33	A10, A33	A10, A33
E16	A06, A18, A19	A18, A19	A18, A19
E17	A12, A20, A21	A20, A21	A20, A21

a relationship may exist between *B* and *C*. On the basis of this hypothesis, we obtain a new supplementary relationship, as shown in Table 8.8.

In Table 8.8, for the different events, A09, A17, A06, and A12 act as the co-leader or middleman in the terrorist incident. However, the remaining two members of the terrorist organization are not related to each other in public information. Here, we suppose that an interaction exists between the remaining two members of the terrorist organization.

Spurious relationship hypothesis based on association differences

In the possible relationship network of members based on an association event, an association relationship is formed, because both of them jointly participate in the same event. But this relationship does not actually exist because of regional and time differences. For this circumstance, we propose the spurious relationship hypothesis: that is, for three members of a terrorist organization in the same chain of command, *A*, *B*, and *C*, if *A* and *C* are at both ends of the chain of command separately, and regional and time difference exists, the possibility of a direct relationship between *A* and *C* is very unlikely.

For example, for A24 and A26, as well as A27 and A26, because A24, A26, and A27 jointly participate in E23, both of them establish the direct relationship shown in Figure 8.6. However, the method of participating in E23 is very different. A26 is instigated by A22 to participate in E23, while A27 actively contacts A22 and A24 and requires participation in E23 after finding A22 and A24 premeditating and planning E23 through a network video. Therefore, in accordance with the different methods of A26 and A27 participating in E23, we can suppose that the relationship between A24 and A26 is a spurious relationship, as well as that of A27 and A26.

8.4.4 Improvement of the Appointment and Interaction Relationship Network of the Members of a Terrorist Organization

On the basis of the entity missing case of action association and the tripartite relationship hypothesis of the event, we can refine the appointment and interaction network of the members of the terrorist organization in Figure 8.3, as shown in Figure 8.7. In the figure, the

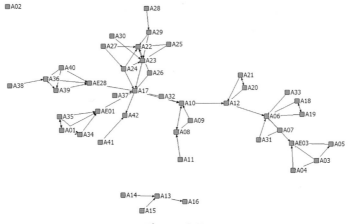

Figure 8.7:
Improved assignment and interaction relationship network.

relationship between the members of terrorist organization with the entity missing is defined as the assumed middleman, and the relationship between the members of terrorist organization with the relationship missing is defined as the interaction relationship. As shown in the figure, A03, A04, A05, and A06 point at AE03 by the arrow, which means that they are the members of AE03, A08, and A10 are connected by a two-way arrow, which shows the interactions between them. Meanwhile, on the basis of the entity missing hypothesis of action association, the tripartite relationship of the event, and the spurious relationship of association differences, we can improve the relationship network (Figure 8.6) based on the event, get rid of the spurious relationship through increasing the entities and missing relationships, and finally get a consistent assignment and interaction relationship network.

8.5 Relationship Network Refinement and Final Relationship Network of Terrorist Organizations and Incidents

In this section, we first construct a possible relationship network between terrorist organizations and terrorist incidents. Then we compare the possible relationship network to the initial social network and obtain the final multi-element terrorist social network by refining the initial social network according to the possible relationship network.

8.5.1 Possible Relationship Network Construction and Perfection of Terrorist Organizations and Terrorist Incidents

As terrorist organization members and instigators of terrorist incidents, the terrorist organization members connect terrorist organizations with terrorist incidents indirectly. The

Table 8.9: Relationship Matrix Between Terrorist Organizations and Terrorist Incidents

	E01	E02	E03	E04	E05	E06	E07	E08	E09	...	E28
G01	1	1	0	0	3	0	0	0	0	...	1
G02	1	0	2	3	0	1	0	0	0	...	0
G03	0	0	0	0	0	1	0	0	0	...	0
G04	0	0	0	0	0	1	0	0	0	...	0
G05	0	0	0	0	0	0	0	0	0	...	0
G06	0	0	0	0	0	0	0	0	0	...	0
G07	0	0	0	0	0	0	0	0	0	...	0
G08	0	0	0	0	0	0	0	0	0	...	0

terrorist organizations provide substantial and spiritual support for terrorist organization members to implement terrorist activities. To a certain extent, the existence of terrorist organizations might be regarded as the source of the occurrence of terrorist incidents. By analyzing the affiliations between terrorist organization members and terrorist incidents, as well as among terrorist organizations, a possible relationship between terrorist organizations and terrorist incidents can be established, which plays an important role in understanding the activities of terrorist organizations.

The relationship matrix between terrorist organization members and terrorist incidents, as well as among terrorist organizations, is shown in Tables 8.1 and 8.2. Multiplication of these two matrices gives the possible relationship matrix between terrorist organizations and terrorist incidents, as shown in Table 8.9.

The relationships that may exist between terrorist organizations and terrorist incidents, on the basis of this matrix, are shown in Figure 8.8. In the figure, the round dots represent eight terrorist organizations, the square dots represent 28 terrorist incidents, and the arrows point to terrorist incidents by terrorist organizations.

Figure 8.8 is a comprehensive illustration of the possible relationships between terrorist organizations and terrorist incidents. However, on analysis, Figure 8.8 was found to contain three obvious spurious relationships, involving E01 and G01, E01 and G02, and E02 and G01. The incidents E01 and E02 happened in 1991 and 1996 respectively, while G01 and G02 were established in 1997 and 1996 respectively. Due to the differences of incident time and the time the organizations were established, we could suppose that there was no direct relationship between E01 and G01, E01 and G02, or E02 and G01. Other incidents happened after the establishment of each terrorist organization, which were made by terrorist organization members affiliated with each terrorist organization. The relationship network between terrorist organizations and terrorist incidents after refinement is shown in Figure 8.9.

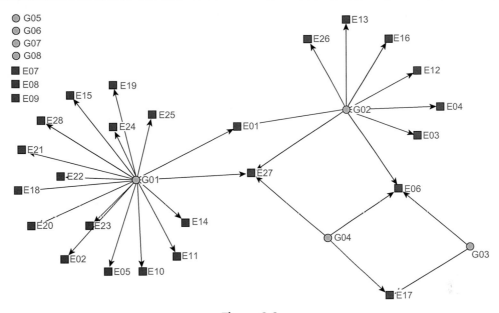

Figure 8.8:
Initial possible relationship figure between terrorist organizations and terrorist incidents.

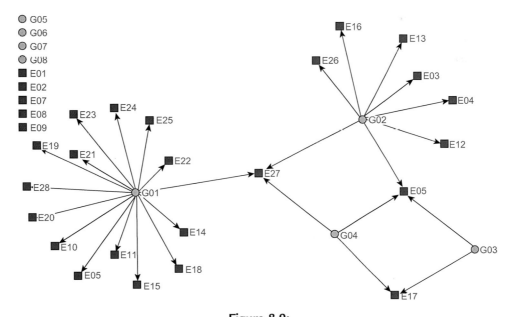

Figure 8.9:
Relationship network refinement between terrorist organizations and terrorist incidents.

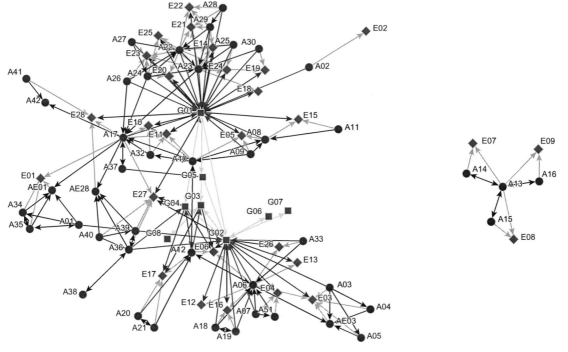

Figure 8.10:
Multi-element network figure of the terrorist organization after refinement.

8.5.2 Final Multi-Element Network Model

Using the above analysis, we can obtain a relatively complete multi-element network model of the terrorist organization members, shown in Figure 8.10. This network provides a thorough representation of the multi-element relationships among organization members, terrorist incidents, and terrorist organizations. Moreover, through this network, we can not only find the perpetrators of terrorist incidents and the terrorist organizations behind them, but also find the designated, interactive relations among members of the terrorist organization, as well as the support relations in the organization.

8.6 Analysis and Verification

In this section, we first analyze some common characteristics of terrorist social networks. We then evaluate the organizations and people within them to find the key entities. Finally, we verify the effectiveness of the model.

8.6.1 Network Characteristics Analysis

On the basis of the social network theory, in this chapter indices, such as scale, density, diameter, and node degree (degree of association), are selected to analyze the general

Table 8.10: Egocentrality Network Calculation Results of the Terrorist Network

	Size	Ties	Pairs	Density	Avg Distance	Diameter	Out Deg	In Deg
A01	3.00	4.00	6.00	66.67			3.000	2.000
A02	0.00	0.00	0.00	0.00	0.00	0.00	0.000	0.000
A03	3.00	2.00	6.00	33.33			3.000	0.000
A04	2.00	1.00	2.00	50.00			1.000	1.000
A05	2.00	1.00	2.00	50.00			1.000	1.000
...	...	...	...	...	...	...	...	...
A42	2.00	0.00	2.00	0.00			0.000	2.000
AE01	4.00	6.00	12.00	50.00			0.000	4.000
AE03	4.00	2.00	12.00	16.67			0.000	4.000
AE28	4.00	4.00	12.00	33.33			0.000	4.000

characteristics of terrorist networks; the results of basic characteristics for the above terrorist network from calculations using UCINET software are shown in Table 8.10.

The results of the calculation show that, from the perspective of scale, 11 people had a direct relationship with more than four people among the network members of terrorists, and most members only had a relationship with one or two other members. This explains the distensibility and invisibility of the network relationship. From the perspective of density, there are two high-density relational members, 16 medium-density relational members, with most members being in the low-density connection relational network, with an overall network density of 0.0389. The network shows the local gang nature and the low density in the overall correlation. From the perspective of dimension, the relational path of the terrorists is rather short. Moreover, from the perspective of the node degree, the average click-in and -out degree is 1.711, the largest click-out degree is 5, and the largest click-in degree is 6, which shows the limitation of individual influence in a decentralized network.

8.6.2 Evaluation of Leading Figures

This refers to members in the network of terrorists who take up important positions and are capable of influencing and controlling the flow of information and resources. Some of them are either the command chiefs of the organization or play the special roles in the organization; thus, the absence of these members may seriously affect the operation of the terrorist organization. To analyze these people, social network analysis usually uses centrality and other methods to carry out positioning. The evaluation indices that are generally used are as follows. The degree centrality measures the active degree of the actors relating to the interactive communication aspects, the closeness centrality measures the distance with others, and the betweenness centrality measures the go-betweens. Because the requirements of closeness centrality to the digraph calculation is rather strict, and considering the positive correlation between this index and point centrality, the point centrality is generally

Table 8.11: Core Figure Measurement and Estimation

Index	Out Degree		In Degree		Betweenness Centrality	
Sequence	Numerical Value	Personnel	Numerical Value	Personnel	Numerical Value	Personnel
1	11.364	A17	13.636	A17	8.192	A17
2	9.091	A10	13.636	A06	7.875	A10
3	6.818	A24	11.364	A10	5.285	A12
4	6.818	A36	11.364	A22	3.647	A06
5	6.818	A03	11.364	A23	2.907	A23
6	6.818	A01	9.091	A12	0.687	A29
7	6.818	A40	9.091	AE01	0.608	A24
8	6.818	A13	9.091	AE03	0.529	A08
9	6.818	A35	9.091	AE08	0.317	A13
10	6.818	A34	6.818	A36	0.211	A36

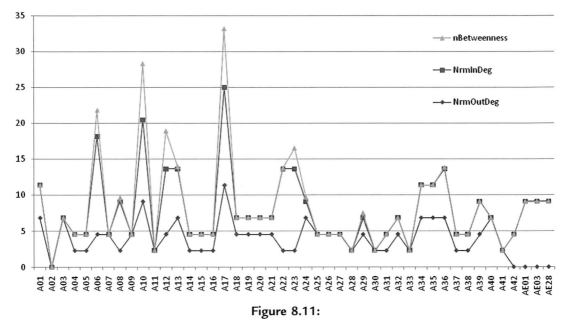

Figure 8.11:
Core index measurement and estimation for terrorist organization members.

considered as the reference; thus, we will omit it. The results of other centrality indices from both calculations using UCINET software and regulative treatment are shown in Table 8.11 (only the top 10 listed) and Figure 8.11.

It appears that, from the evaluation, the leading figures in the member network are A17, A10, A06, A23, A12, etc.

Table 8.12: Importance Measurement and Estimation of Terrorist Organization

Organization Scale			Ability of Destruction			Centrality of Organization		
Scale	Orgs	No. of Persons	Scale	Orgs	Destruction	Scale	Orgs	Centrality
1	G01	14	1	G01	15	1	G02	0.8571
2	G02	10	2	G02	8	2	G01	0.5714
3	G04	2	3	G04	3	3	G03	0.5714
4	G03	1	4	G03	2	4	G04	0.4286
5	G05	1	5	G05	0	5	G05	0.2857
6	G06	0	6	G06	0	6	G06	0.1429
7	G07	0	7	G07	0	7	G07	0.1429
8	G08	0	8	G08	0	8	G08	0.1429

8.6.3 Important Organization Evaluation

Similarly, we can also measure and estimate the importance of the terrorist organization. Here, we use the number of members of the terrorist organization to represent its scale, the number of terrorist incidents perpetrated by the organization to represent the destructiveness of the organization, and the betweenness centrality to represent the centrality of the organization. The measured and estimated results are shown in Table 8.12 and Figure 8.12.

8.6.4 Result Verification

The evaluation results of the missing figures and network key figures are found according to the assumption and deduction through confirmation conforming to the facts. The intermediary roles AE01, AE03, and AE08 and the missing relations exist in the deductions

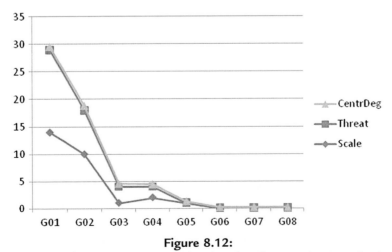

Figure 8.12:
Important index measurement and estimation for terrorist organization.

and assumptions. So, during the individual missing case, E03 stands for the Guns' Secrete Transport Case in 1998, and by verification of the subsequent information, in that incident, several people have played the role of AE03 and have been responsible for contacts both at home and abroad. Moreover, during the relation missing case, taking incident E05 (Arms Private Manufacture Case in 1998) as an example, A09 was seized by the Public Security Organ, and during the trial proceedings, A09 confessed that he was designated by A08 and A10 to carry out terrorist activities; however, in available public information, there was no mention of the relation between A08 and A10.

The evaluation results for the leading figures agree with the facts; for example, A17 organized and established the "East Turkistan Islamic Movement," and he was the chairman of this organization. Moreover, he had certain connections with al-Qaeda. The terrorist A23 took the place of A17 after A17 was shot dead. In 2005, A23 became a member of a leading organization of al-Qaeda, "Ijtima'al-Shurra," and terrorist A10 became vice-chairman of the "East Turkistan Islamic Movement," etc.

8.7 Conclusions

Much previous research on network models of terrorist organization members took the viewpoint of interaction relationships among terrorist organization members available in public information. However, due to missing data problems, it may contribute to the outcome of the analysis deviating from the real-world situation. Thus, in this chapter, to obviate the missing data problem in the invisible network model construction of terrorist organization members, a type of terrorist construction method has been proposed based on the combination of interactive relation records and deductions and assumptions. Firstly, the initial relation network of the members is established according to the interactive relation in available public information. Secondly, a possible relation network of the members is established using the incidence relation. Based on these relation networks, we identify the missing data phenomenon by comparison of the two networks. We then propose the interactive relation assumption as a characteristic of theoretical activities, and thus improve the initial network. Finally, its effectiveness is proved via empirical research. The network construction method of terrorists based on the combination of the interactive relationship records and deductions and assumptions is found to be an effective method to refine social network model construction for terrorist groups.

It is also worth pointing out that this chapter has also studied the network construction method of terrorist organization members based on the interactive relation hypothesis, and that the source of these data is public interactive information. With the current availability of a huge quantity of information, there are many problems needing solutions. For example, there may be a large amount of false information in the relational network established on the basis of network and open source intelligence information, so how can we carry out the missing data and spurious analysis? Another example, relating to terrorist organization members in a particular terrorist incident, is how to carry out relationship deduction by analysis of the roles, knowledge, resources, skills, and other factors of terrorist organization members? Therefore, in the future, we still need to introduce several new means of analysis, such as the combination of the interactive relation assumption, the probability transition, and statistical inference. The combination of data mining and machine learning should also be a potential development direction in the future.

Acknowledgments

This research is supported by the National Natural Science Foundation of China under Grant No. 70973138.

References

[1] M. Sageman, Understanding Terror Networks, University of Pennsylvania Press, Philadelphia, 2004.
[2] B.H. Erickson, Secret societies and social structure, J. Soc. Forces 60 (1) (1981) 188–210.
[3] M. Sparrow, The application of network analysis to criminal intelligence: An assessment of the prospects, J. Soc. Netw. 13 (3) (1991) 251–274.
[4] W.E. Baker, R.R. Faulkner, The social organization of conspiration: Illegal networks in the heavy electrical equipment industry, J. Am. Sociol. Rev. 58 (6) (1993) 837–860.
[5] V.E. Krebs, Mapping networks of terrorist cells, J. Connect. 24 (3) (2002) 43–52.
[6] A. Basu, Social network analysis of terrorist organizations in India. the North American Association for Computational Social and Organizational Science (NAACSOS) Conference 2005, Notre Dame, IN, June 26–28, 2005.
[7] R. Rothenberg, From whole cloth: Making up the terrorist network, J. Connect. 24 (3) (2001) 36–42.
[8] K.M. Carley, Estimating vulnerabilities in large covert networks using multi-level data, Proceedings of the 2004 International Symposium on Command and Control Research and Technology, 2004.
[9] K.M. Carley, M. Dombroski, M. Tsvetovat, J. Reminga, N. Kamneva, Destabilizing dynamic covert networks, Proceedings of the 8th International Command and Control Research and Technology Symposium, Vienna, VA, 2003.
[10] J.A. Rodriguez, The March 11th terrorist network: In its weakness lies its strength, Department of Sociology and Analysis of Organizations. Working Paper EPP-LEA:03, Barcelona (in Spanish), 2005.
[11] J. Kennedy, G. Weimann, The strength of weak terrorist ties, Terror. Polit. Viol. 23 (2) (2011) 201–212.
[12] D. Cartwright, F. Harary, Structural balance: A generalization of Heider's theory, J. Psychol. Rev. 63 (5) (1956) 277–293.
[13] M.S. Granovetter, The strength of weak ties, Am. J. Sociol. 78 (6) (1973) 1360–1380.

CHAPTER 9

Incorporating Data and Methodologies for Knowledge Discovery for Crime

Fatih Ozgul

Counter-Terrorism Department, Turkish National Police Headquarters, Ankara, Turkey

Chapter Outline

Intelligent Systems for Security Informatics.
http://dx.doi.org/10.1016/B978-0-12-404702-0.00009-4

9.1 Introduction

Knowledge discovery is the process of extracting useful knowledge from data [1]. Application of criminal intelligence that is extracted from crime data is used in many ways for investigation of individual crimes, as well as criminal networks [2,3]. Skillicorn [4] states that knowledge discovery can take place in two different ways. In traditional law enforcement the role of knowledge discovery is retrospective: when a crime has been committed, an investigation gathers data in a needs-driven way, and both humans and potentially algorithmic tools examine these data, looking for patterns that might give an indication of the perpetrators. He also states that, increasingly, knowledge discovery is also used in a prospective way to try and prevent something bad happening, such as in counter-terrorism efforts and crime prevention projects. In many ways knowledge discovery and crime investigation are similar. The aim of knowledge discovery is to extract useful knowledge, whereas the aim of crime investigation is to solve and shed light on unknown aspects of what really happened. To focus on the use of knowledge discovery in crime investigation, we initially need to look further into the steps involved in crime investigation. Then, the data sources used for crime investigation are considered. By using these data sources, four types of knowledge discovery are produced. These four knowledge discovery types are applied to the most suitable type of crime investigations and the most suitable methodologies, since each crime investigation focuses on different types of findings and knowledge discovery. The question is which type of crime investigation works best with which methodology and knowledge discovery using which type of data.

9.2 Steps Involved in Crime Investigation

McCue [5] states that the steps in a crime investigation are similar to those in crime data mining and knowledge discovery. Crime data are used to extract operationally actionable output for solving crimes or explaining criminality. She also points out that the police methodology for investigation also implements case-based reasoning techniques. Each individual case teaches investigators about the type of events and *modus operandi* of crime. According to McCue, all data sources used by the police can also be used as the source for crime data mining. The crime investigation process therefore can be organized into the following five steps:

- **Collecting crime data.** When a crime occurs, patrol officers and detectives usually work at the scene to collect and record crime information in various documents. Information collection also includes the information that detectives acquire from victims, witnesses, and suspects during the investigation process.

- **Processing and storing crime data and documents.** Documents are then collected and managed by a special unit inside the police department and part of the recorded information is entered into one or more computer-based systems.
- **Searching, retrieving, and collecting additional information.** When investigating a case, more information about the suspects and crimes is needed and is retrieved from various data resources and databases. For instance, after a police officer or a detective is assigned to a case, he or she searches for the necessary information, or may ask a crime analyst for help to search for such information. There are many possible sources for collecting information, including obtaining records from various institutions such as other police departments; numerous utility companies on water, gas, and electricity; phone companies; and various cities, state, and federal government branches.
- **Analyzing information to find clues.** In order to find more complete evidence to charge a criminal or to find clues for an investigation, sophisticated and logical crime analyses need to be conducted in order to find links between criminals and/or among crimes. Such analyses include crime pattern analysis, data analysis, etc. A crime analyst must type and print out a report after the analysis stage. The report is delivered to the requester by hard copy, not by email. Although crime analysts are encouraged to enter the findings into a database to share with others, they usually do not do so because they are too busy.
- **Using information to prosecute criminals.** Detectives use information collected from the crime scene, the suspects, victims, and witnesses of the crime, and crime analysis reports to generate formal documents in order to prosecute criminals. In addition, detectives also need to perform many data-intensive tasks such as completing supplementary reports, requesting lab reports from crime lab technicians, and obtaining transcripts of all interviews from transcribers. Furthermore, this stage often involves the collaboration of detectives from several departmental units, county attorney offices, and courts to combine all the information into a complete file that becomes the basis for the prosecution. It is beneficial for data-mining practitioners to know the difficulties of crime data mining according to the investigation process.

9.3 Data Sources for Crime Data Mining and Investigation

In order to determine the right type of knowledge discovery and successful investigation, it is essential to identify the available data sources. The police commonly use the following data sources during an investigation.

9.3.1 Offender Demographics Information

This comprises name, surname, date of birth, place of birth, social security number, etc. These records are generally stored in electronic databases but this does not mean that the police can easily access it. Sometimes the police are authorized to see similar people's records as it is very beneficial to have an idea about a possible suspect. For instance, people generally use the same password for credit cards, emails, pin numbers, etc. The police can recover evidence if they think they are on the right path to spot the clue. Offender demographics information comes in relational or text format.

9.3.2 Criminal Background Information

It is important to know whether a person has previously been involved in crimes, possibly together with other criminals. This co-offending knowledge can be essential to the police for detecting members of criminal networks. Criminal background information comes in relational or text format.

9.3.3 Previous Investigation Files

After identifying a previously convicted suspect, the police ask for previous investigation files of intended suspects. Previous investigation files come in text, photo, video footage, CCTV (closed circuit television) video files, bank account and credit card statements, phone and email send—receive records, flight and travel itineraries, forensic reports, witness and victim statements, call for service files, lawyer and criminal statements, and confessions. Previous investigation files come in text format.

9.3.4 Police Arrest Records

Upon general checks and patrol queries, or due to calls for service inquiries, police officers arrest suspects temporarily and keep them in police custody. Most of the time, these people are released without conviction and the records are destroyed within 4—5 years. These records are mainly in relational format or text format. Police can use this arrest record information to identify important relationships.

9.3.5 Photographs

Photographs as data sources include images taken by professional photographers during observations or — most of the time — amateur photos or pictures captured from video files. CCTV footage must be edited in order to use it as evidence. Generally, photos are available in various digital image formats.

9.3.6 Video Files

Like pictures, video files are taken by professionals or amateurs. Videos are stored on various media, such as CDs, DVDs, or on old-fashioned VHS or beta cassettes. Sound files from physical or technical surveillance are treated like video files. Transcriptions of these files are partly available.

9.3.7 Bank Accounts and Credit Card Statements

Bank accounts and credit card statements are available in digital or paper format. From a police perspective, it would be beneficial to find matching suspected transactions between suspects' bank accounts and credit cards. Usually, the police make use of specialized software, such as i2 Analyst Notebook [6], to visualize suspected transactions over thousands of records.

9.3.8 Call Detail Records (CDRs) and Email Records

Call detail records (CDRs) and email records contain information about "who called whom" and "who sent an email to whom" respectively. Furthermore, they may contain email messages with or without attachments, SMS message bodies, or sound files of suspects' phone calls. Like bank accounts, phone call and email sender/recipient records (e.g. "To:", "Cc:", or "Bcc:") are essential and valuable for investigators when matched and visualized.

9.3.9 Travel and Flight Itineraries

Travel and flight itineraries are given by travel companies, insurance companies, or directly from passport or visa record databases of state institutions. These records come in relational or text format.

9.3.10 Open Source Intelligence Findings

Open source intelligence findings are provided from the Web, such as from search engines (e.g. 123people), utility payment records, information gathered from social networking sites (e.g. Facebook, LinkedIn, MySpace), comments of suspects written on web forums and on popular e-commerce sites such as in Amazon or eBay accounts and wish-lists. This information is available in various digital formats.

9.3.11 Call for Service Records

Call for service records are records about calls to the police, asking for service. They may contain information and personal comments about people and events. Call for services are generally in text format.

9.3.12 Hotel and Hospital Records

Since people stay in hotels for vacations and in hospitals for medical treatment, their contact and staying information are entered into logbooks. These are important for proving alibis and possible meetings. They come in both tabular and text format.

9.3.13 Police and Intelligence Service Reports

Police reports contain information about the crime and the suspects. Mostly they are written on paper by police staff. Similar intelligence reports are provided by intelligence services and both reports come mainly in text format.

Data sources that are used both for crime investigation and for knowledge discovery are shown in Table 9.1, along with the knowledge discovery and best practices they are used for. According to McCue [5], these knowledge discovery algorithms can be categorized into two general groups: rule induction models (i.e. decision trees) and unsupervised learning (i.e. clustering) techniques. What can be found using these data sources is explained in the following section.

9.4 The Four Types of Knowledge Discovery

As pointed out in Table 9.1, there are various practices for knowledge discovery. Data for knowledge discovery come mainly in text form, and sometimes in a more structured relational form. The relational form is preferable because it is easier to manipulate relational data in sets. But data that come in text form are also used in text-mining techniques. Combined sources of data include web page, image, stream, and various signal data. Various knowledge engineering techniques are possible but the final aim of knowledge discovery is delivery of operationally actionable output [5]. Skillicorn [4] classifies knowledge discovery into four types: prediction, clustering, understanding connections, and understanding the internal world of others.

9.4.1 Prediction

Prediction is the first type of knowledge discovery for crime data mining. Skillicorn [4] explains prediction as deciding the outcome or meaning of a particular situation by collecting and observing its properties. In the crime domain, crime prediction is realized either retrospectively or prospectively. Retrospective crime prediction is made in order to solve crimes and detect criminals after the crime is committed. This can also be done by minimizing the target group of possible criminals. Prospective crime prediction is made in order to forecast an emerging threat or prevent criminality that has not been detected before.

Table 9.1: Data Sources for the Four Types of Knowledge Discovery

	Data Sources for Knowledge Discovery	Type Used in KD	Best Practices
1	Offender demographics information	Prediction	Criminal prediction
		Prediction	Crime network member prediction
		Clustering	Crime network prediction
2	Criminal background information	Understanding the connections and world of others	Visualizing co-offending networks
		Prediction	Unsolved crime prediction
		Clustering	Crime network detection
3	Previous investigation files	Clustering	Spatial, temporal, *modus operandi* clustering of similar crimes
		Prediction	Unsolved crime prediction
4	Police arrest records	Understanding the connections and world of others	Visualizing co-offending networks
		Clustering	Crime network detection
		Prediction	Crime network member prediction
5	Photographs	Understanding the connections and world of others	Visualizing crimes and criminals
6	Video files	Understanding the connections and world of others	Visualizing crimes and criminals
7	Bank accounts and credit card statements	Understanding the connections and world of others	Visualizing crimes and criminals
8	Call detail records (CDRs)	Clustering	Crime network detection
		Prediction	Crime network member prediction
		Understanding the connections and world of others	Visualizing relationships between criminals
9	Email records	Understanding the connections and world of others	Visualizing relationships between criminals
		Clustering	Crime network detection
		Prediction	Crime network member prediction
10	Travel and flight itineraries	Understanding the connections and world of others	Visualizing activities of criminals
11	Open source intelligence findings	Understanding the connections and world of others	Visualizing activities of criminals
12	Call for service records	Understanding the connections and world of others	Visualizing co-offending networks
		Clustering	Crime network detection
13	Hotel and hospital records	Understanding the connections and world of others	Visualizing relationships between criminals
14	Police and intelligence service reports	Clustering	Crime network detection
		Prediction	Unsolved crime prediction
		Understanding the connections and world of others	Visualizing relationships between criminals

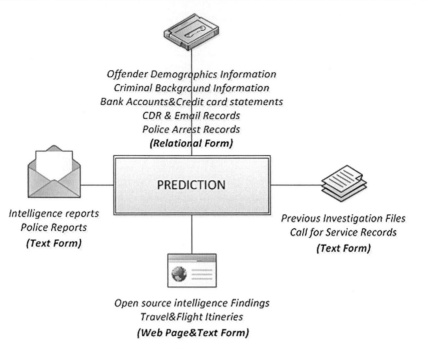

Offender Demographics Information
Criminal Background Information
Bank Accounts&Credit card statements
CDR & Email Records
Police Arrest Records
(Relational Form)

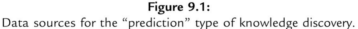

PREDICTION

Intelligence reports
Police Reports
(Text Form)

Previous Investigation Files
Call for Service Records
(Text Form)

Open source intelligence Findings
Travel&Flight Itineries
(Web Page&Text Form)

Figure 9.1:
Data sources for the "prediction" type of knowledge discovery.

One example of retrospective prediction is prediction of an unsolved crime, whereas the prediction of a new member of a criminal network is an example of prospective prediction. Best data sources for crime prediction are previous investigation files, offender demographics, a criminal's background information, and police arrest records, most of which are in text format and therefore suitable for text mining. Data sources for prediction are shown in Figure 9.1.

9.4.2 Clustering

Clustering is the second type of knowledge discovery for crime data mining. Clustering means putting information into groups of objects or situations whose members resemble each other and are usefully different from the members of other groups [7]. Gaining knowledge of such clusters allows investigators to decide effectively how to handle a new and unforeseen situation. Clustering techniques are used to uncover natural patterns or relationships in the data when group membership or category has not been previously identified. For example, similar crimes in which perpetrators resemble a known profile can be detected and grouped. A special type of clustering is outlier detection, which means a person, case or object such as evidence that has not been allocated to a cluster, behaving differently than others. Detecting outliers helps investigators to focus on extraordinary

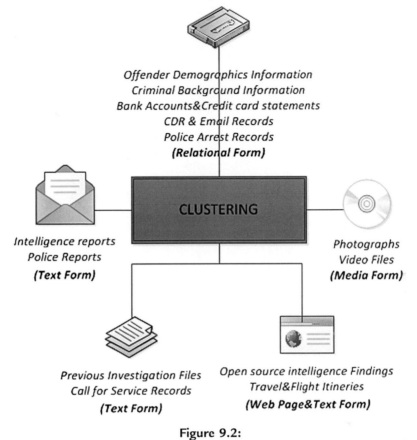

Figure 9.2:
Data sources for the "clustering" type of knowledge discovery.

persons, cases or objects in the overall dataset, thereby questioning what went wrong with these outliers. This approach can help to find whistleblowers, unhappy members of the gang, and the piece of evidence in order to spot the clue. Similar outliers in different clusters might be signaling of new unexplored clusters of criminals or crimes. Data sources for clustering are shown in Figure 9.2.

9.4.3 Understanding Connections

Understanding connections means understanding how objects, processes, and especially people are connected. In the crime domain, this includes knowledge about who is a friend of whom, recognizing the collaboration between criminals. Analysts use data visualization tools to find such connections. Various social network analysis algorithms and visualization software are available for the use of law enforcement community. Data sources for understanding connections are shown in Figure 9.3.

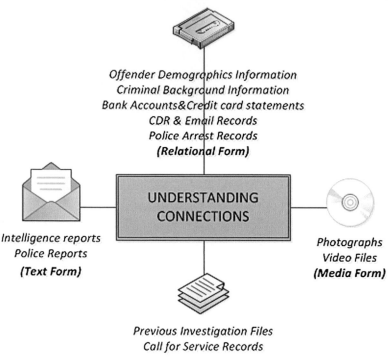

Offender Demographics Information
Criminal Background Information
Bank Accounts&Credit card statements
CDR & Email Records
Police Arrest Records
(Relational Form)

UNDERSTANDING
CONNECTIONS

Intelligence reports
Police Reports
(Text Form)

Photographs
Video Files
(Media Form)

Previous Investigation Files
Call for Service Records
(Text Form)

Figure 9.3:
Data sources for the "understanding connections" type of knowledge discovery.

9.4.4 Understanding the World of Others

Understanding the internal world of others enables us to assume what other persons may think or feel. In the crime domain, this includes frame analysis, sentiment analysis, and learning a criminal's mental state as revealed by his/her writing and conversation [4]. Frame analysis is about a targeted person's intentions, his/her ideas and arguments, and how they think about their world and their activities. For instance, many terrorists believe that their crimes have religious aims or they consider themselves to be freedom fighters. Sentiment analysis aims to learn about opinions and attitudes towards other persons, groups, objects, or ideologies. For instance, an organized crime network may call its members "brothers and sisters" and their organization a "mob." Identifying these words in their speech and writing can help investigators to gain a profile of these people. Learning about the mental state of a criminal is another technique. For instance, negotiations conducted by professionals with hostage takers are based on assumptions about the mental state of criminals. Perhaps the criminal may be depressed or elated during conversations. Another way of understanding the world of others, including terrorists and organized crime networks, might be gained by connection, cooperating and exchanging knowledge, skills, and tools. This can also be found by how

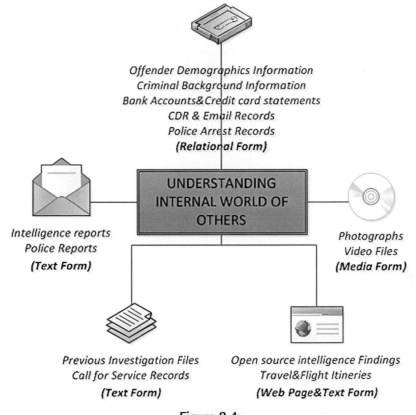

Offender Demographics Information
Criminal Background Information
Bank Accounts&Credit card statements
CDR & Email Records
Police Arrest Records
(Relational Form)

UNDERSTANDING
INTERNAL WORLD OF
OTHERS

Intelligence reports
Police Reports
(Text Form)

Photographs
Video Files
(Media Form)

Previous Investigation Files
Call for Service Records
(Text Form)

Open source intelligence Findings
Travel&Flight Itineries
(Web Page&Text Form)

Figure 9.4:
Data sources for the "understanding the world of others" type of knowledge discovery.

similar such targeted crime networks are, by comparing their *modus operandi*, retired old skilled members recruited by new networks, using similar supply lines, etc. Many scoring algorithms or decision tree models have been developed and are being used by the law enforcement community. To understand the world of others, text mining and web content mining techniques have been developed and these technologies are offered to the law enforcement and intelligence communities. Data sources for understanding the world of others are shown in Figure 9.4.

These four types of knowledge discovery can be applied to criminal cases, to individual criminals, and to crime networks, as shown in Table 9.2. They can be applied to single crime cases as prediction of unsolved crimes, to compare similar and dissimilar crimes, to detect an interrelated series of crimes, and to detect common attributes of crimes. They can be applied to crime cases to predict the next attack of a serial criminal, to detect similarly behaving criminals, to detecting friendship links of criminals, and to detect relationships between criminals.

Table 9.2: The Four Types of Knowledge Discovery in Criminal Cases

	Prediction	Clustering	Understanding Connections	Understanding the World of Others
Crime	Prediction of unsolved crimes	Finding similar and dissimilar crimes	Detecting interrelated and series of crimes	Detecting common attributes of crimes
Criminal	Prediction of next attack of a serial criminal	Detecting similarly behaving criminals	Detecting friendship links of criminals	Detecting relationships of criminals
Criminal networks	Prediction of a missing member in a criminal network	Detecting cliques and subgroups in a criminal network	Positional analysis of criminal network members	Detecting similarity of groups, finding emerging networks

9.5 Knowledge Discovery Methodologies for Crime Data

After considering the available data sources and knowledge discovery forms, we now look into methodologies that are available in the current literature. There are four known methodologies. CRISP-DM [8] methodology (CRISP-DM: Cross-Industry Standard Process for Data Mining), like SEMMA [9] methodology (SEMMA: Sample, Explore, Modify, Model, Assess), refers to the more general process of data mining. CIA intelligence methodology refers to the life cycle of converting data into intelligence, which is also a well-known methodology. Van der Hulst's methodology [10] is specifically developed for criminal networks, including specific steps for identifying and analyzing criminal networks. Last but not least, AMPA (Actionable Mining and Predictive Analytics) methodology was developed by McCue [5] to give a better understanding of crime data mining. They are briefly introduced in the following section, and how to apply which type of knowledge discovery to which methodology is outlined below.

9.5.1 CRISP-DM Methodology

Several years ago, representatives from a diverse array of industries gathered to define the best practices or standard methodology for data mining. The result of this was the Cross-Industry Standard Process for Data Mining (CRISP-DM). CRISP-DM consists of six steps [8]:

1. **Business understanding.** In the business understanding phase, the analyst determines the objectives of the task.
2. **Data understanding.** In this phase, data are collected and the analyst becomes familiar with it, considering form, content, and structure.

3. **Data preparation.** After the data have been examined and characterized during the data understanding step, they are then prepared for subsequent mining. The data preparation phase includes data cleaning, recording, selection, and production of training and testing data. Additionally, datasets or elements may be merged or aggregated in this step.

4. **Modeling.** In this phase of the project, specific modeling algorithms are selected and run on data. The selection of specific algorithms employed in the data-mining process is based on the nature of the question and outputs desired.

5. **Evaluation.** In the evaluation phase, the models created are reviewed to determine their accuracy as well as their ability to meet the goals and objectives. This phase reveals whether the model is accurate and appropriate to the question posed.

6. **Deployment.** This phase includes the dissemination of the information.

9.5.2 CIA Intelligence Methodology

The Central Intelligence Agency (CIA) of the USA has developed a methodology for intelligence processing that is also used for mining crime data. It is divided into six stages [11]:

1. **Needs.** Intelligence information priorities are determined during the needs or requirements phase.

2. **Collection.** The CIA methodology specifies four basic types of collection data: (a) Signals intelligence that includes information obtained from intercepted signals. Subdisciplines within this category include communications intelligence and electronic intelligence. (b) Imagery intelligence includes information obtained through satellite, aerial, and ground-based collection methods. (c) Human-source intelligence includes intelligence gathered from human sources. This collection discipline has been divided further for clandestine activities as well as overt collection efforts, debriefing, and official contacts. (d) Open-source information includes information available publicly and can include, but is not limited to, newspapers, radio, television, and the Internet.

3. **Processing and exploitation.** The processing and exploitation phase includes the separation, preparation, and transformation of data into a format that can be analyzed.

4. **Analysis and production.** In this phase, raw data and information are converted into intelligence products. These finished intelligence studies may also include the integration of multiple sources of information, which affords a greater depth of analysis and insight.

5. **Dissemination.** Dissemination means the distribution of intelligence products to the intelligence community.

6. **Feedback.** The feedback step ensures the continuous and iterative nature of intelligence methodology.

9.5.3 Van der Hulst's Methodology

Van der Hulst's methodology [10] is designed specifically for analysis of criminal networks. It is comprised of three main steps:

1. **Data preparation.** This step includes accessing the network data and defining the network boundaries, i.e. defining a meaningful social category of the target group (e.g. which actors, ties, or events are included or excluded from analysis). Research questions are formulated and the required analysis routines identified. Furthermore, assumptions are formulated before coding (e.g. which ties are considered as friends?). Finally, a coding system is developed, considering the actors' attributes, activities, and affiliations, which ensure data reliability and change over time.
2. **Data processing.** In this step information on the social ties of actors is gathered. This often requires handling of time-intensive large datasets related to the target group. Then, the attributes, activities, and affiliations associated with the actors are identified and a database of individual attributes (e.g. sex, age, skills, and criminal records) is built. Adjacency matrices of ties between actors (e.g. tasks, logistics, and resources) and an incidence matrix of affiliations that associate actors to events (e.g. locations) are created. Finally, names of actors are sorted (e.g. in alphabetic order) and the overall data are tightened and cleaned.
3. **Data analysis and reporting.** This step considers which routines are robust measures to analyze the data and deal with missing data. Analysis routines are performed and the results properly stored in a database. Finally, the results are interpreted and reported.

9.5.4 Actionable Mining and Predictive Analysis (AMPA) Methodology

To address the requirements and challenges for operationally relevant data preprocessing and output, a new methodology was developed by McCue [5]: Predictive Analytics and Crime Data Mining. Her methodology includes eight steps:

1. **Question or challenge.** To which problem are you looking for an answer? In this stage, current procedures and reports are reviewed to understand the nature of the question. It is imperative to collaborate directly with the anticipated recipient or end-user of the output, especially the operational personnel.
2. **Data collection and fusion.** Using various data sources is beneficial in designing models for particular questions. Depending on the nature of the question, the required data are put into the same format, such as relational or text.
3. **Operationally relevant processing.** This process requires recoding and variable selection. Data preprocessing and preparation make up as much as 80% of the data-mining process [5,7].

Table 9.3: Comparison of Available Criminal Data-Mining Methodologies

CRISP-DM Methodology	CIA Methodology	Van der Hulst's Methodology	AMPA Methodology
Business understanding	Needs	Data preparation	Question or challenge
Data understanding	Collection	Data preparation	Data collection and fusion
Data preparation	Processing and exploitation	Data preparation	Operationally relevant processing Recoding
Data preparation	Processing and exploitation	Data preparation	Variable selection
Modeling	Analysis and production	Data processing	Identification, characterization, and modeling
Evaluation	Dissemination	Data analysis and reporting	Public safety specific evaluation
Deployment	Feedback	Data analysis and reporting	Operationally actionable output

4. **Recoding.** This phase includes the transformation and cleaning of data. Furthermore, the user becomes familiar with the data and gains a rough idea of its patterns.

5. **Variable selection.** This step requires significant expertise on existing crime domains and ensures the usefulness of variables. Some variables may only be producing noise over the best results given by models.

6. **Identification, characterization, modeling.** In this step descriptive and heuristics of available data are applied to identify, characterize, and model the data.

7. **Public safety specific evaluation.** In this phase, the created models are reviewed in order to decide whether they answer the question raised in the initial step.

8. **Operationally actionable output.** The output is prepared for end-users to satisfy their expectancy for operational output.

Based on these definitions and explanations, crime data-mining methodologies are summarized in Table 9.3. As can be seen, these methodologies include steps that are much the same, to do the same job. CRISP-DM applies six steps, CIA applies six steps, and Van der Hulst applies only three steps, whereas AMPA applies eight steps. The CRISP-DM and CIA methodologies are very similar and they approach the problem in a more general manner, not specific for crime data. Since it is more detailed and focused, AMPA turns out to be better than the previous methods. The AMPA methodology also differs from the others in its specialty to public safety and security domains, security specifics, as well as the inclusion of operationally actionable relevant processing and output [5]. Van der Hulst's methodology, on the other hand, is stronger than the others when working on criminal networks [10], because it specializes in criminal network detection and analysis problems.

9.6 Methodologies Applied to Knowledge Discovery Types

Now that we have investigated the available methodologies and use of data sources for the four types of knowledge discovery tasks, we can look further into how we can decide which methodology is most suitable for which type of knowledge discovery. As indicated in Table 9.4, the more general methodologies such as CRISP-DM and CIA are most suitable for prediction and clustering tasks, because tasks such as prediction of unsolved crimes, prediction of the next step of a serial criminal, finding similar crimes and criminals requires more data than the other tasks; the CRISP-DM and CIA methodologies require less data preparation and less public safety-specific evaluation time and steps. For instance, much off-the-shelf data-mining software such as SAS Enterprise Miner [9] and SPSS Clementine [8] easily prepares data for mining, and they do not require domain experts' feedback; they rather use computerized evaluation metrics.

Knowledge discovery tasks for understanding connections and understanding the internal world of others are more amenable to the Van der Hulst and AMPA methodologies, because these tasks require a considerable amount of time for data preparation, public safety-specific evaluation, and detailed visualization tools such as databases, graphs and diagrams. For instance, Van der Hulst's methodology is particularly suited to analyze criminal networks, with more emphasis on data preparation and processing. It also offers to create a database to evaluate results, thereby querying and plotting results using various approaches. Similarly, AMPA methodology is also focused on data preparation with operationally relevant

Table 9.4: Methodologies Applied to the Four Types of Knowledge Discovery

CRISP-DM	CIA	Van der Hulst	AMPA
Prediction			
More suitable for prediction tasks	More suitable for prediction tasks	Less suitable for prediction tasks	Less suitable for prediction tasks
Clustering			
More suitable for clustering tasks	More suitable for clustering tasks	Less suitable for clustering tasks	Less suitable for clustering tasks
Understanding Connections			
Less suitable for understanding connection tasks	Less suitable for understanding connection tasks	More suitable methodology for criminal networks	More suitable methodology for criminal networks
Understanding the World of Others			
Less suitable for understanding world of others tasks	Less suitable for understanding world of others tasks	More suitable for understanding world of others tasks	More suitable for understanding world of others tasks

processing, and targeting operationally actionable output with public safety-specific evaluation. The AMPA methodology ensures that public safety professionals can engage in data preparation and evaluation of results, which is desirable for criminal network identification and understanding the world of criminals tasks.

In general, the CRISP-DM and CIA methodologies are suited to large datasets with more predictive analytic tasks, and the Van der Hulst and AMPA methodologies are more amenable to small datasets that require more preparation, specific evaluation, and detailed visualization.

9.7 Conclusion

We have considered the steps involved in a criminal investigation and their similarity to criminal data-mining steps. Data sources for investigation and data mining have also been explained in detail. Four types of knowledge discovery and their applications in using crime data are discussed, and which types of knowledge discovery to be used for criminal cases, persons, and criminal networks have been discussed. Based on these knowledge discovery tasks, the available methodologies have been studied as to which methodologies are suitable for which types of knowledge discovery tasks. Prediction and clustering tasks are suitable for CRISP-DM and CIA intelligence methodologies, whereas cases involving understanding connections and the world of others with more data preparation and specific evaluation are more amenable to the AMPA and Van der Hulst methodologies.

References

[1] H. Chen, W. Chung, J.J. Xu, G. Wang, Y. Qin, M. Chau, Crime data mining: A general framework and some examples, Computer, IEEE Comput. Soc. 37 (4) (2004) 50−56.
[2] C. Morselli, Inside Criminal Networks, Springer Science Business Media LLC, New York, 2009.
[3] M.K. Sparrow, The application of network analysis to criminal intelligence: An assessment of the prospects, Soc. Netw. 13 (3) (1991) 251−274.
[4] D. Skillicorn, Knowledge Discovery for Counterterrorism and Law Enforcement, Taylor & Francis Group, Boca Raton, FL USA, 2009.
[5] C. McCue, Data Mining and Predictive Analysis: Intelligence Gathering and Crime Analysis, Elsevier, Butterworth-Heinemann, Oxford, 2007.
[6] i2, i2 Analyst's Notebook, i2 Ltd., Cambrige, UK, 2011.
[7] M. Kantardzic, Data Mining: Concepts, Models, Methods, and Algorithms, Wiley-IEEE Press, 2002.
[8] P. Chapman, J. Clinton, R. Kerber, T. Khabaza, T. Reinartz, C. Shearer, R. Wirth, CRISP-DM 1.0 step-by-step data mining guide, Technical Report, The CRISP-DM Consortium, August 2000. Available at <http://www.crisp-dm.org/CRISPWP-0800.pdf>.
[9] D.L. Olson, D. Delen, Advanced Data Mining Techniques, Springer, Berlin, 2008.
[10] R.C. van der Hulst, Introduction to social network analysis (SNA) as an investigative tool, Trends Organ. Crim. 12 (2) (2009) 101−121.
[11] R.M. Clark, Intelligence Analysis: A Target Centric Approach, CQ Press, Washington, DC, 2007.

Index

Edwards Brothers Malloy
Ann Arbor MI. USA
July 26, 2013